MOODS OF
RUTLAND WATER

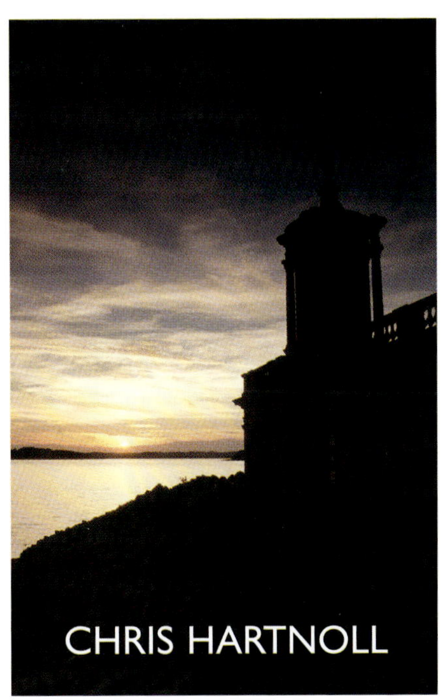

CHRIS HARTNOLL

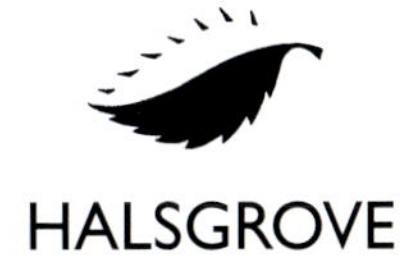

HALSGROVE

DEDICATION

For Jamie and Alex
Because, as we say: 'I can'

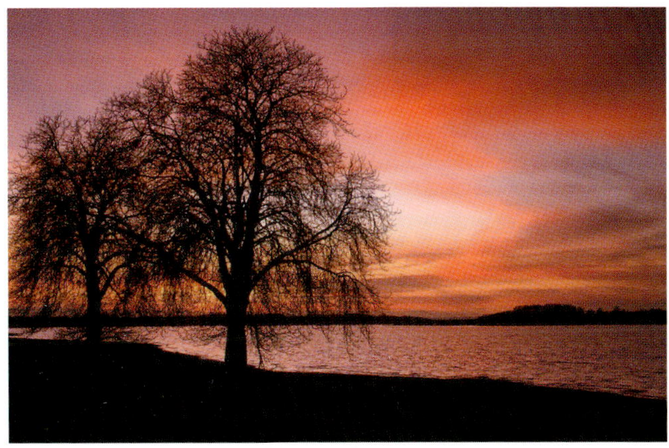

'Three Trees' near Mowmires Reach

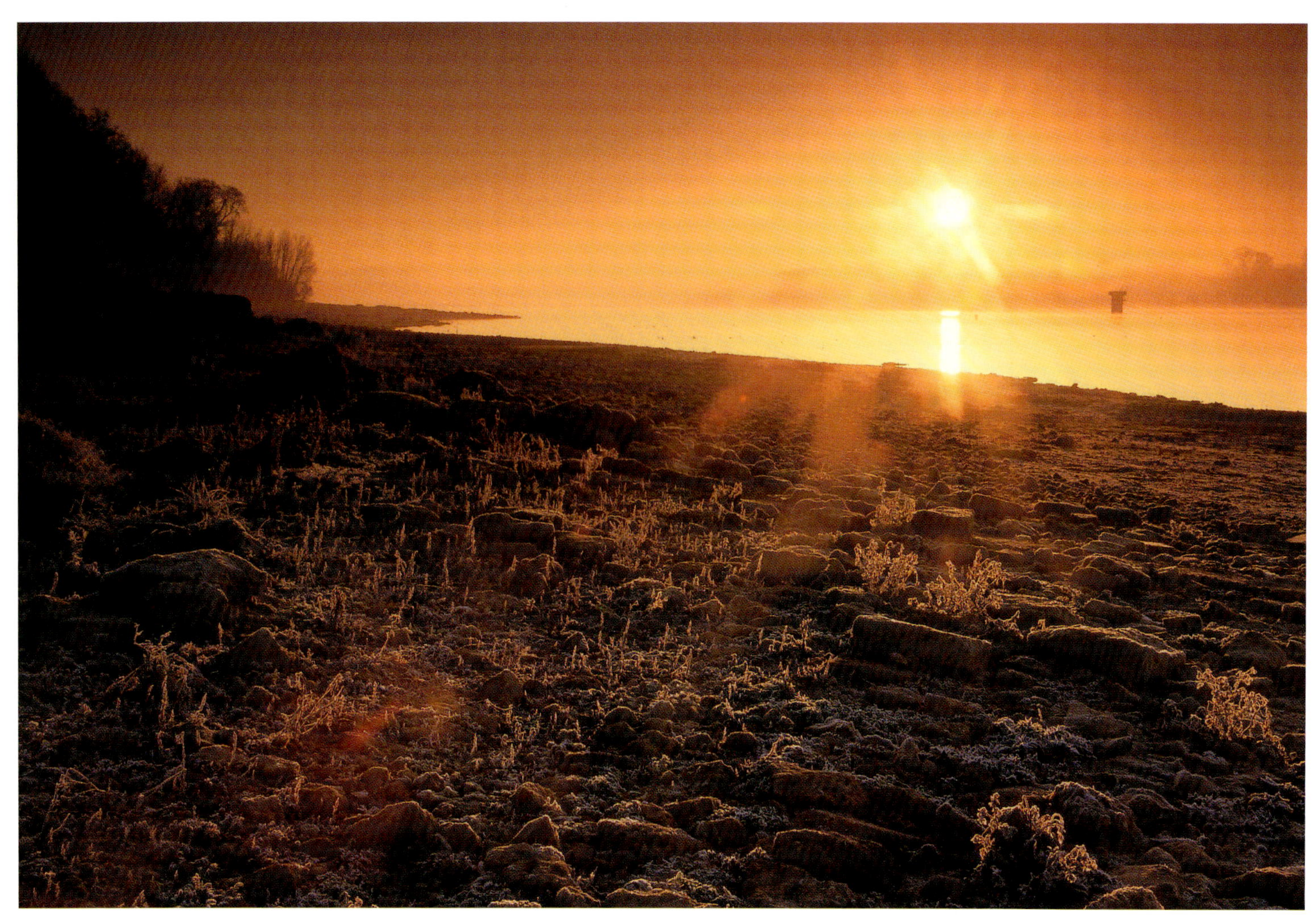

The beginning of a bright and crisp December day.

CONTENTS

ACKNOWLEDGEMENTS

I did not start out with the intention of publishing a book, but after I had rejected the vast majority of the images that I had taken, I was left with a small number that other people also seemed enthusiastic about. From there it was a relatively small leap of the imagination to consider publication.

However without the encouragement and support of local people this book would never have moved on from that idea stage. I am therefore especially grateful to Tim Hart, proprietor of Hambleton Hall (Hotel); Ed Burrows, General Manager of Barnsdale Lodge Hotel, and David Bagshaw, General Manager of Castle Cement for their committed support.

From all of the fantastically able team at Halsgrove, I specifically need to mention Simon Butler for his initial and continued support and Karen Binaccioni and Sharon O'Inn for their professionalism and great design work.

Finally, but by no means least, thanks to Jamie and Alex for their belief, to Petra for her unselfish enthusiasm and to Bri for consistently pulling the duvet cover off.

Just after sunset, low light gives extra
emphasis to the rising crescent moon.

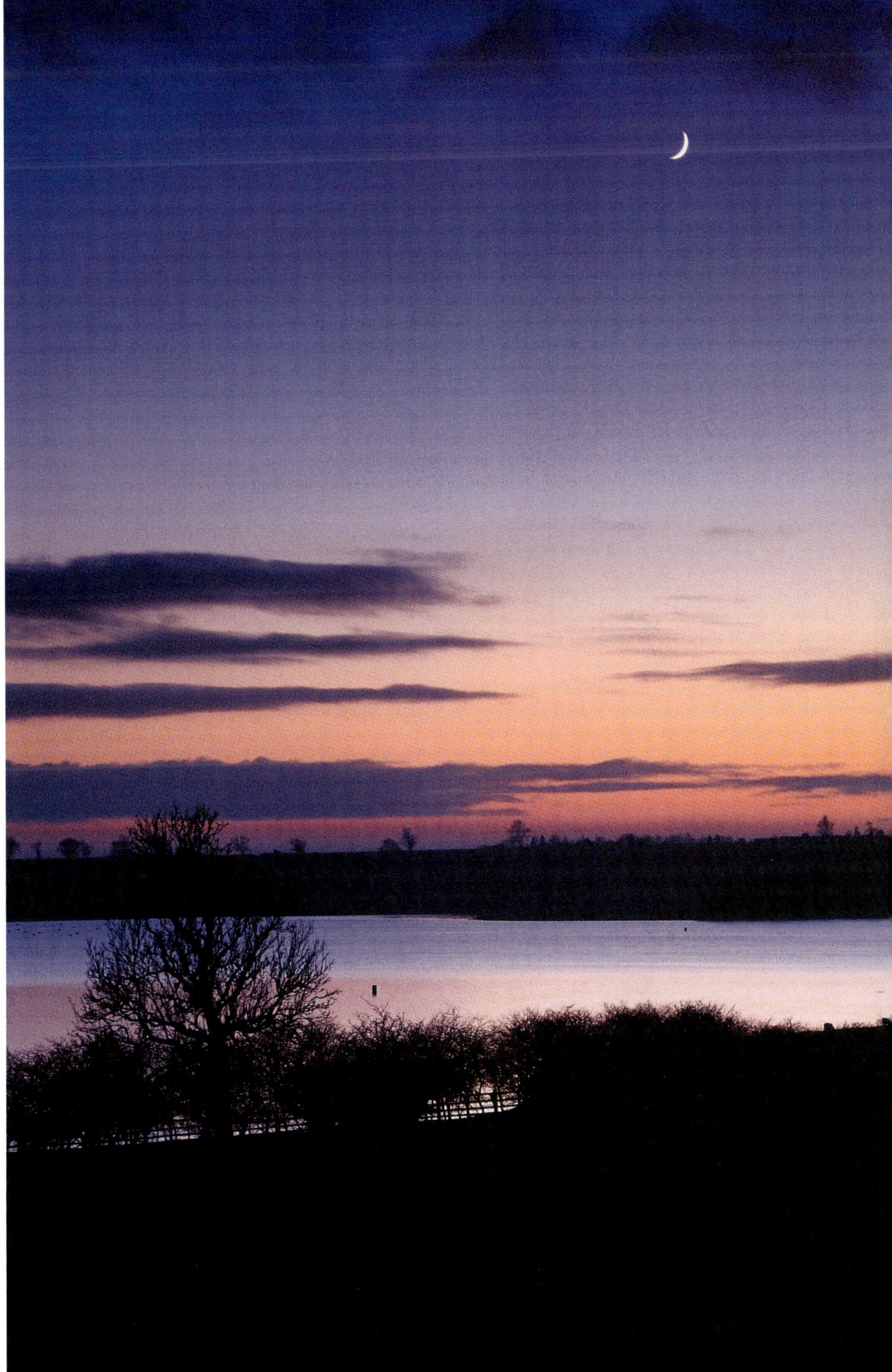

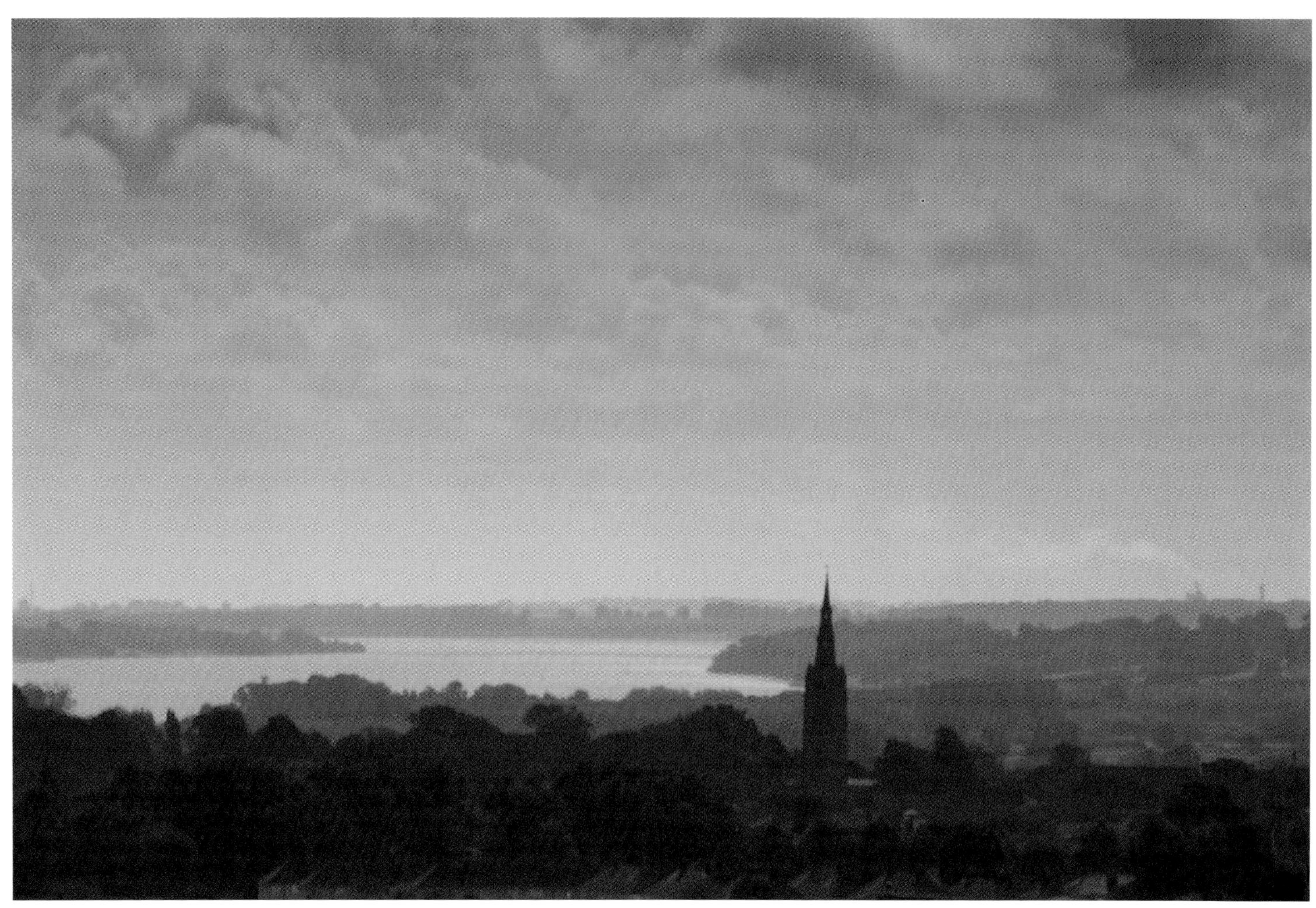

Morning haze adds atmosphere to this view of the northern leg of the Water, taken from above Barleythorpe.

RUTLAND WATER

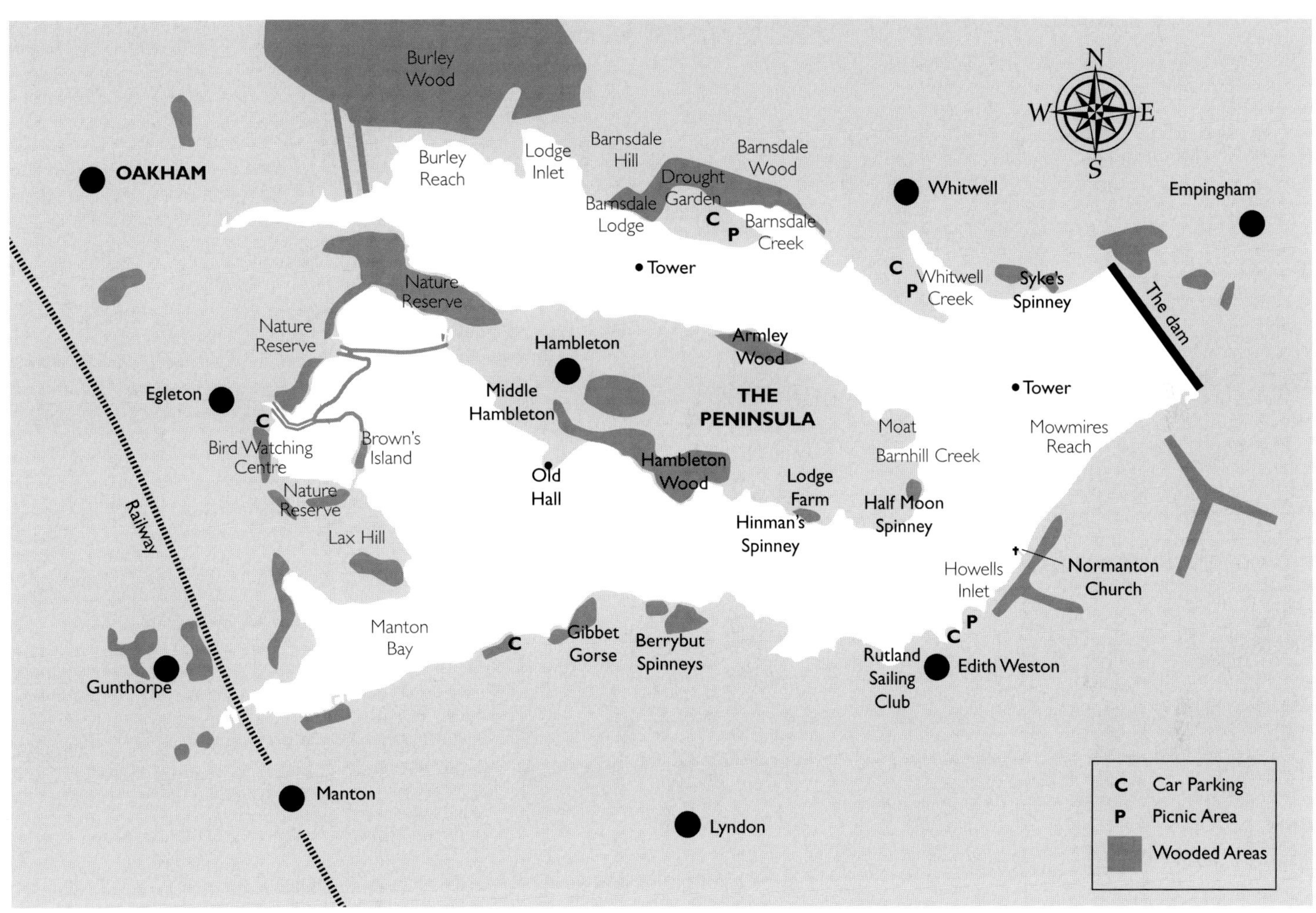

INTRODUCTION

A large part of landscape photography is being in the right place at the right time. The question, of course, is how to achieve that. In the time that it took me to collect the images for this book and in the months before that when I was teaching myself the basic skills, I have learned at first hand the frustration of our unpredictable weather.

As I became more familiar with the detail of the reservoir landscape, the times of the sunrise and sunset, the arc of the sun during the day throughout the year and the compass bearings of the images that I wanted to capture, I originally assumed it was then simply a matter of waiting for the weather forecast to predict the kind of conditions I needed. I have lost count of the number of times I left the house at (for me) an ungodly hour, in the pitch black, only to return home later without having taken a single shot. On those rare occasions when the weather was kind and all my detailed planning came together, it was still not unusual for the image to be disappointing.

In fact my frustration became so great that I have virtually given up this method of working and have adopted the 'let's go and see' approach. I simply choose the specific location and make the most of whatever conditions I find when I arrive there, at whatever time. This works so much better for me – I am no longer frustrated at not being in the right place at the right time, or distracted by the worry of missing a better image to be had elsewhere. I simply commit to making the most of where I am. As a result I look harder, study the place more conscientiously, and almost always end up with something I could never have envisaged with all the planning in the world.

It is therefore true for me that there is always something to appreciate in the landscape if I look hard enough.

I hope that these images will illustrate just how differently Rutland Water can appear at different times of the day through the seasons of the year, and therefore encourage others to see the area around the Water in a new light, or preferably many new lights in many different conditions.

THE PHOTOGRAPHS

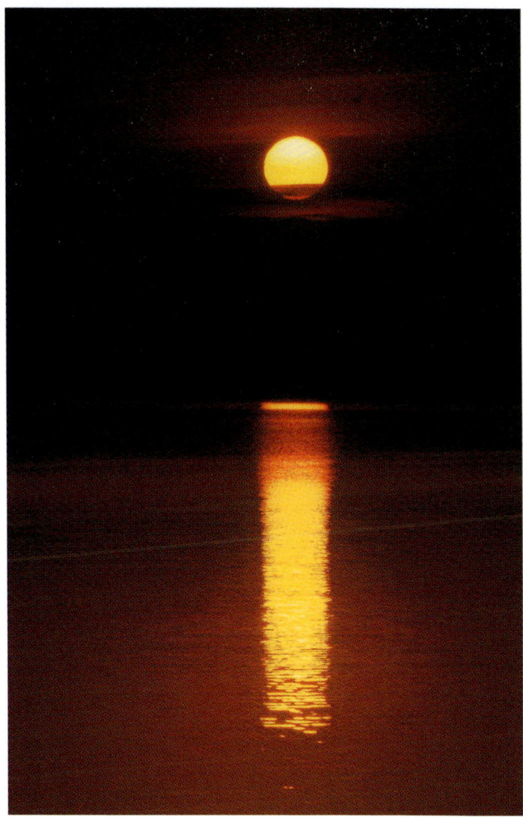

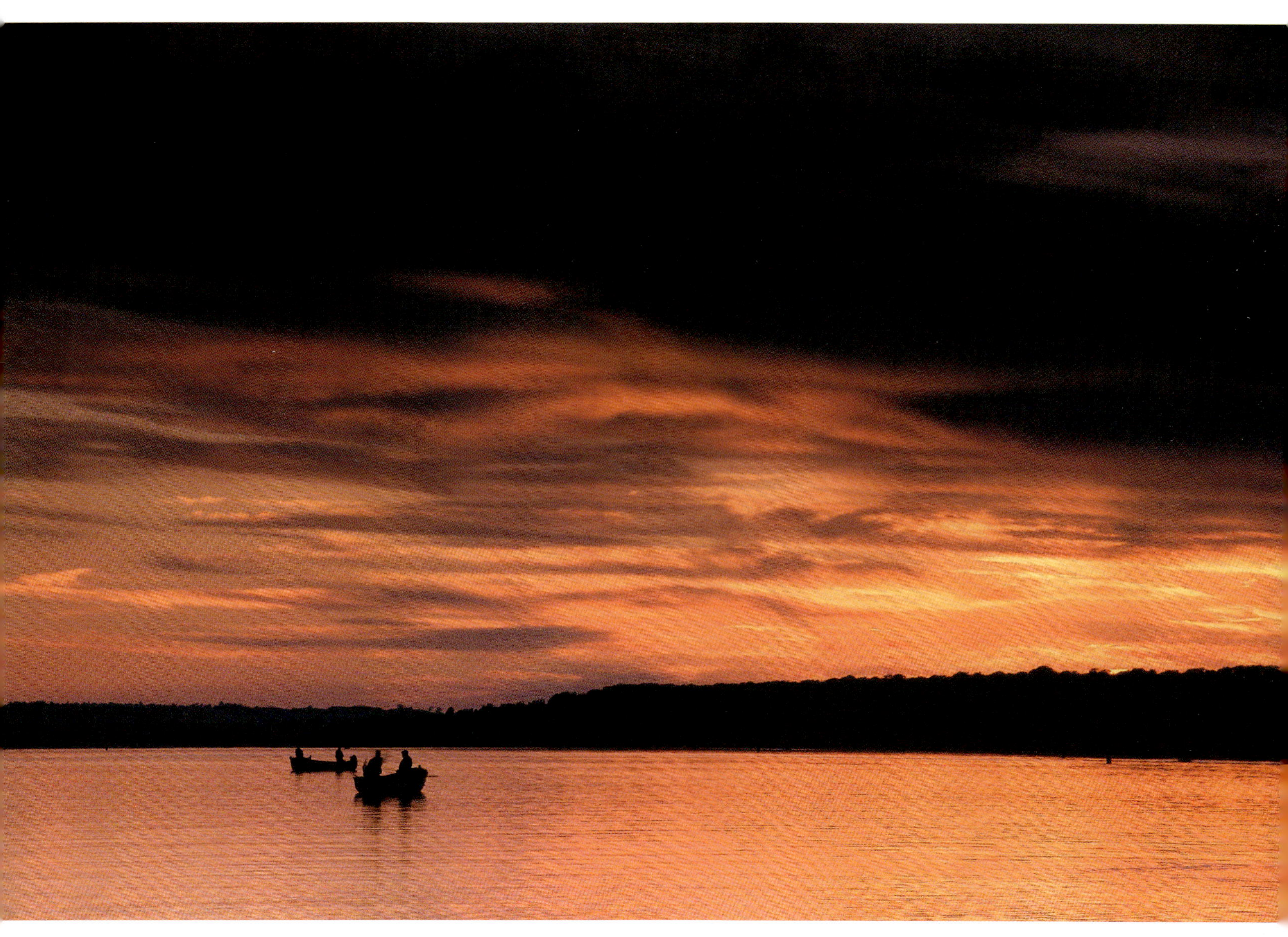

A classic early summer sunset.

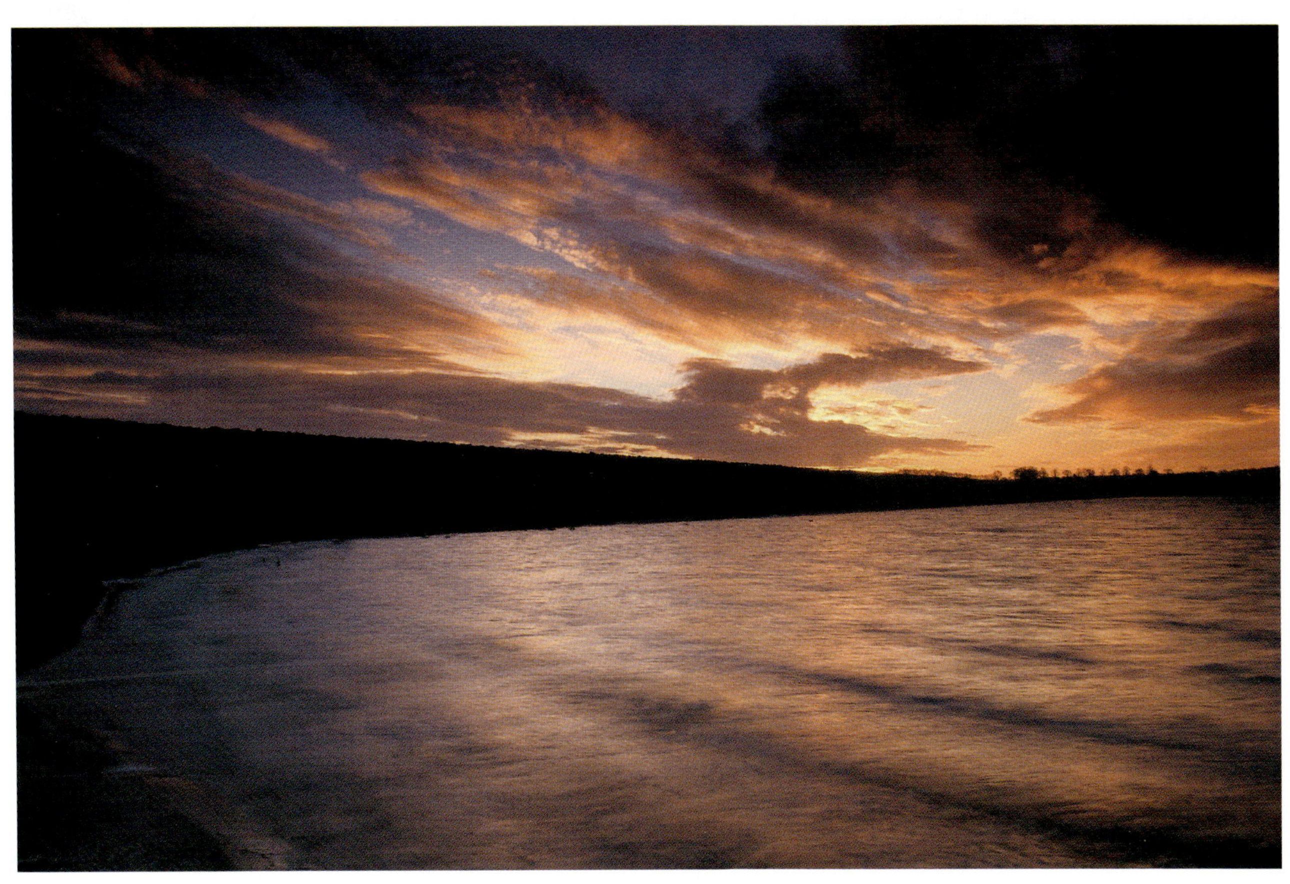

Sunrise over the southern end of the Dam.

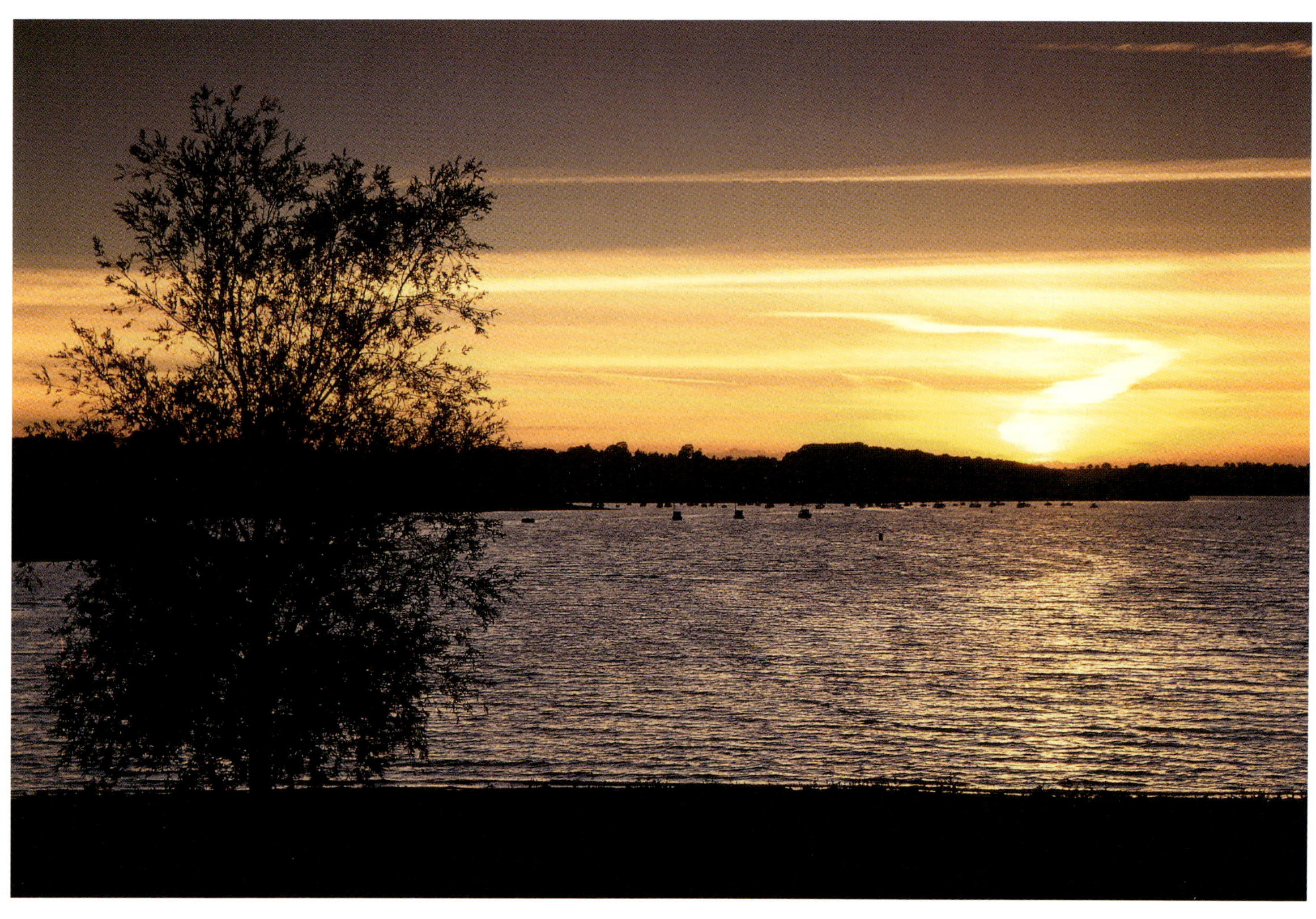

Sunset at Rutland Water Sailing Club, my daughter's choice for the front cover.

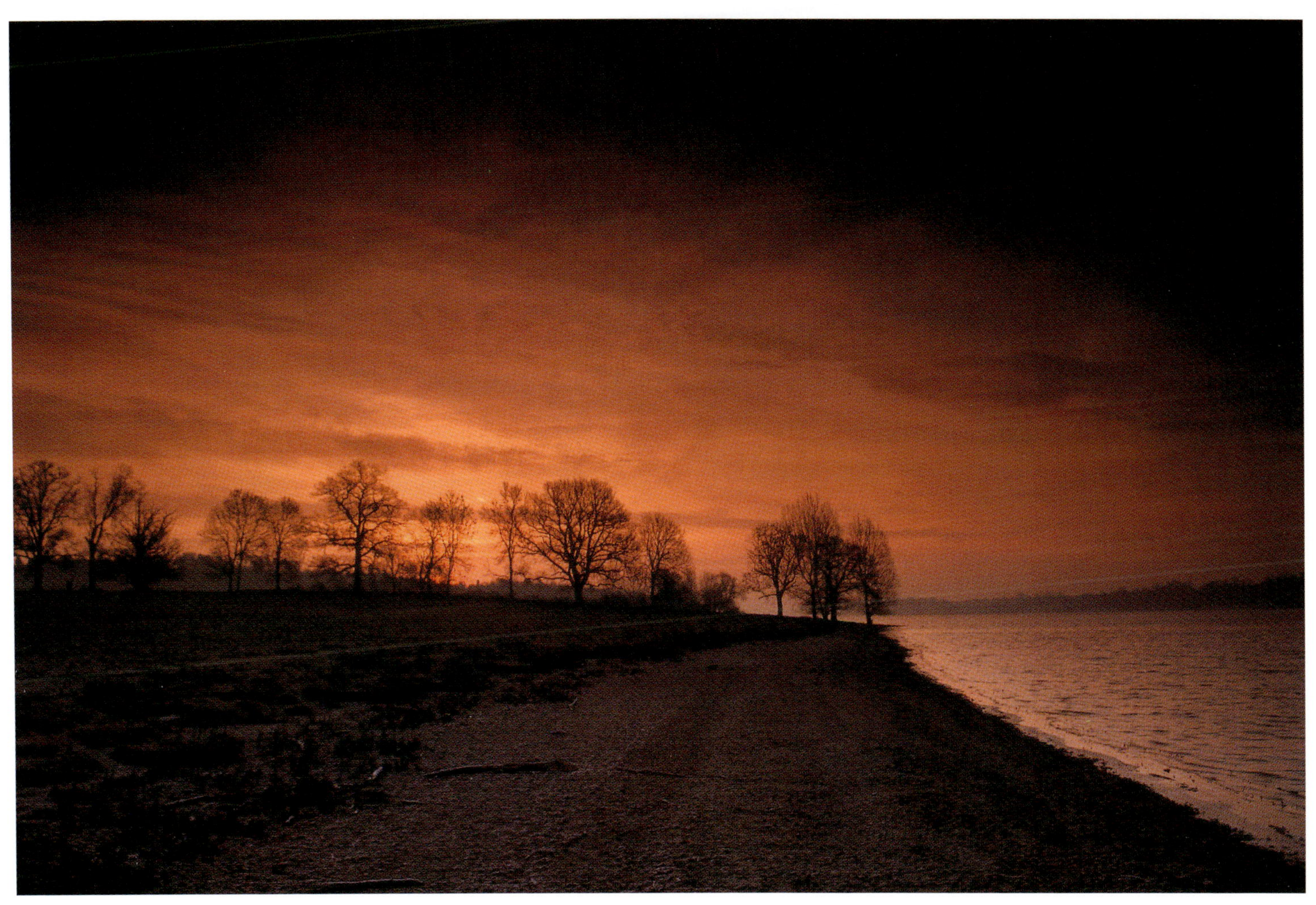

Dawn at Burley Reach.

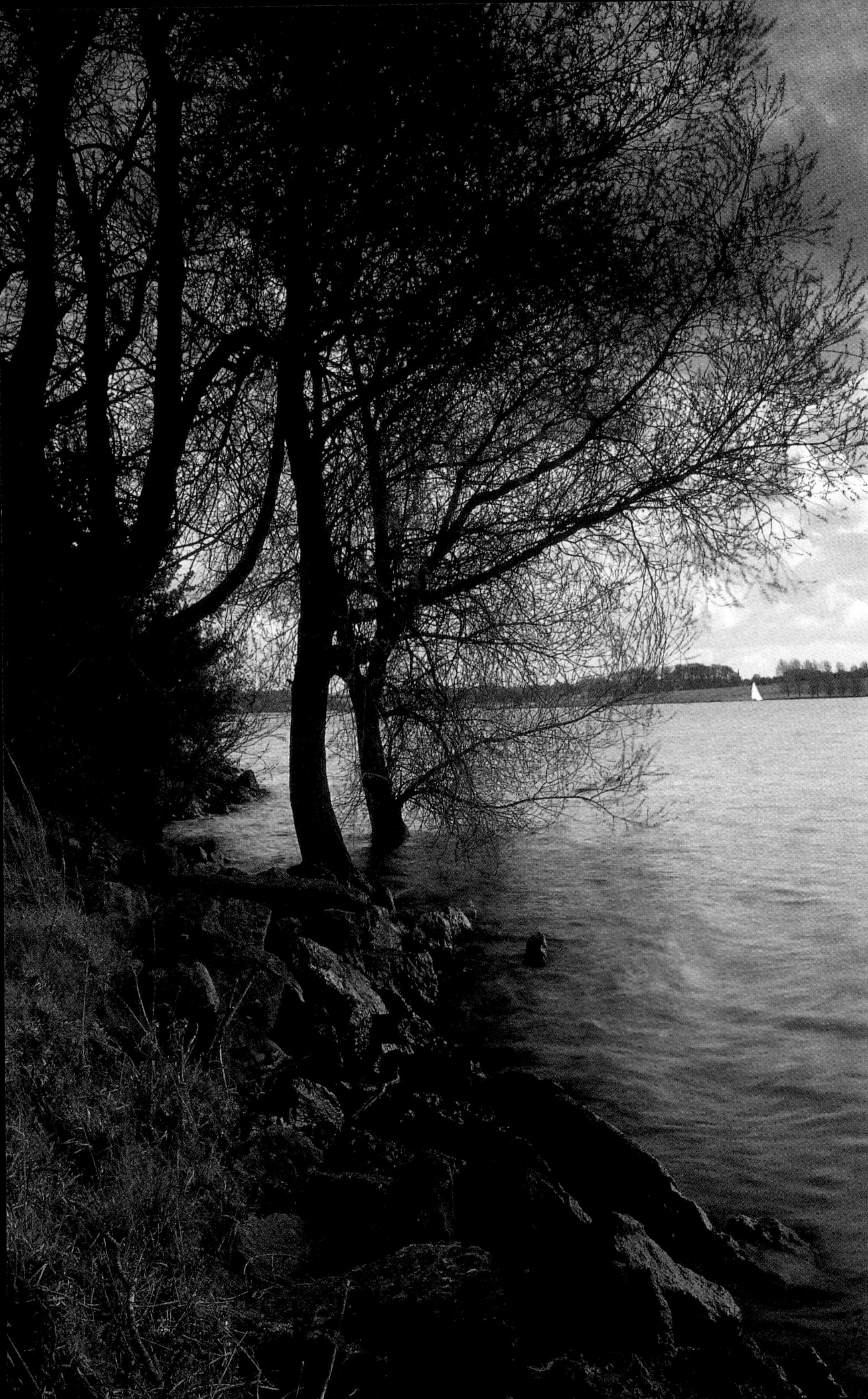

Sailing at Whitwell.

Lifting fog at Syke's Spinney.

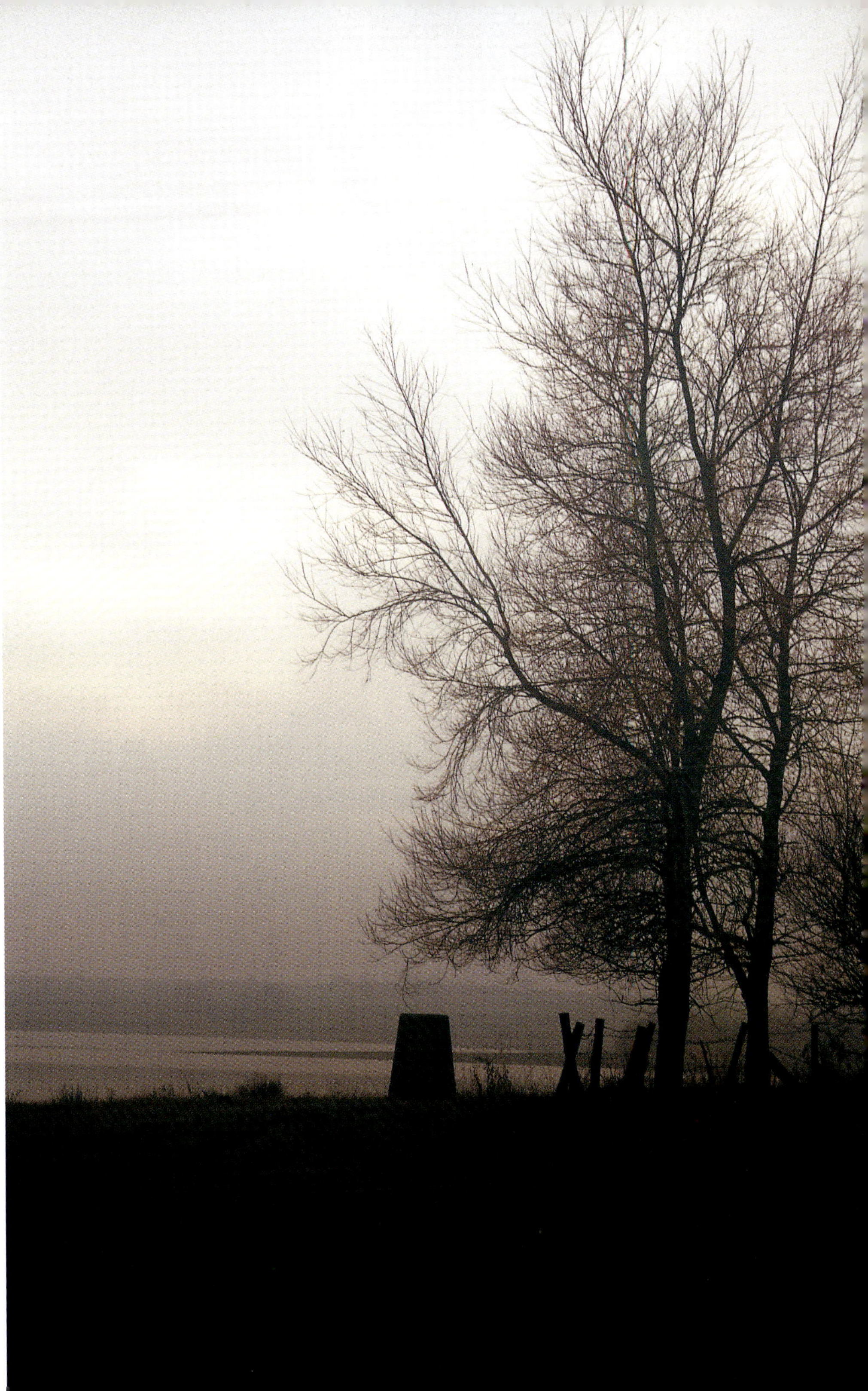

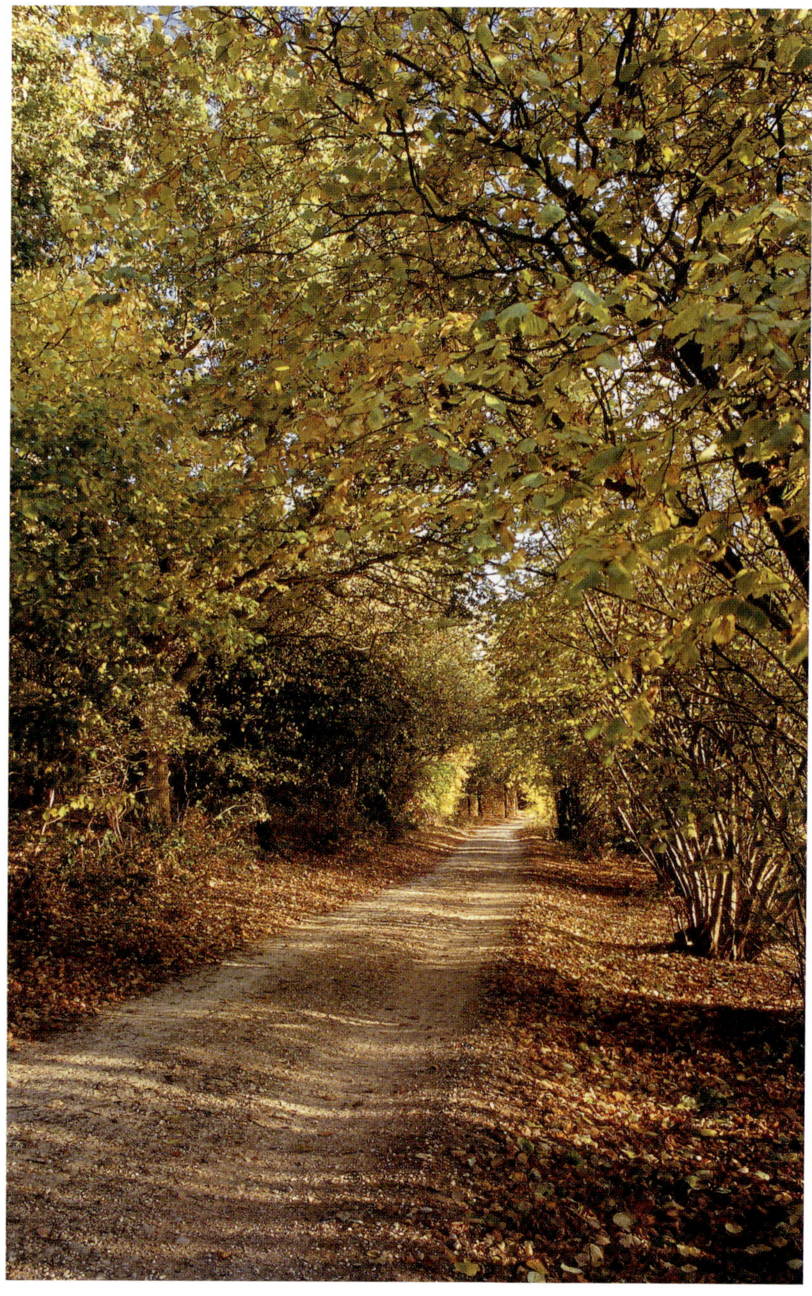

An invitation to follow the path through Hambleton Wood.

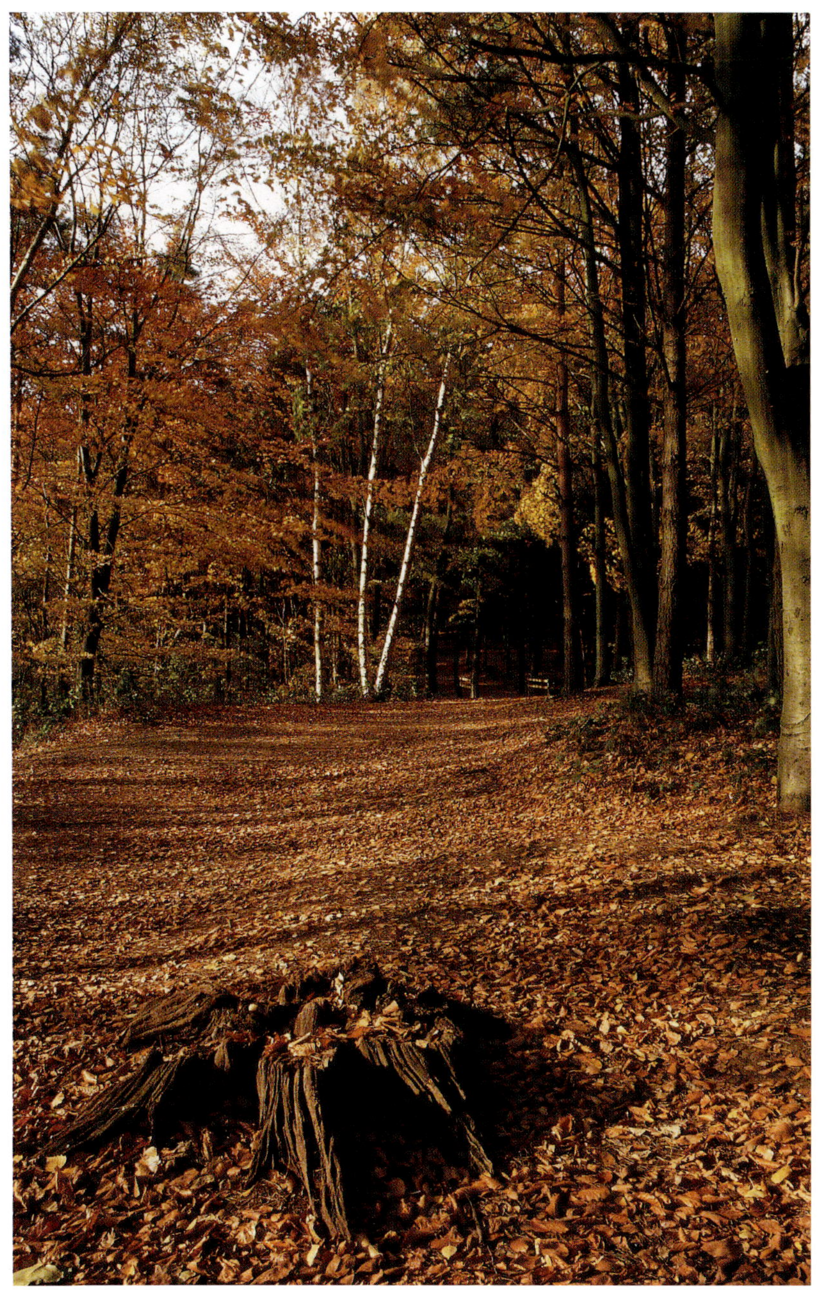

Barnsdale Wood on a glorious
November day.

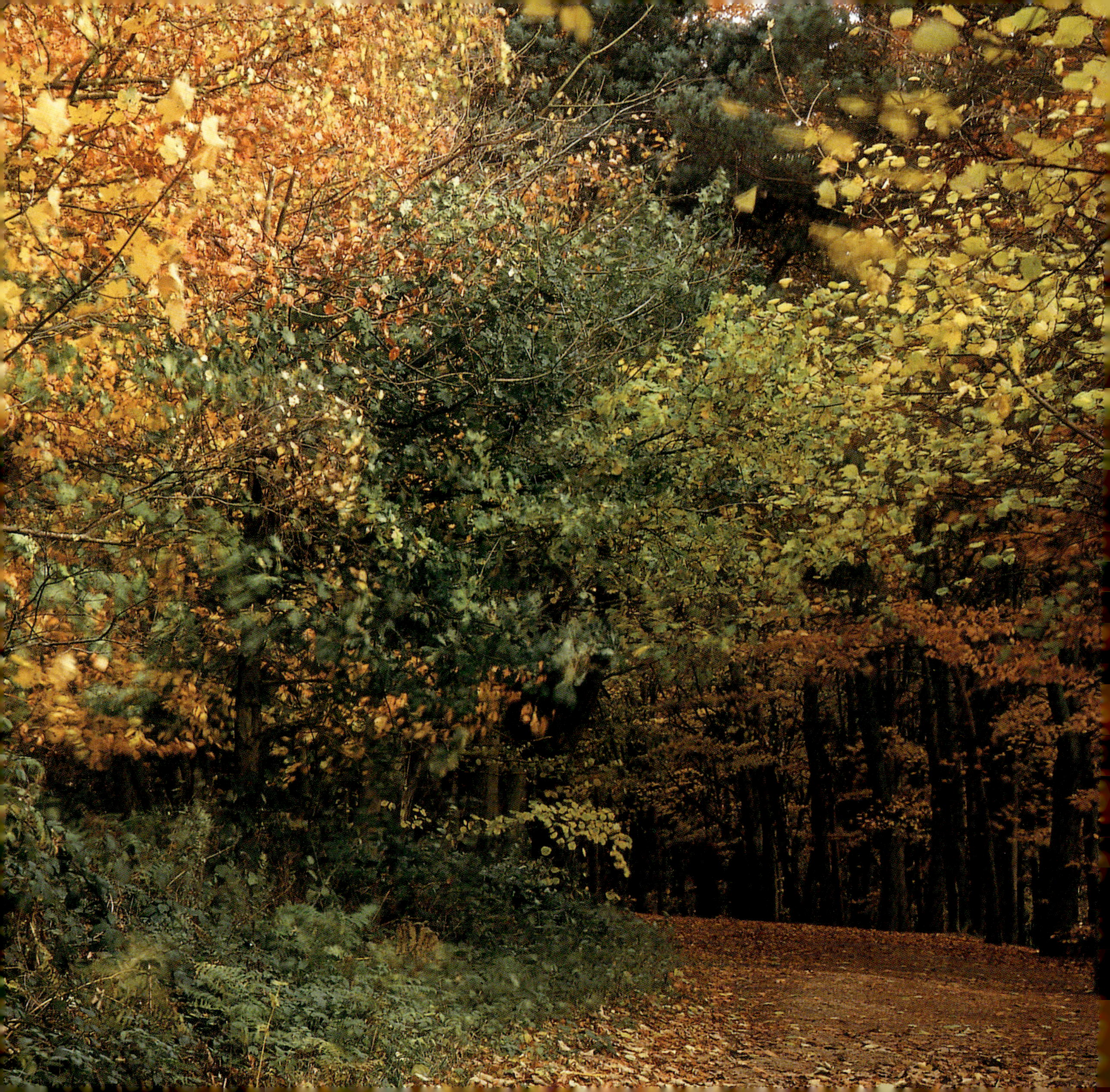

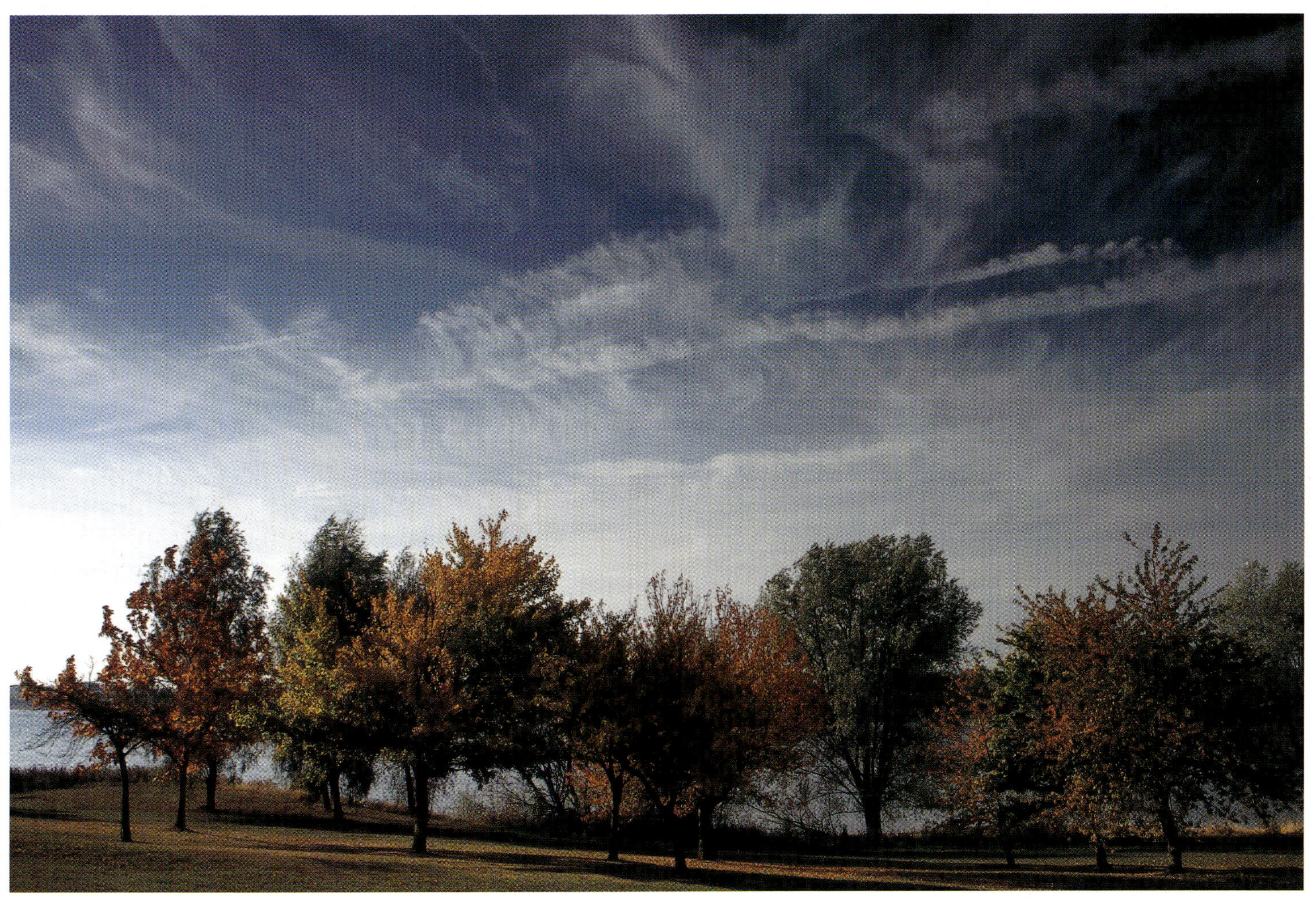

The busy, whispy sky complements the Autumn colours of the trees.

Opposite page: Autumn colours.

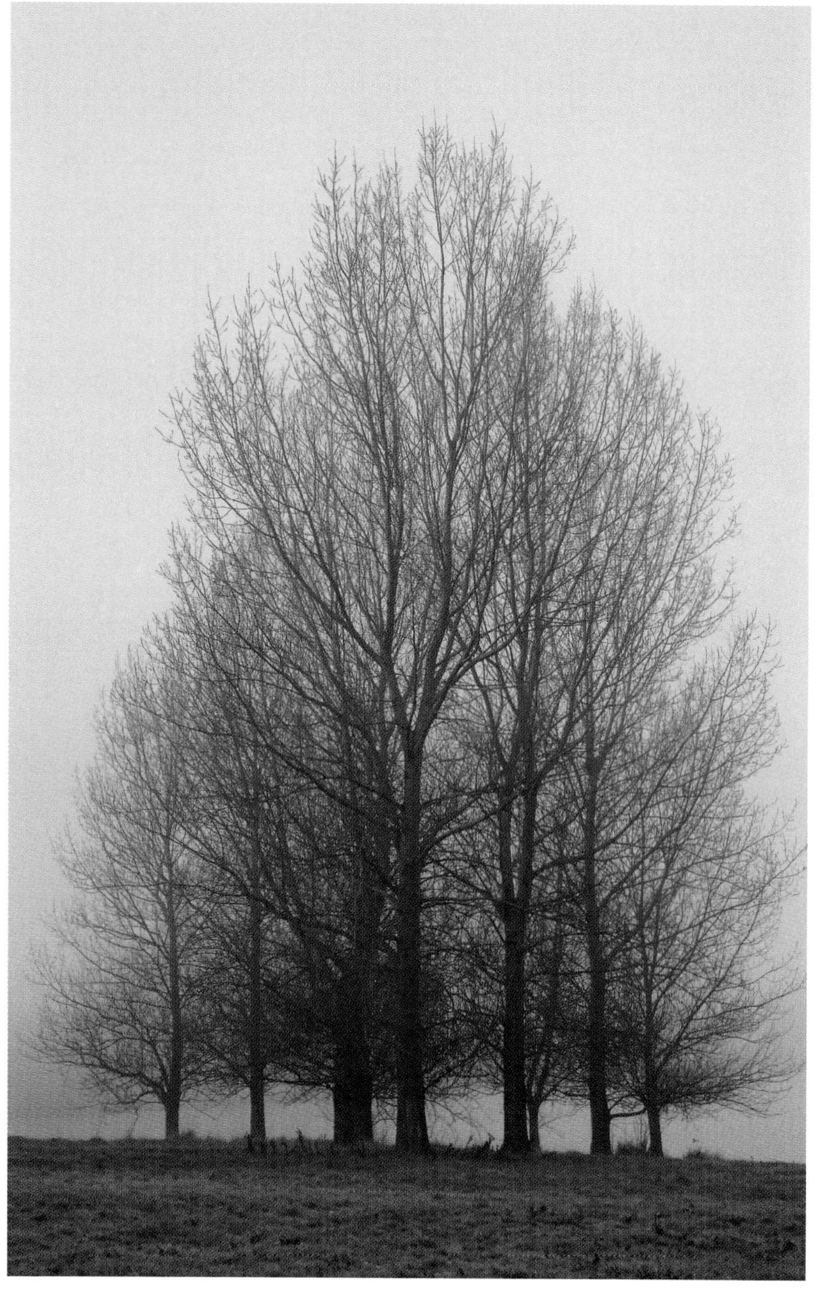

The effect of the heavy fog is to isolate
these trees from their surroundings.

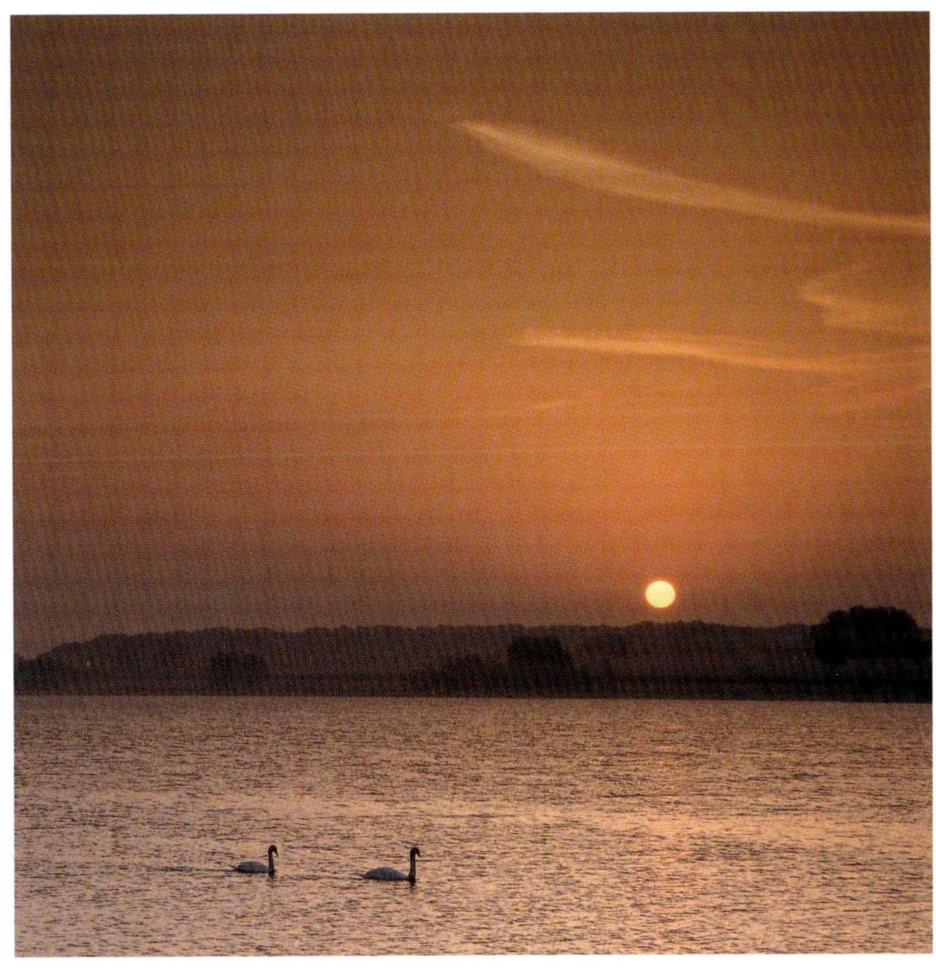

The swans drifting into the picture just as the sun cleared the horizon
don't just make the composition – they become the subject itself.

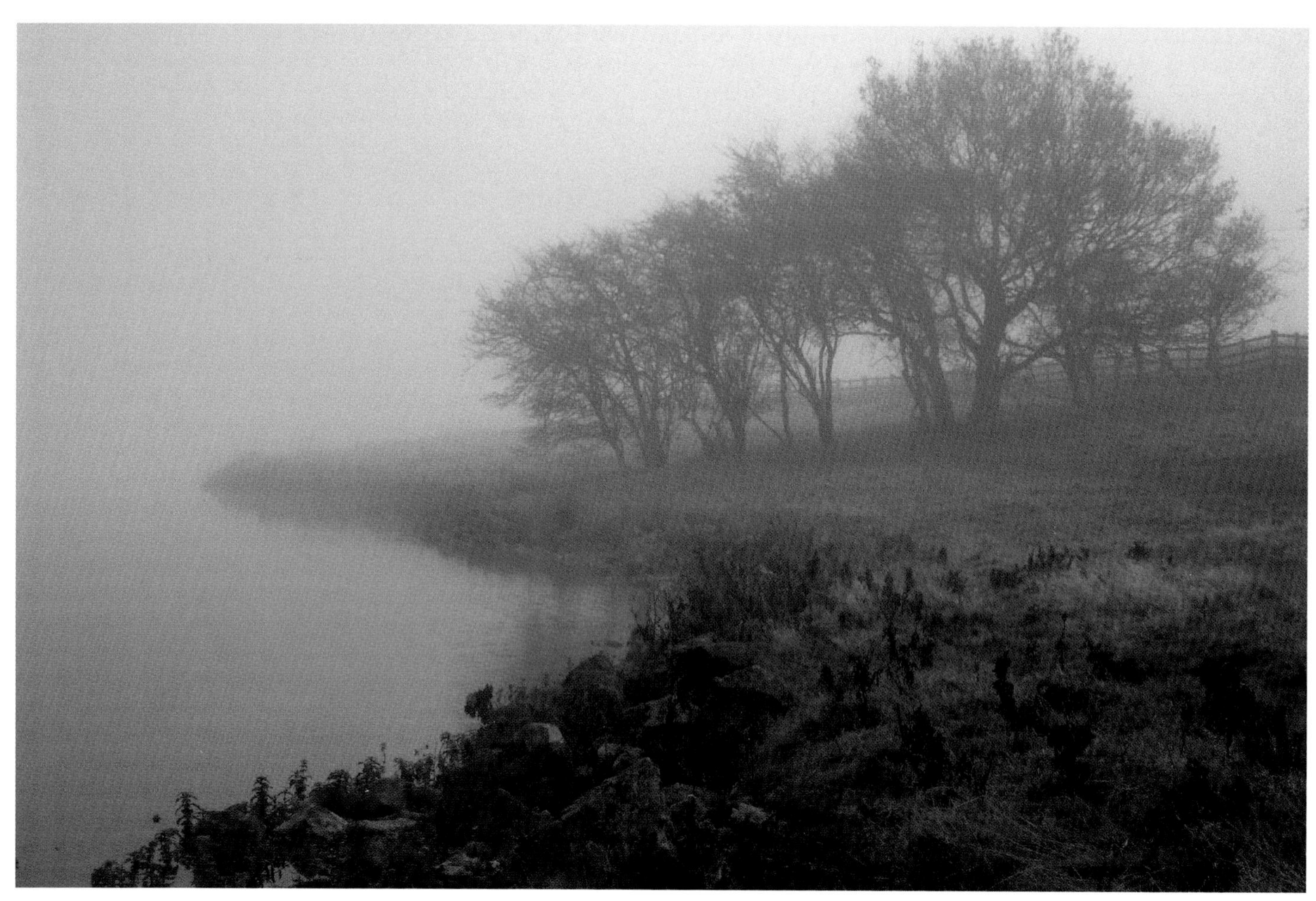

A cold and foggy morning on the peninsula.

Only a slight ripple in the foreground water
disturbs an almost surreal symmetry.

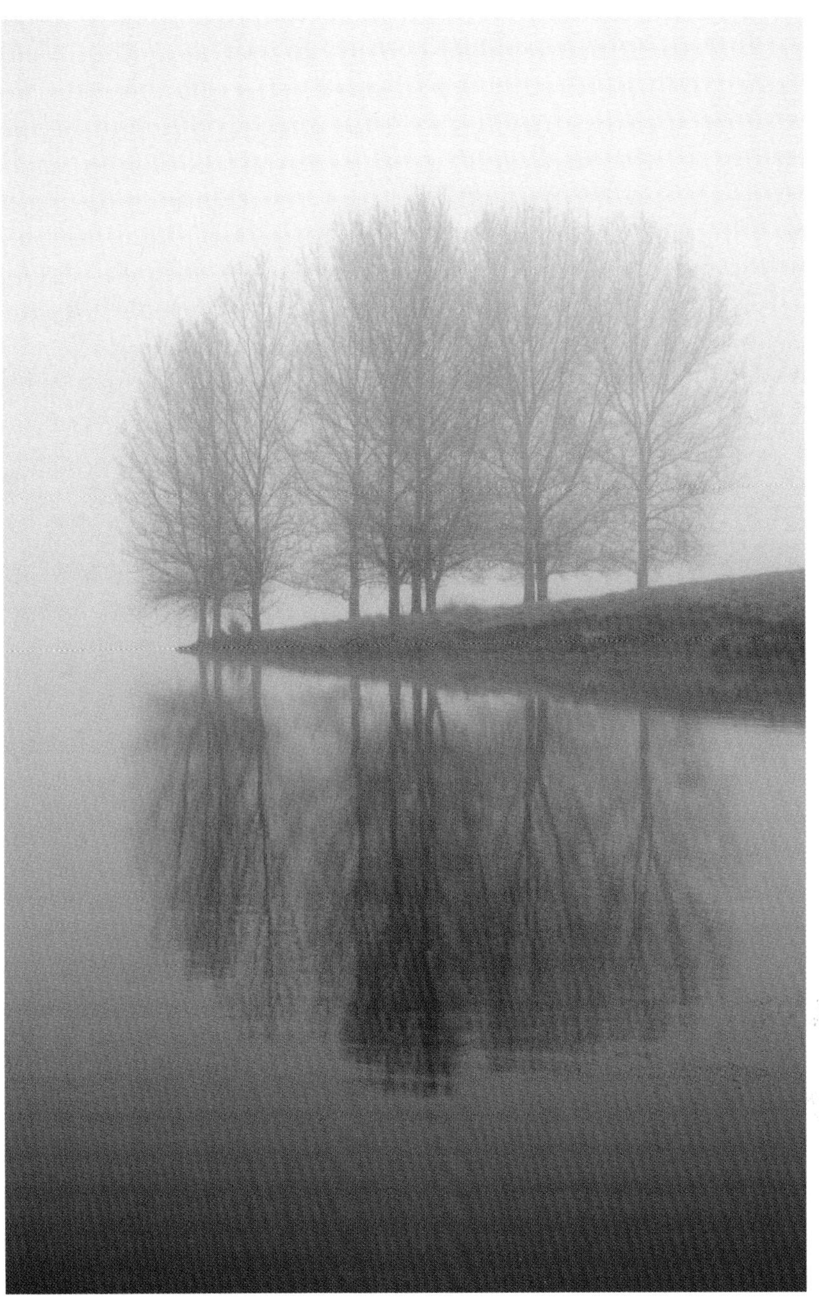

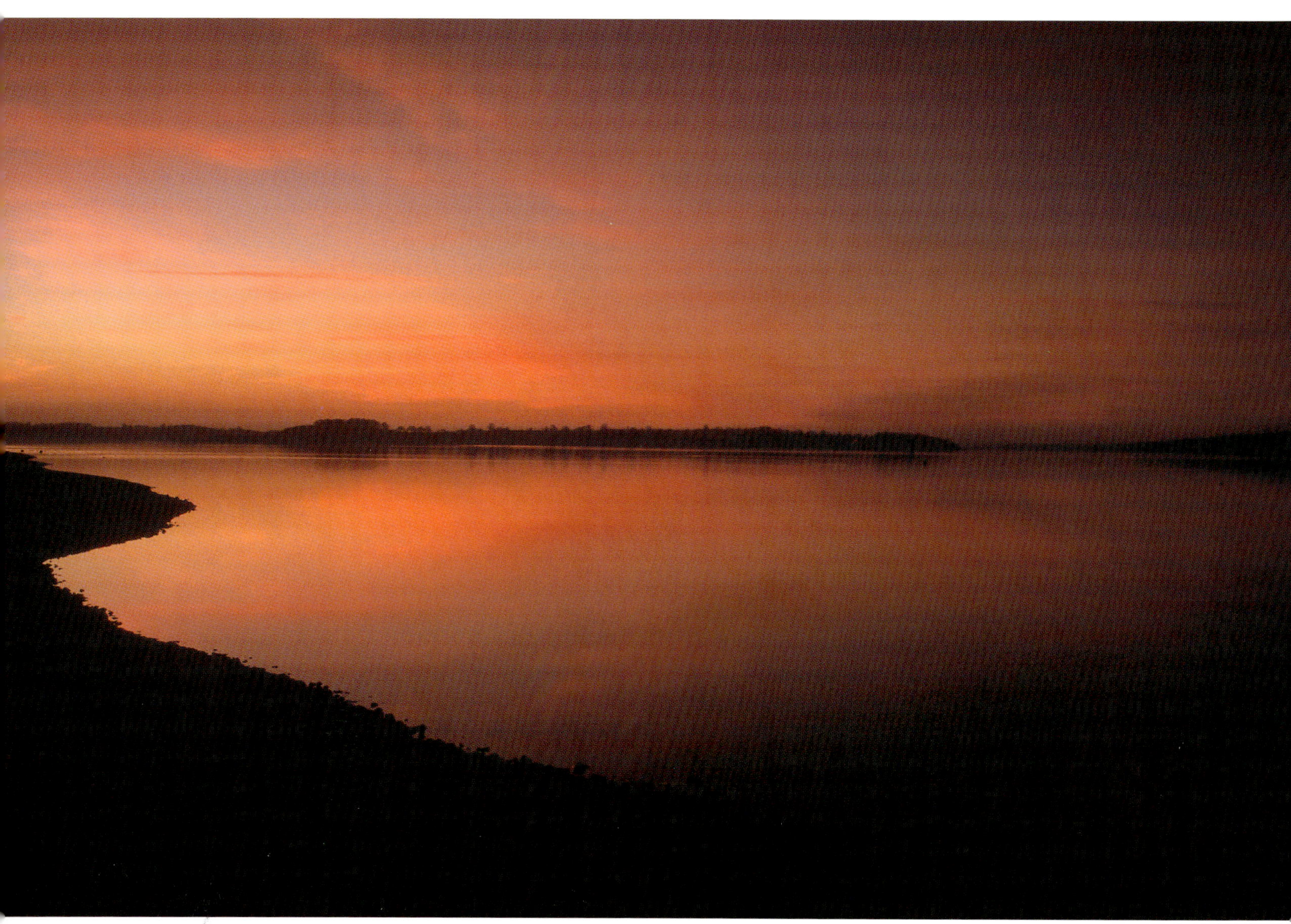

The water was so still on this evening, the reflection is mirror-like.

'...communicating with an awareness
outside the range of everday life.'

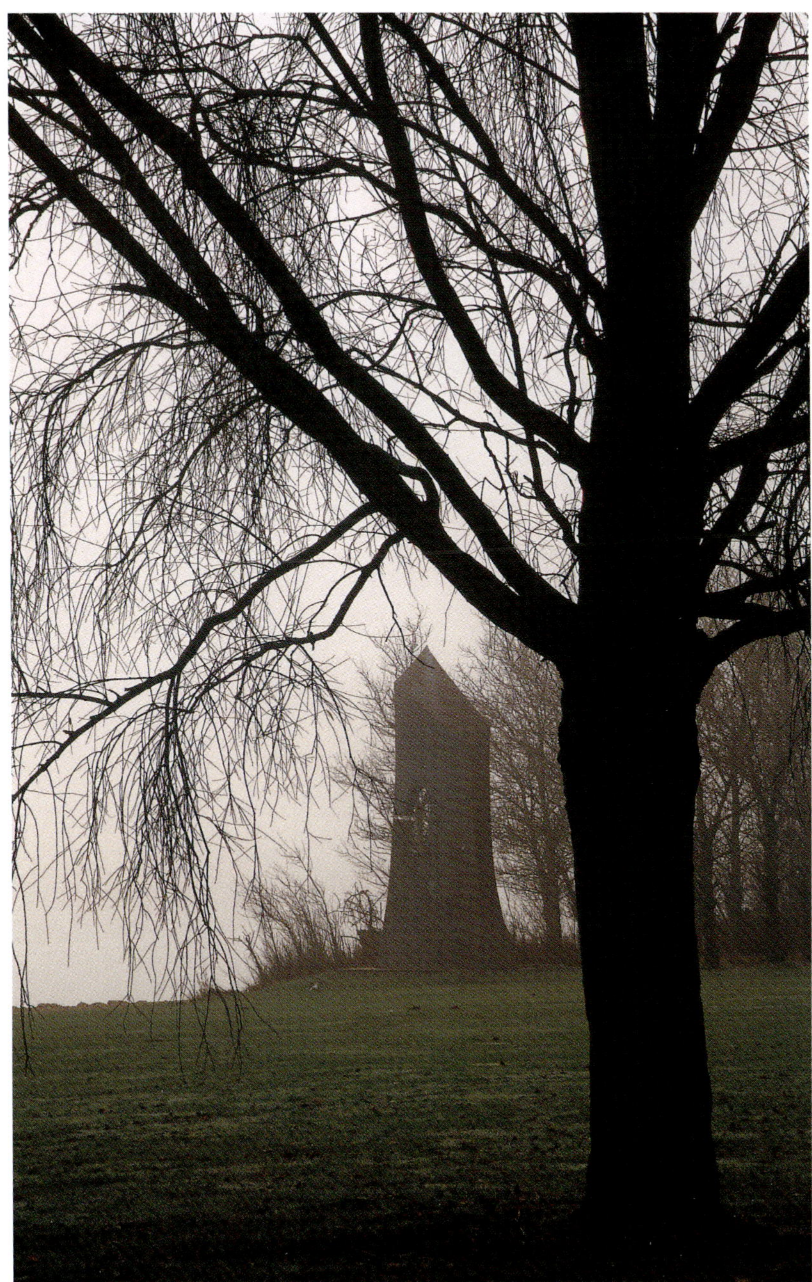

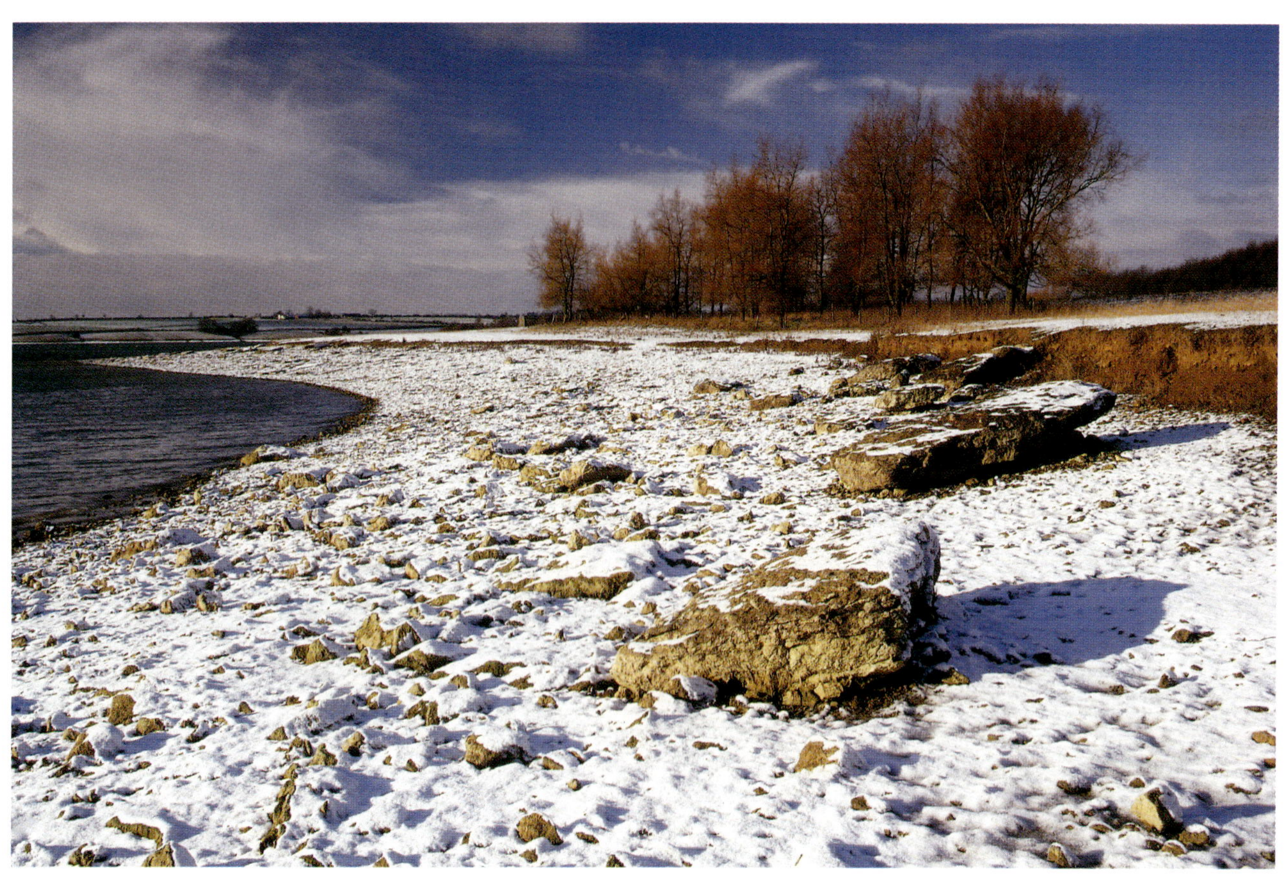

All the lines in this view lead towards the distant house on the peninsula…

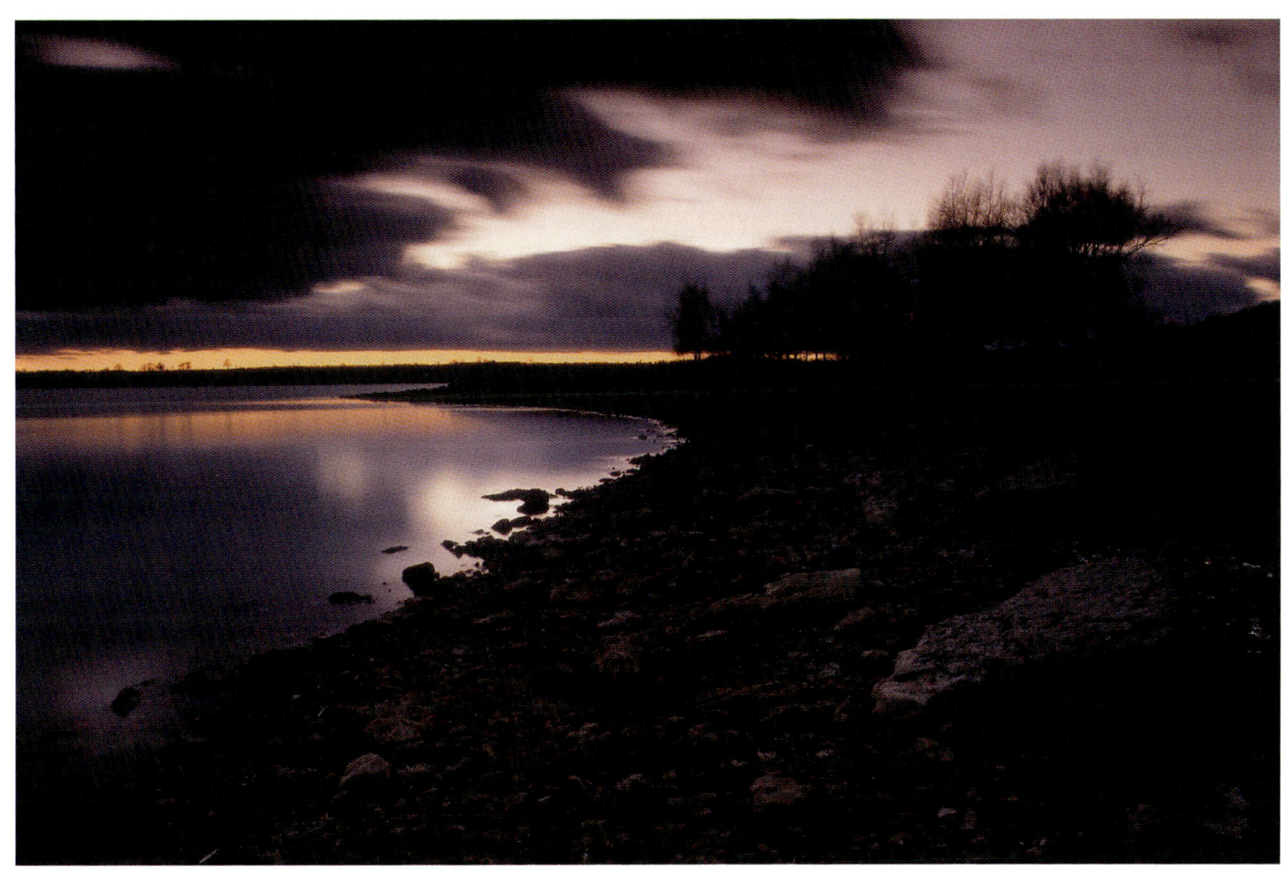

...and towards the fast-moving clouds.

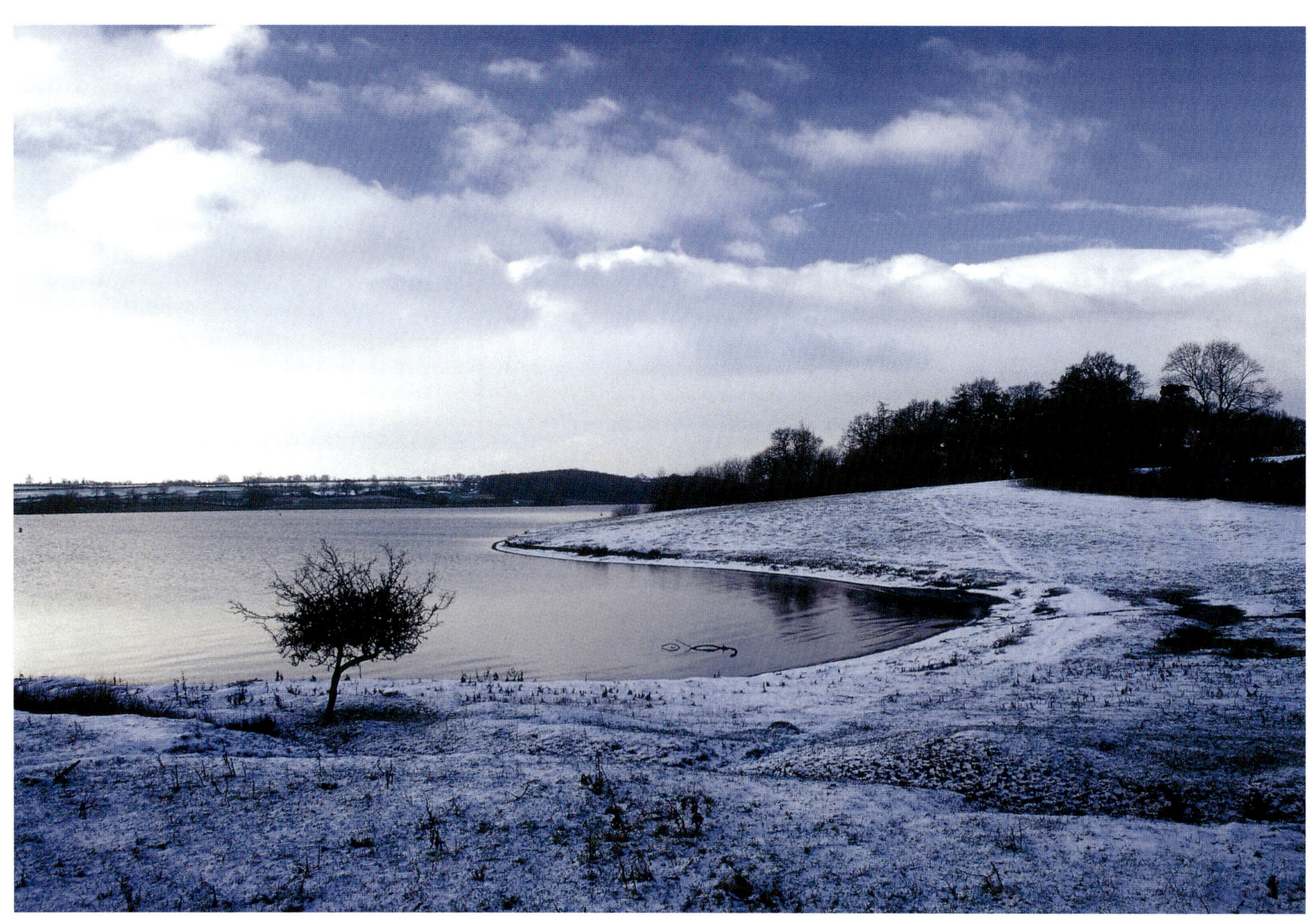

A bright January day on Hambleton Peninsula.

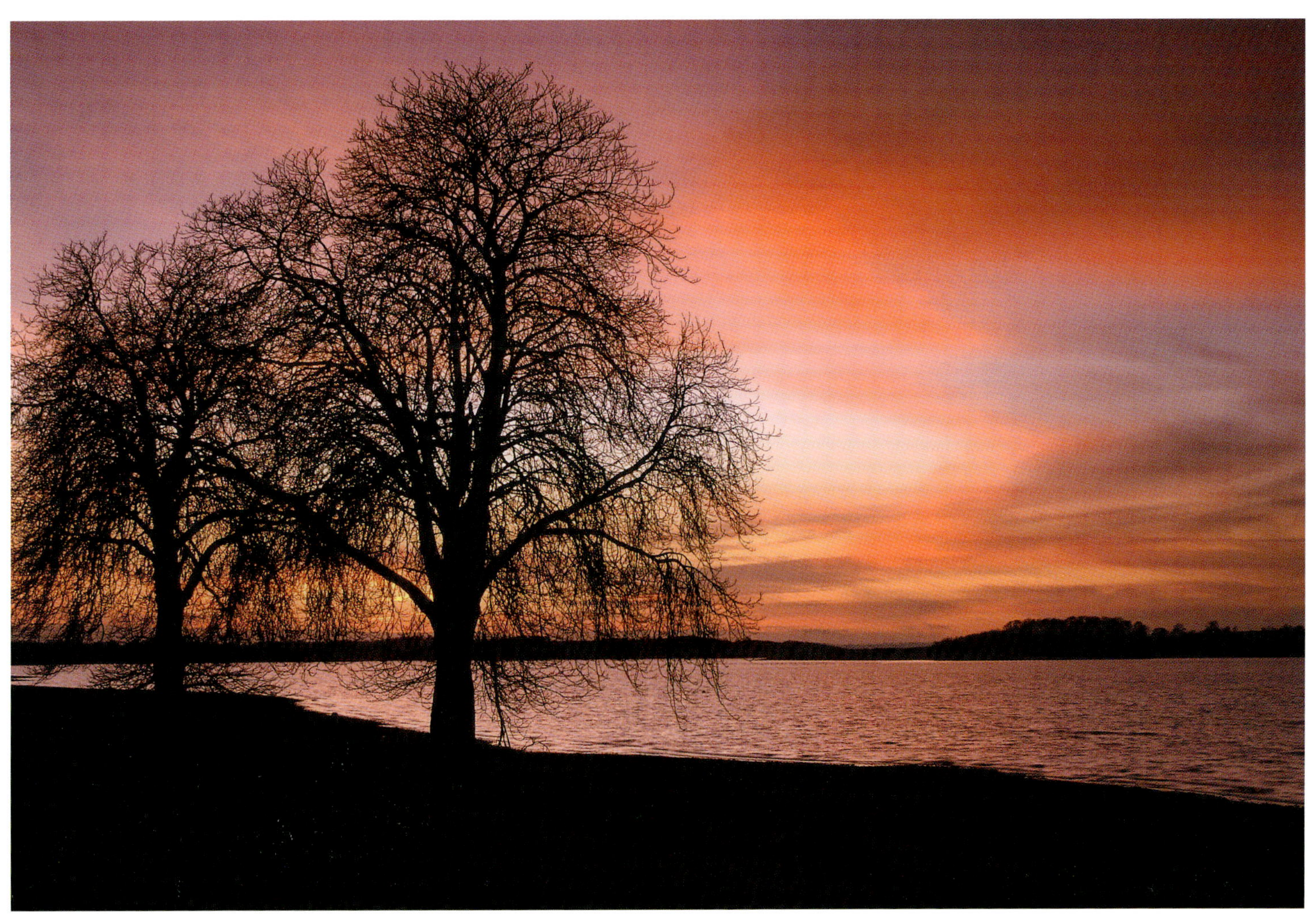

Rather here than…?

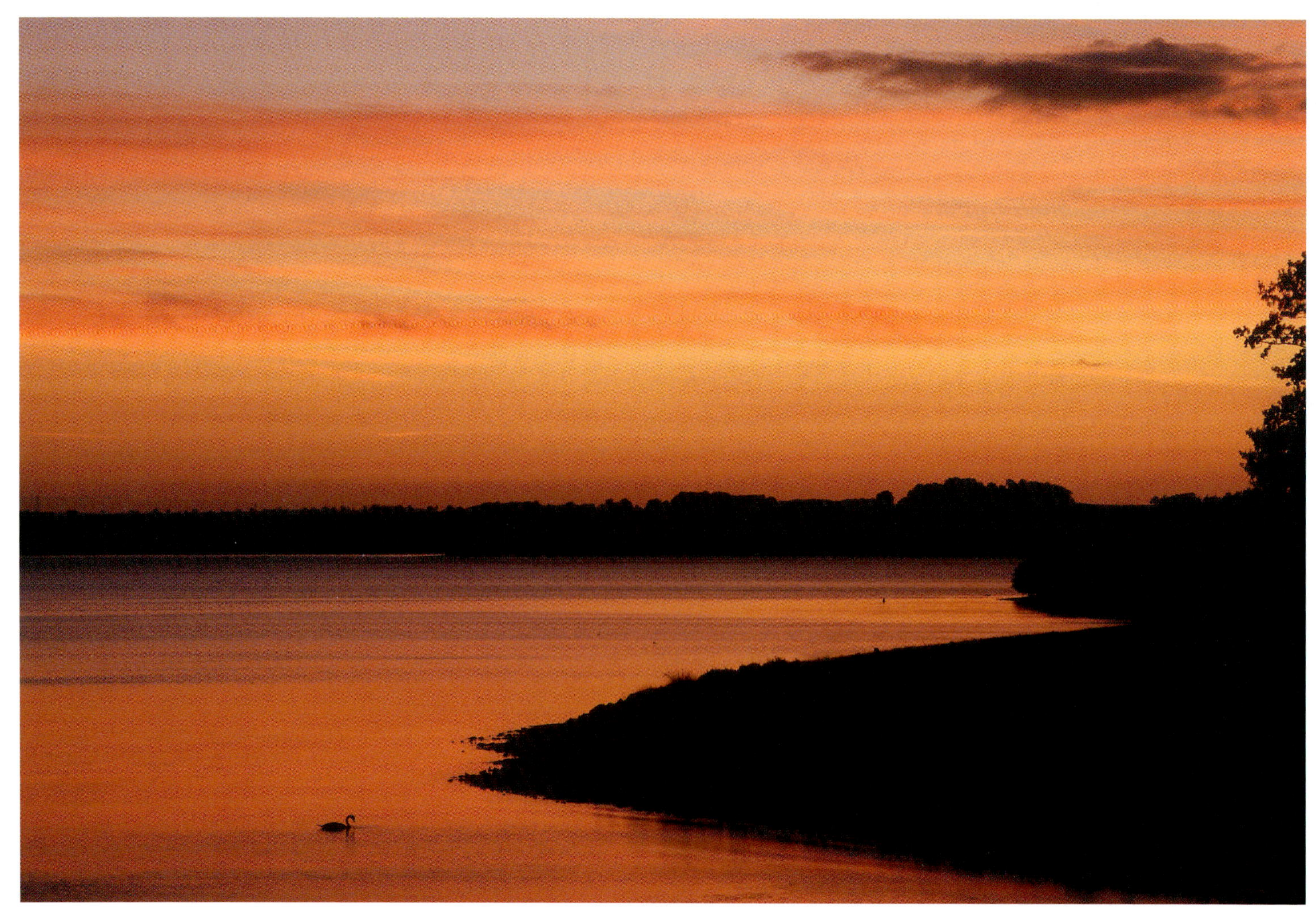

Solitude.

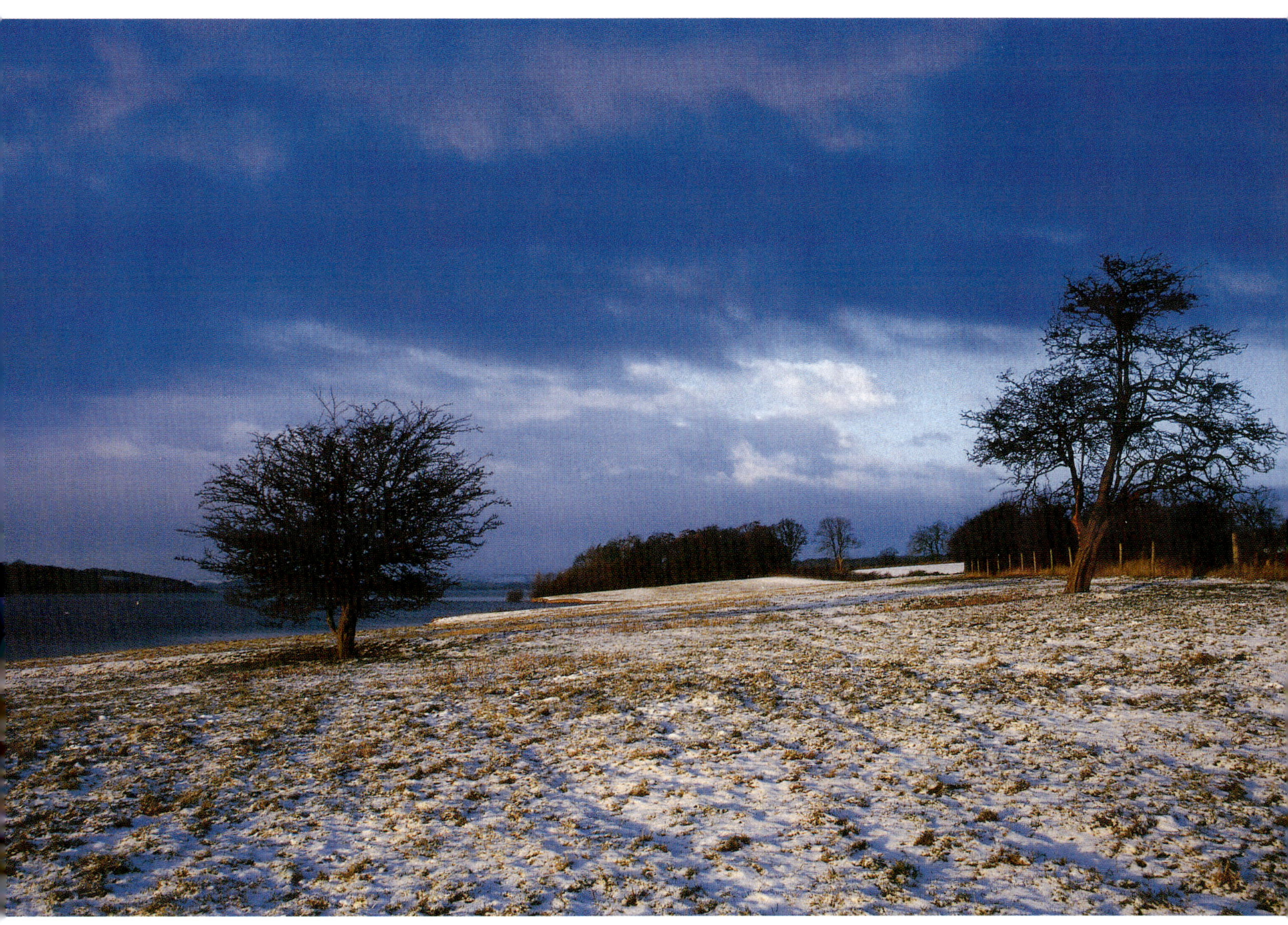

The blue sky reflected in the snow emphasizes the coldness of this January morning.

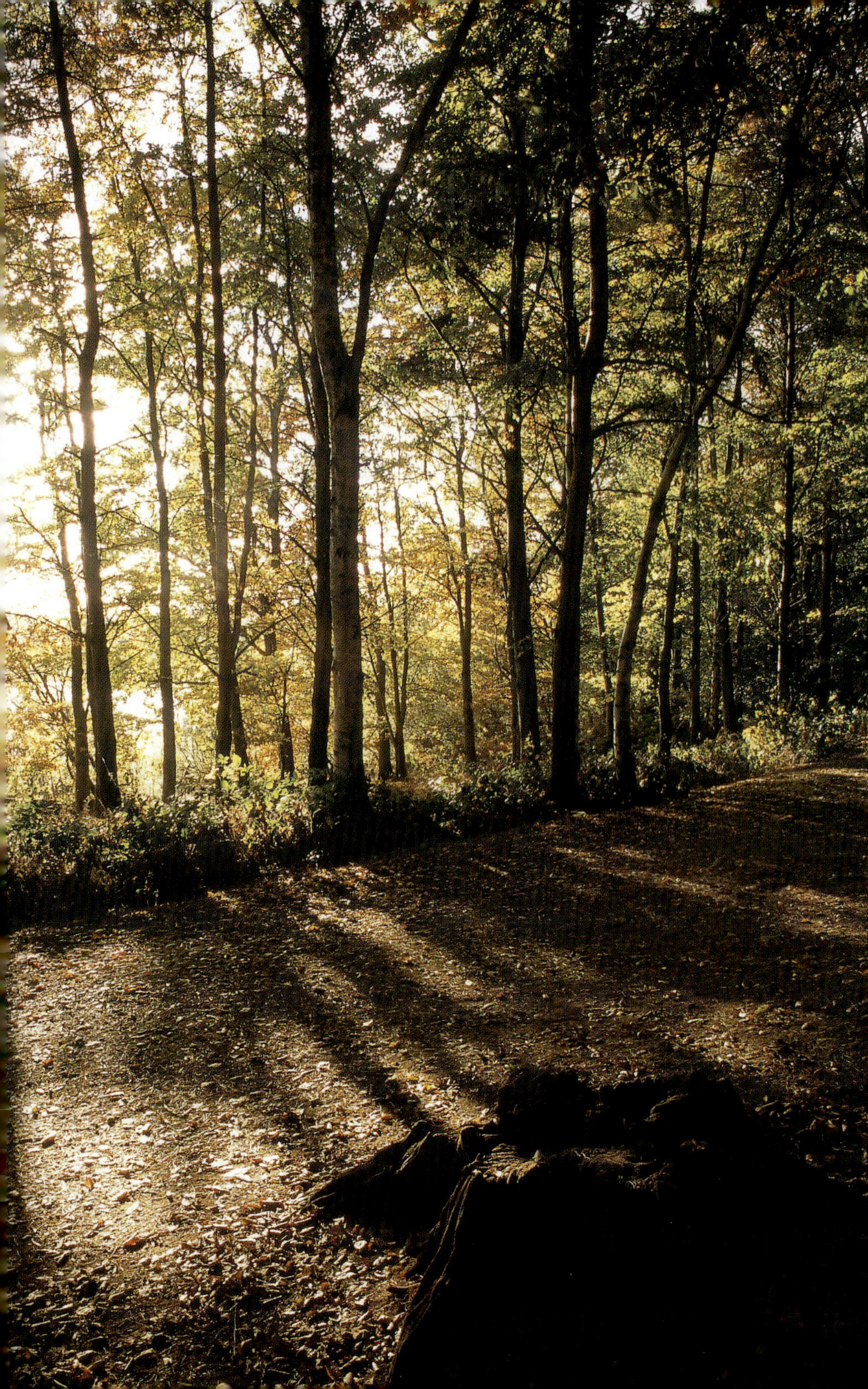

Along the path through
Barnsdale Wood.

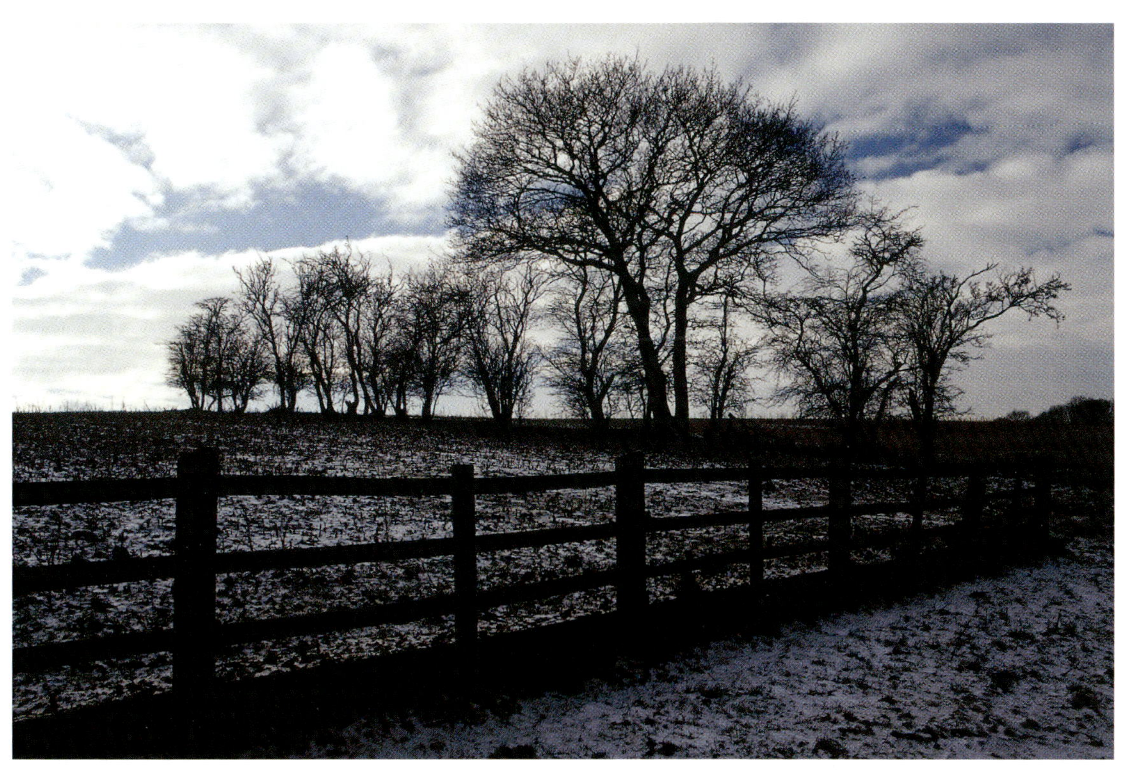

Winter at Barnhill Creek.

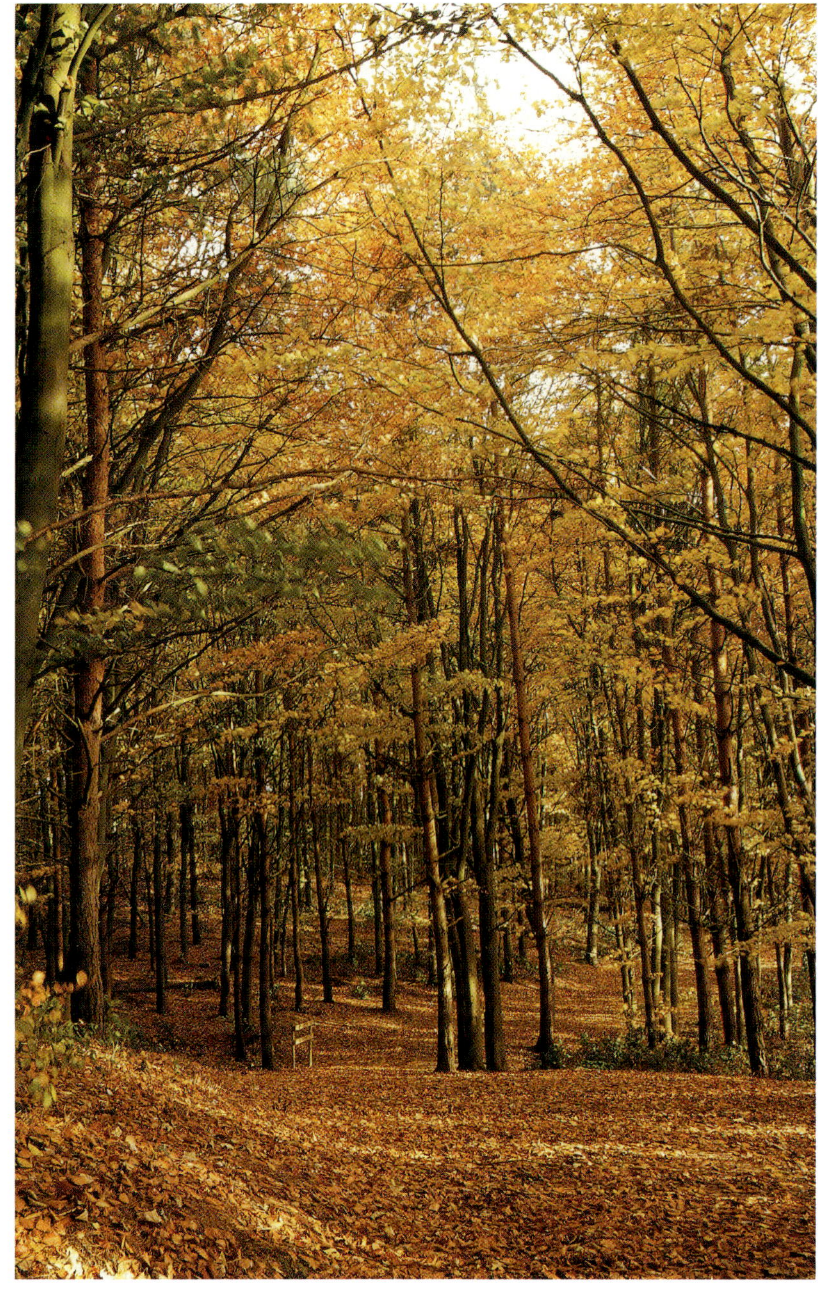

A leafy carpet in
Barnsdale Wood.

Autumn in
Berrybut Spinneys.

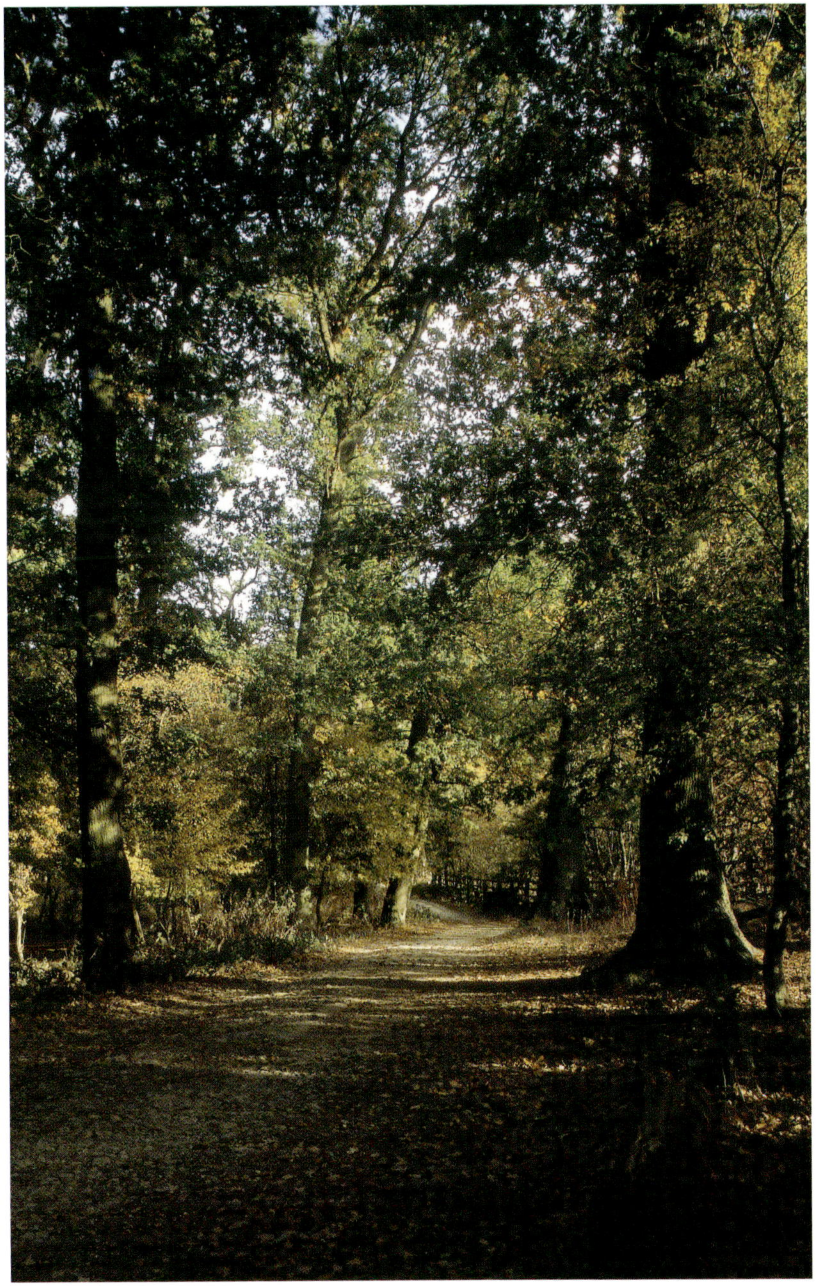

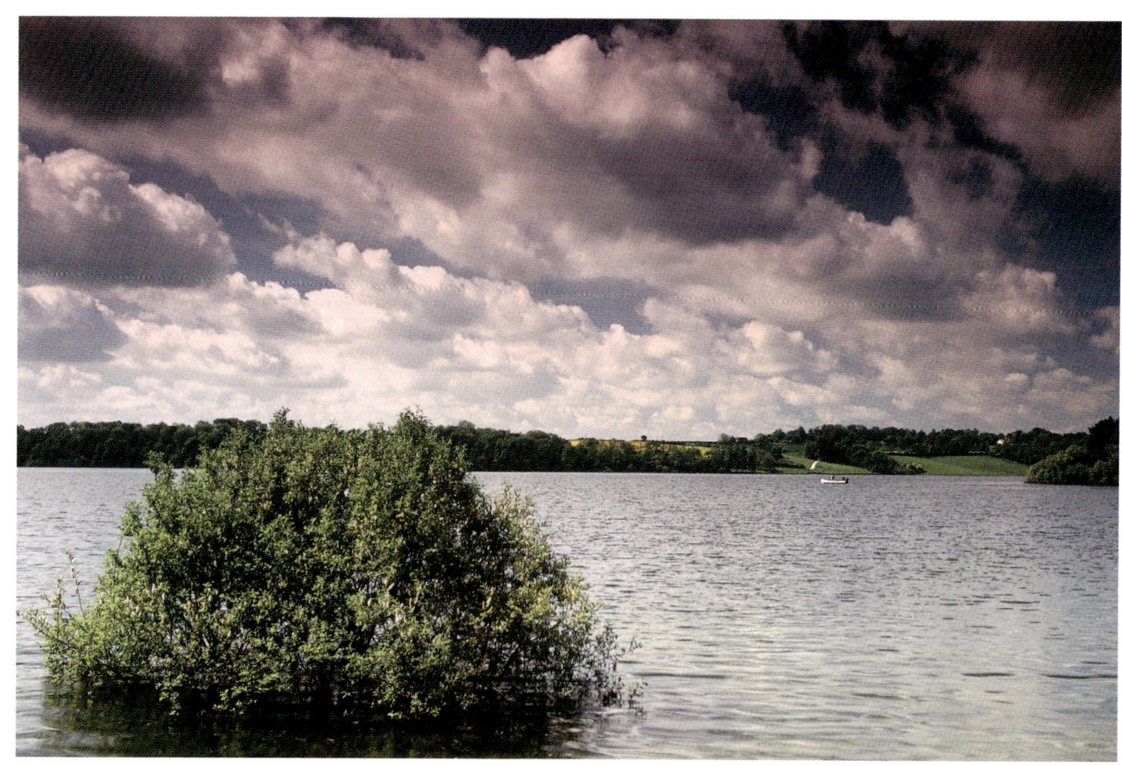

Clouds' illusions.

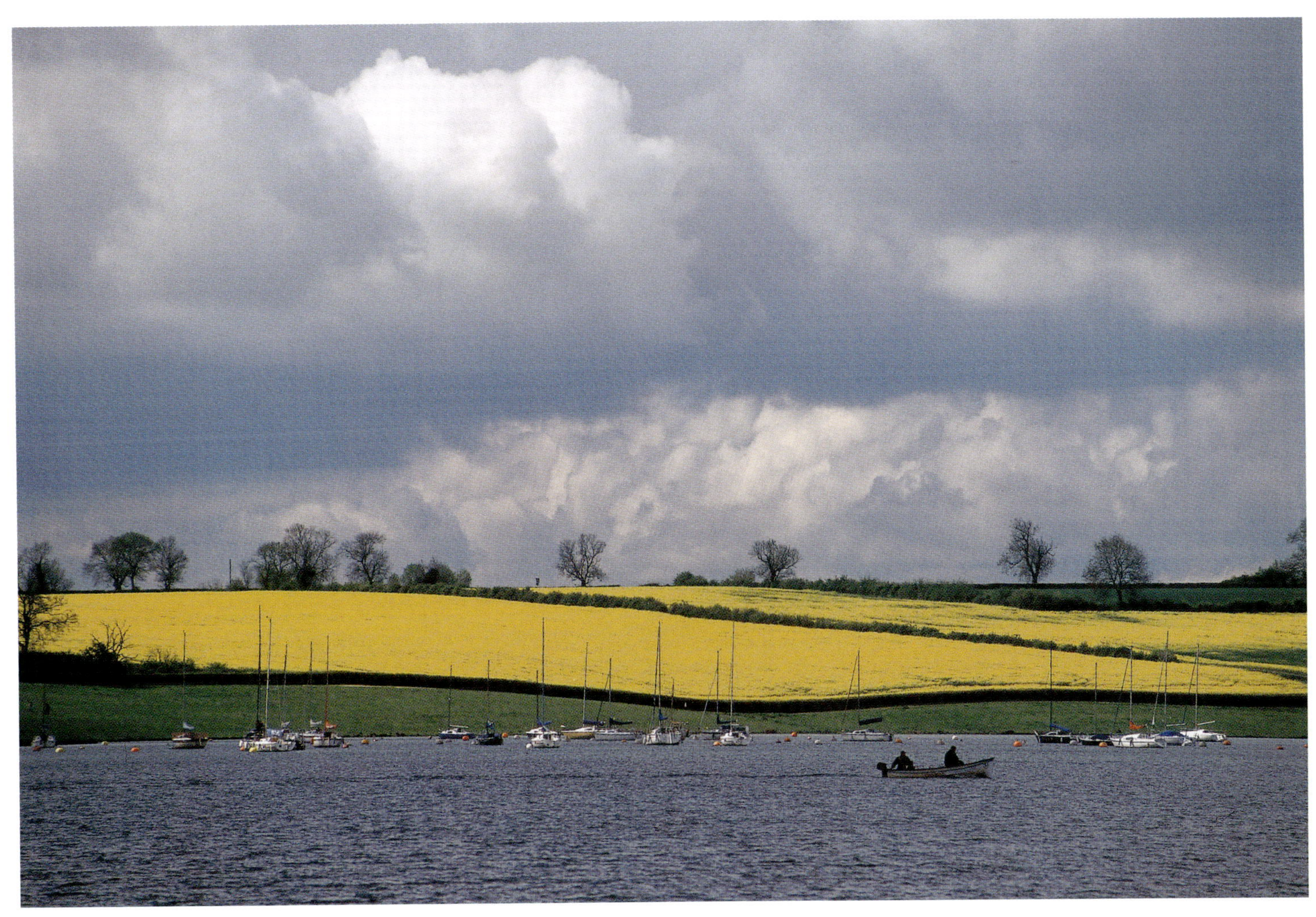

Going fishing.

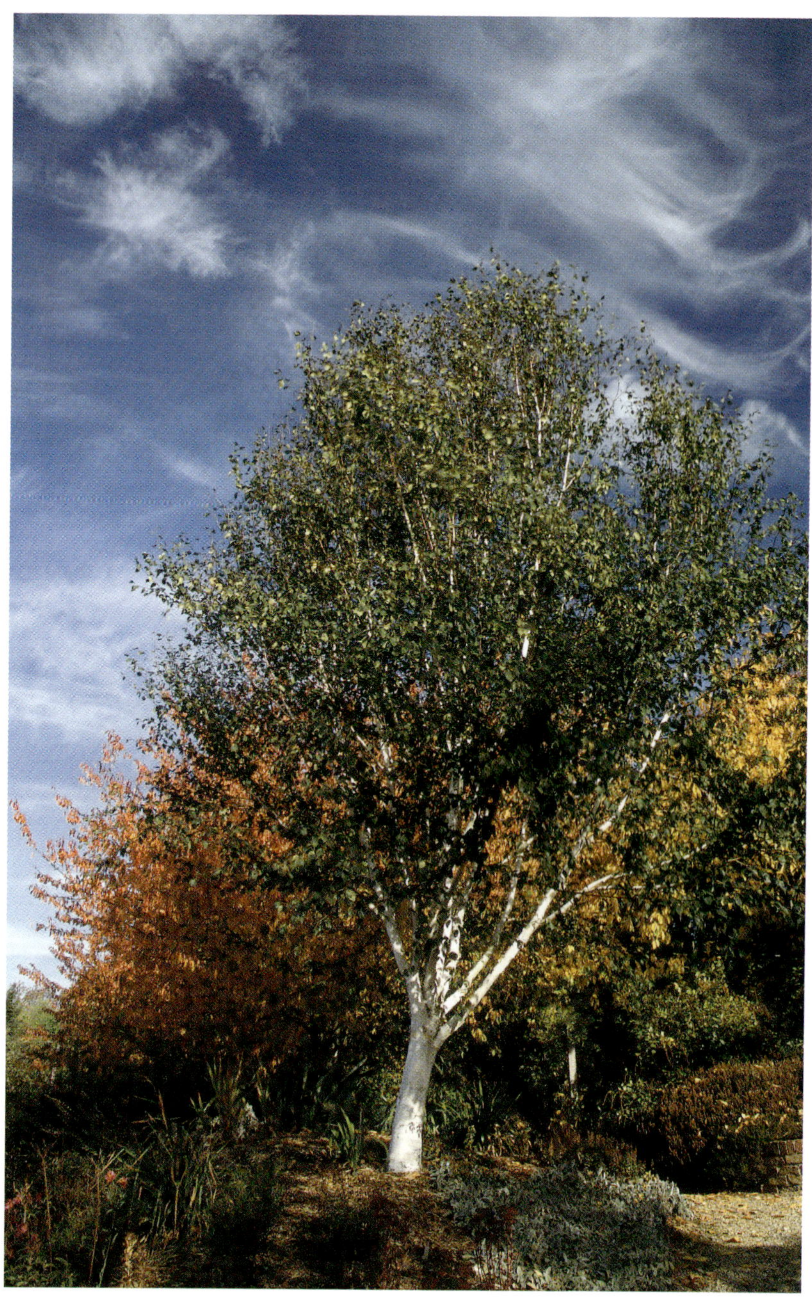

The Drought Garden at Barnsdale.

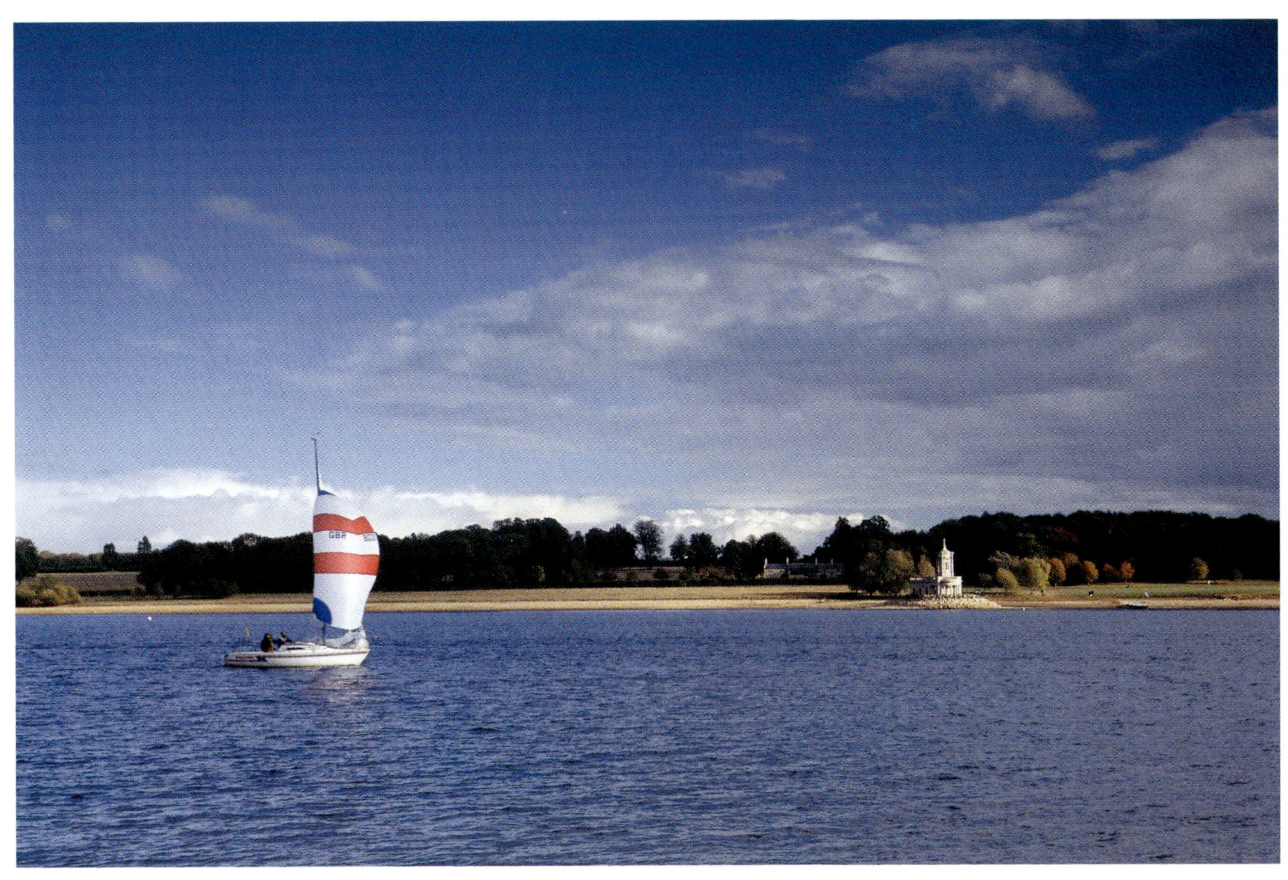

A classic 'postcard' view of Normanton Church, enhanced by the sun highlighting its westerly aspect.

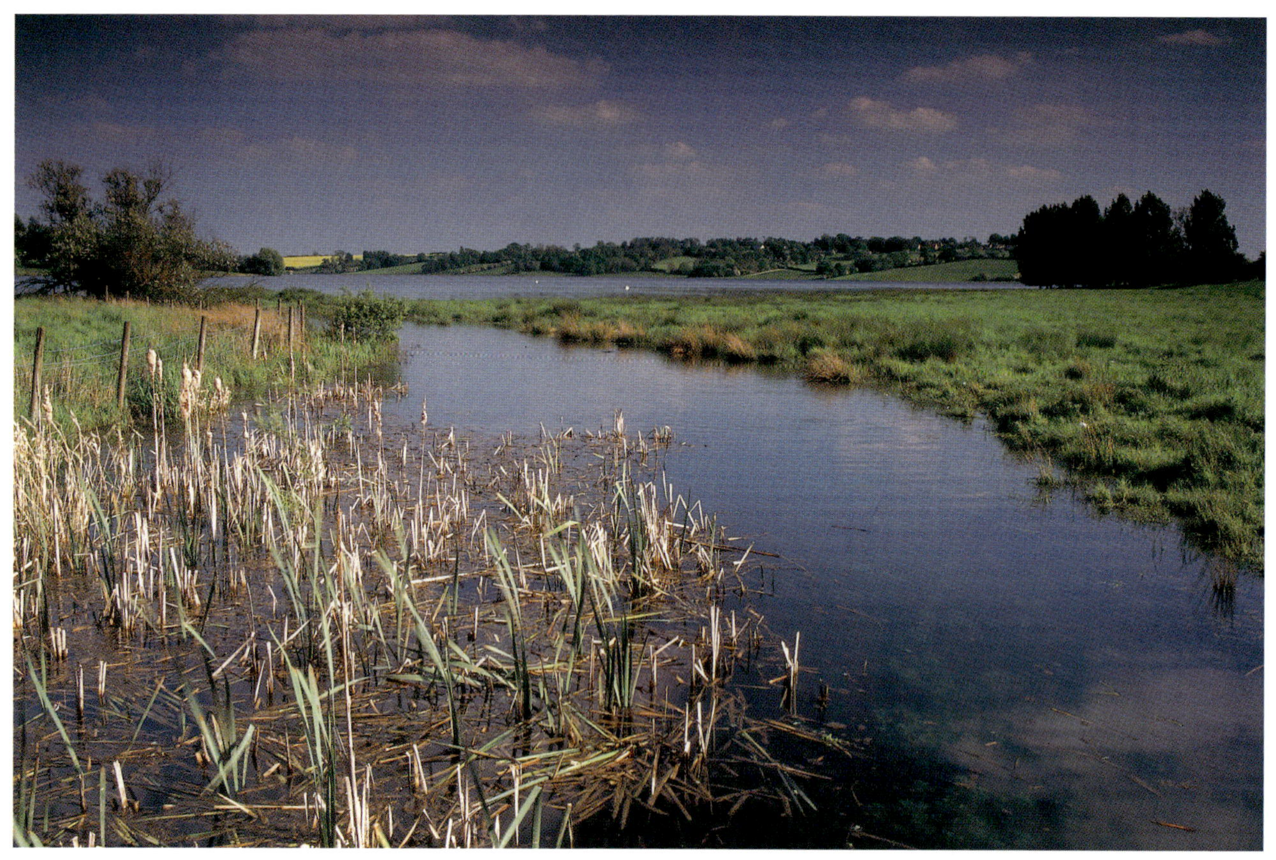

Lodge Inlet.

Opposite page: Barnsdale Creek in Spring.

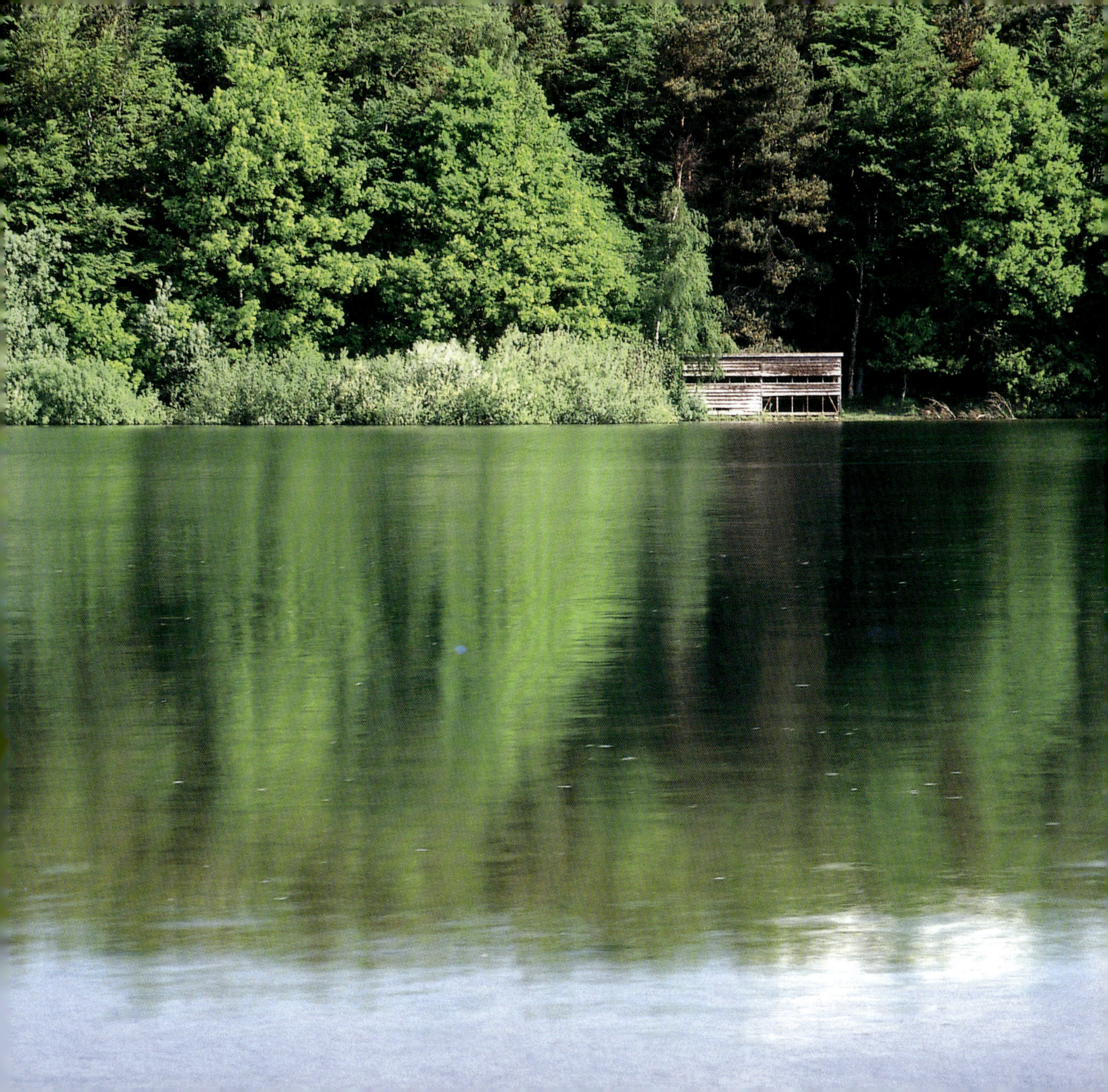

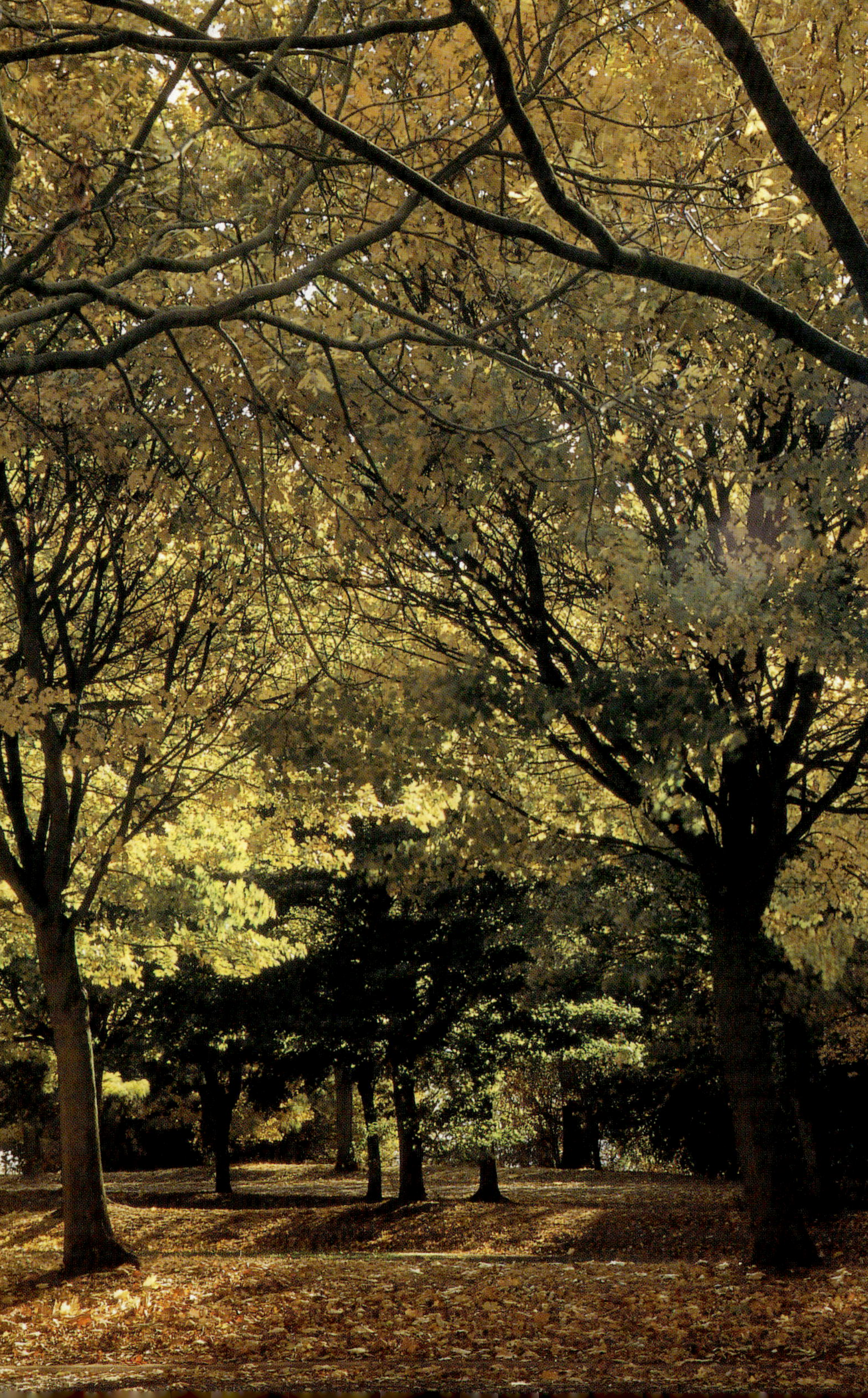

The car park at Whitwell.

One of those fabulous Autumn days
when it was almost impossible
to take a bad shot.

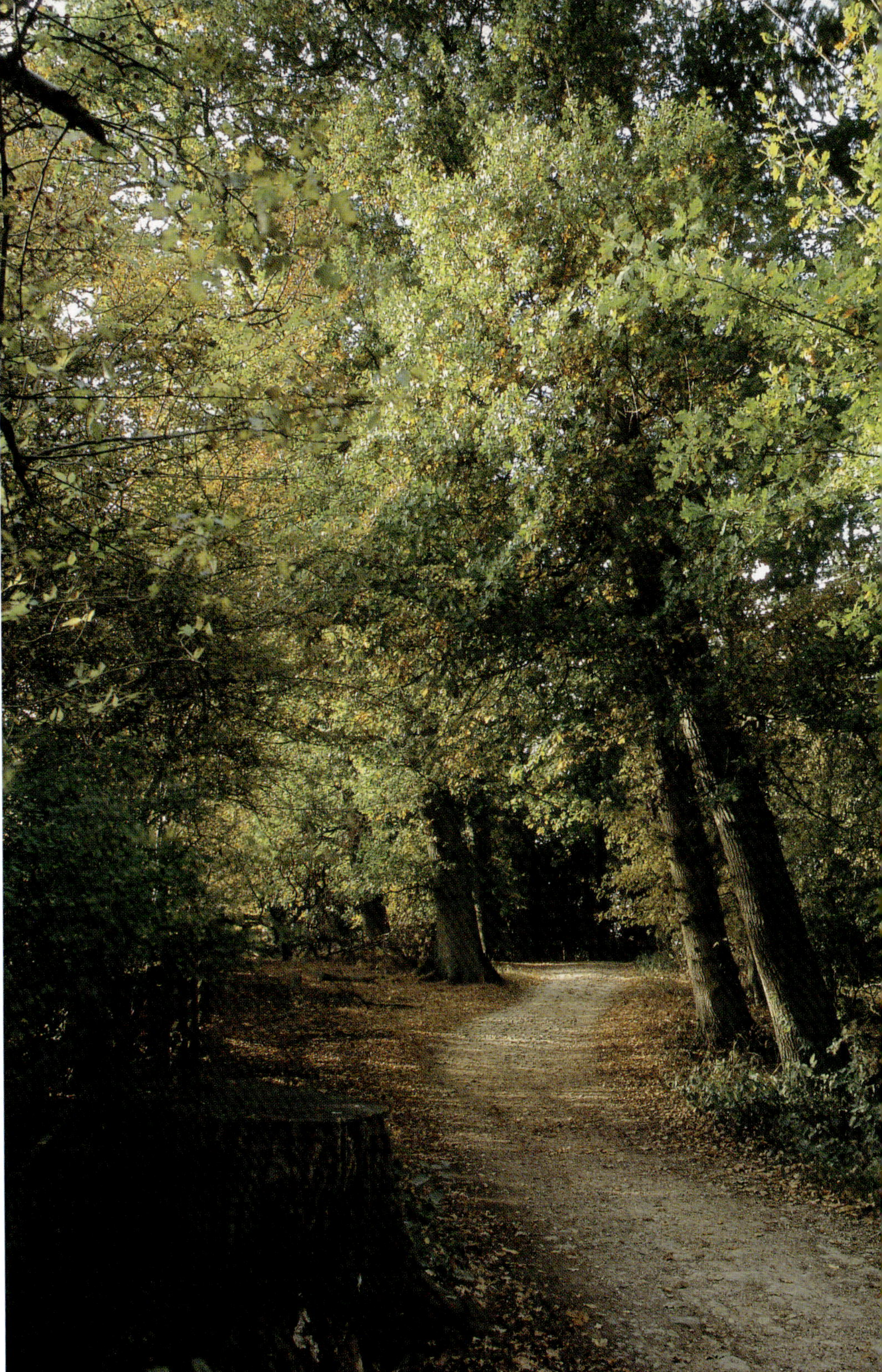

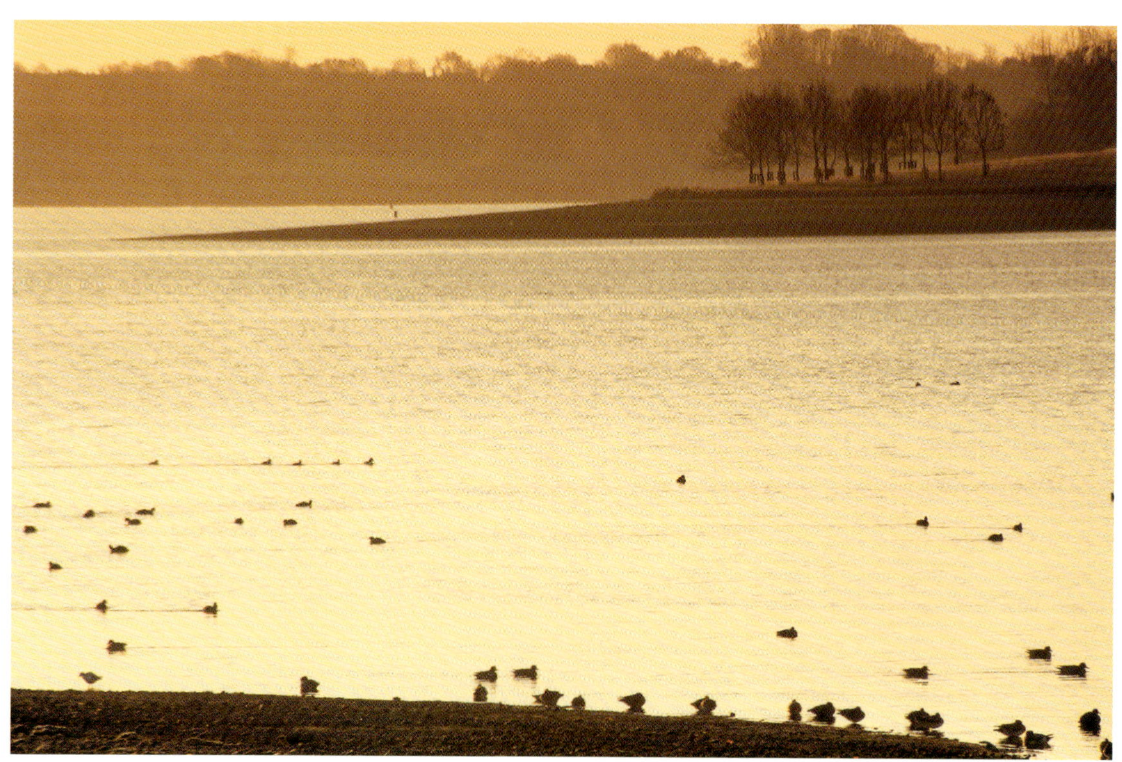

A peaceful December morning at Barnsdale Creek.

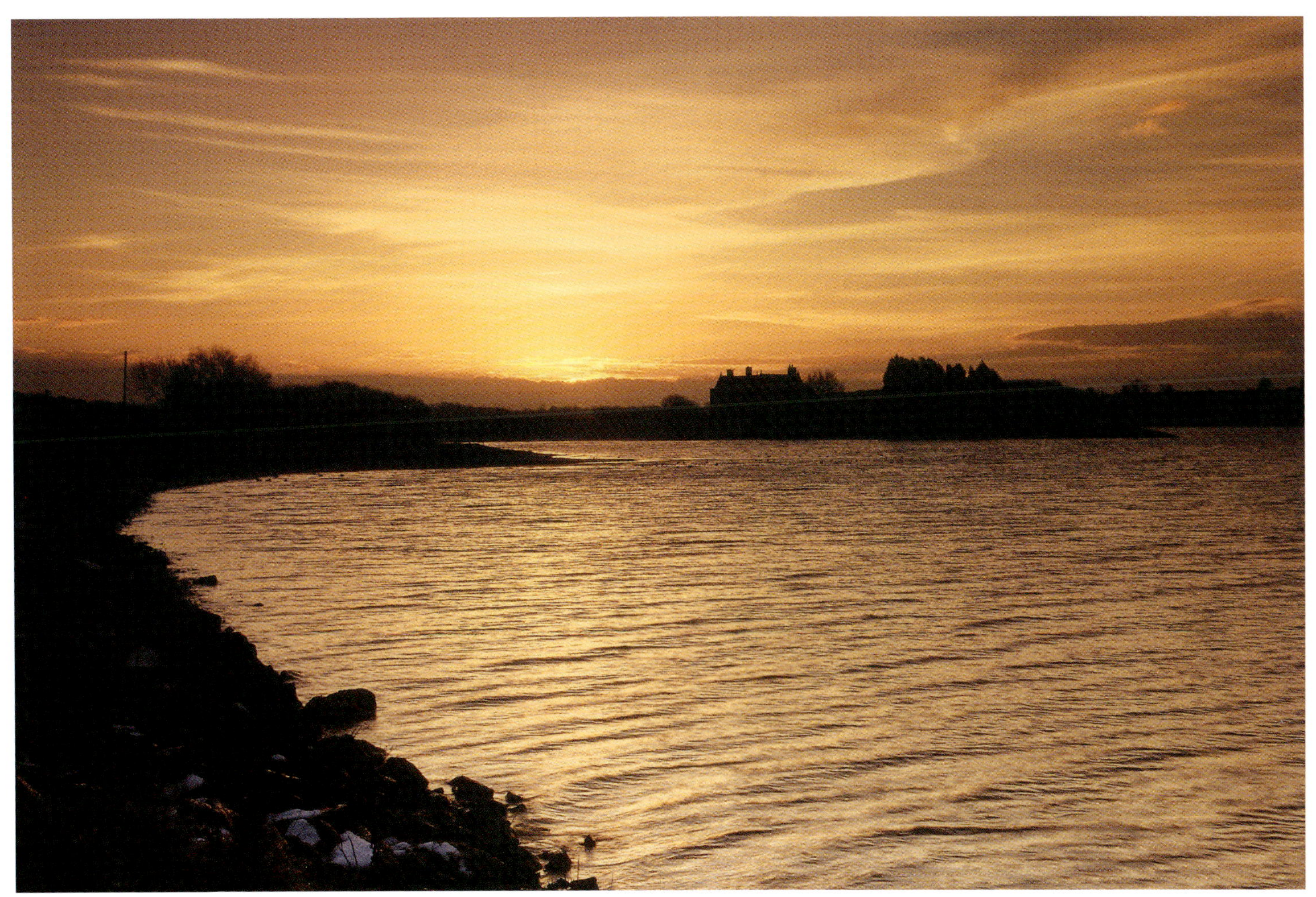

The Old Hall.

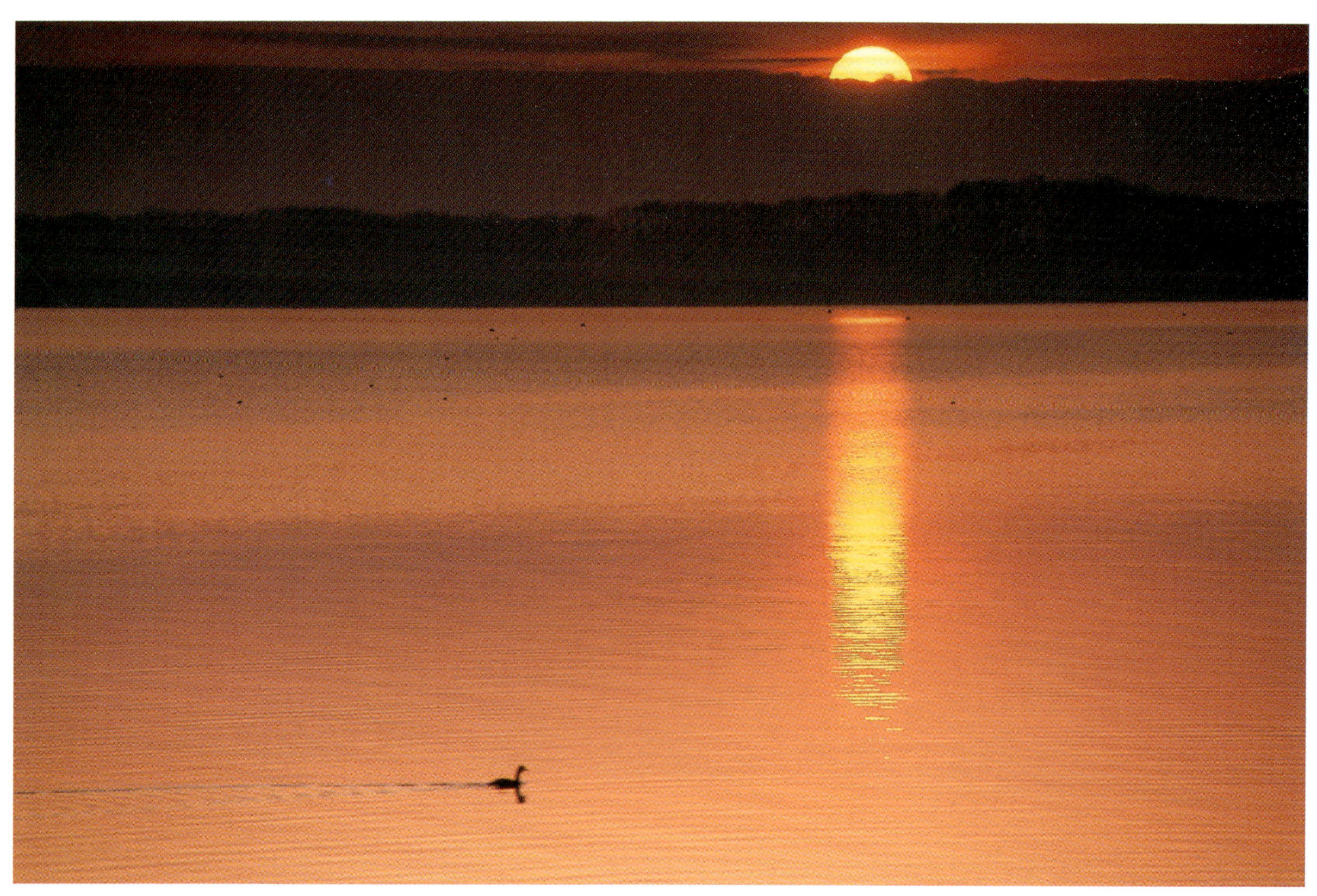

The dawn of this new day makes a peaceful landscape or...

...a powerful graphic.

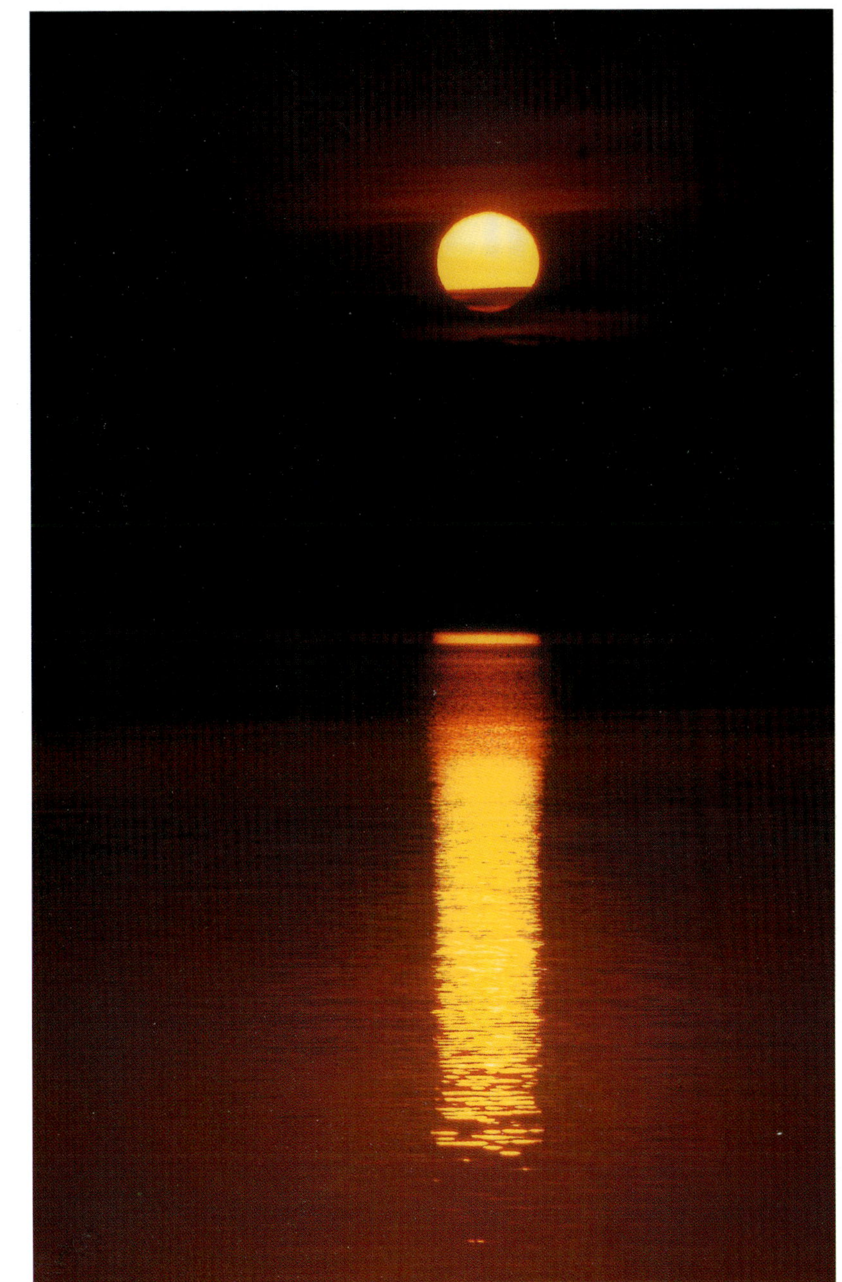

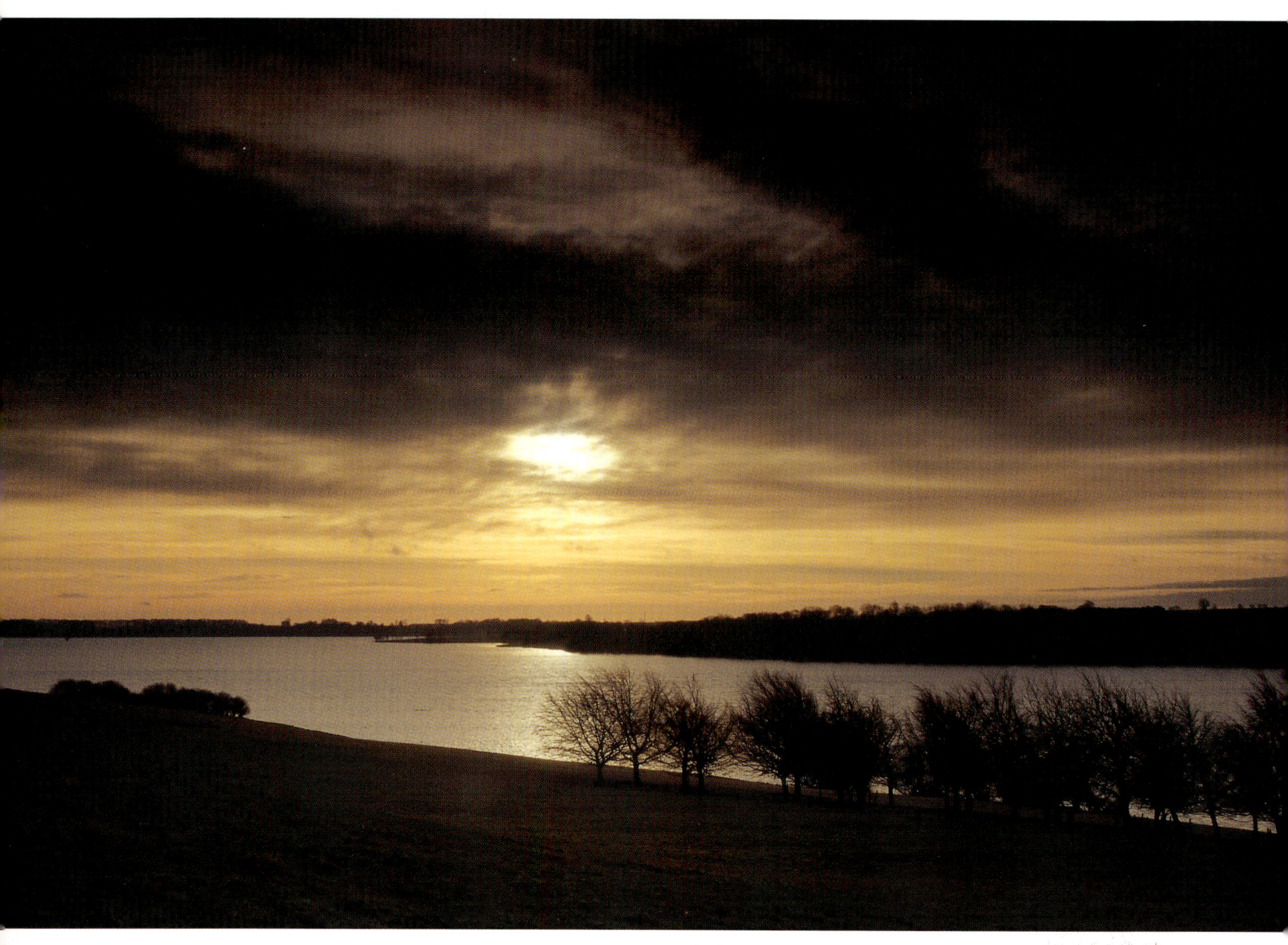

On this occassion the morning was well worth getting up early for.

As the sun set, it was only for a short moment
that there was both colour in the sky and a
clear reflection on the church windows.

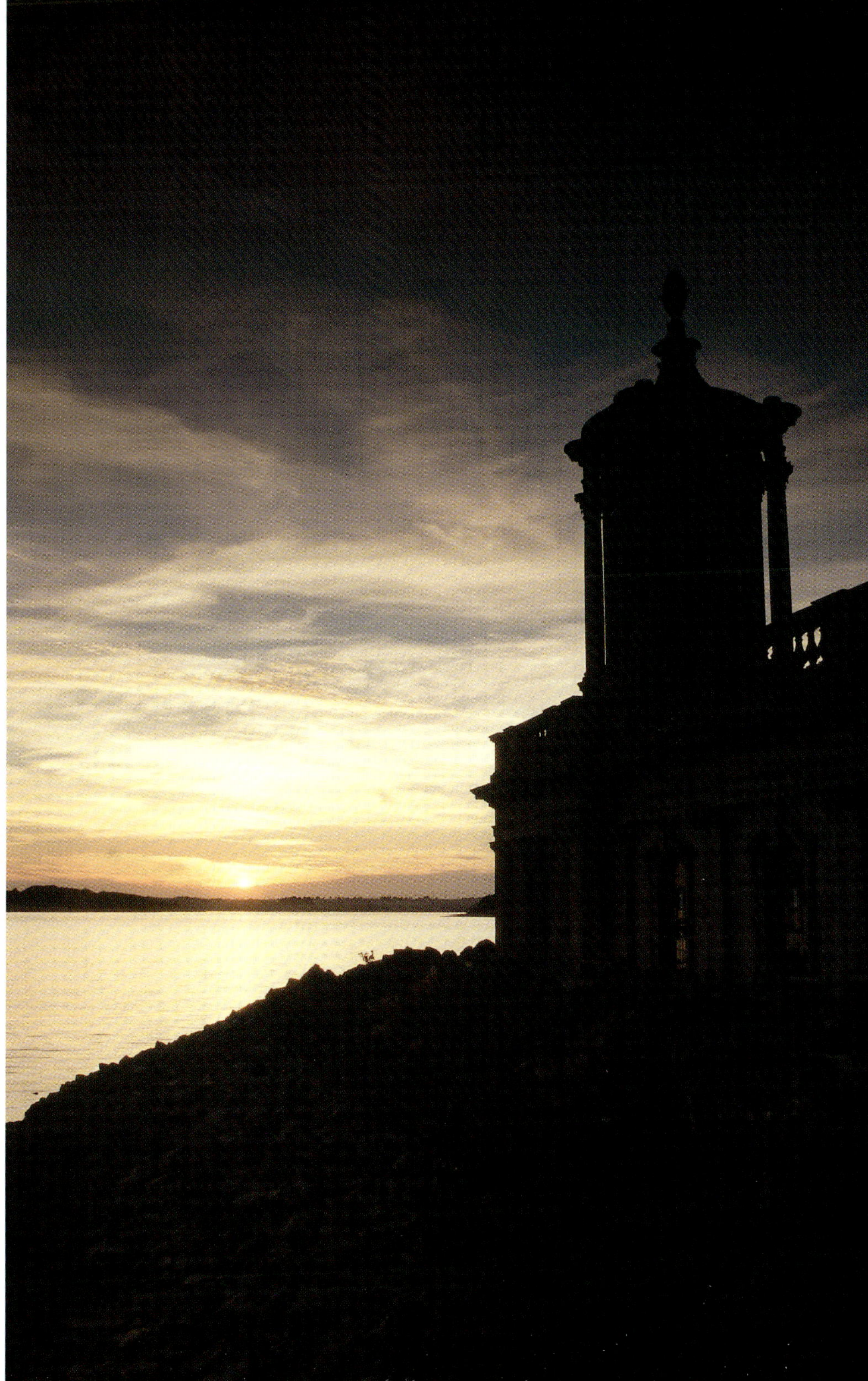

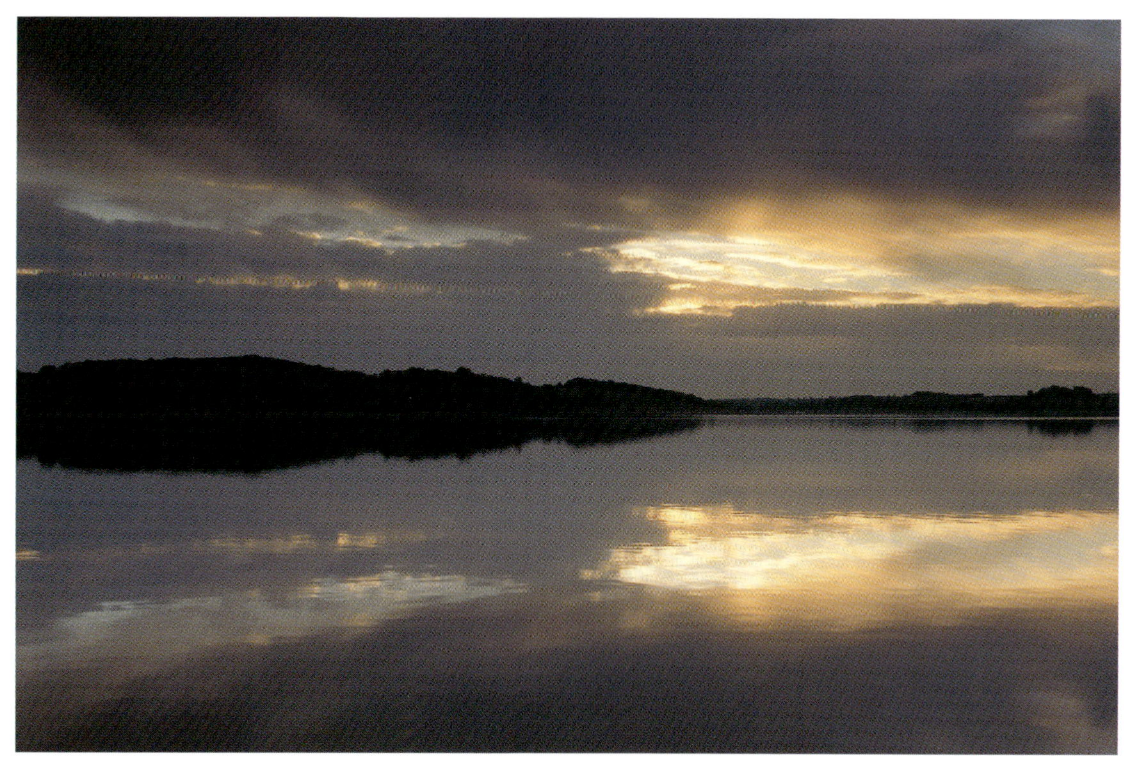

Looking west along the southern arm of the Water.

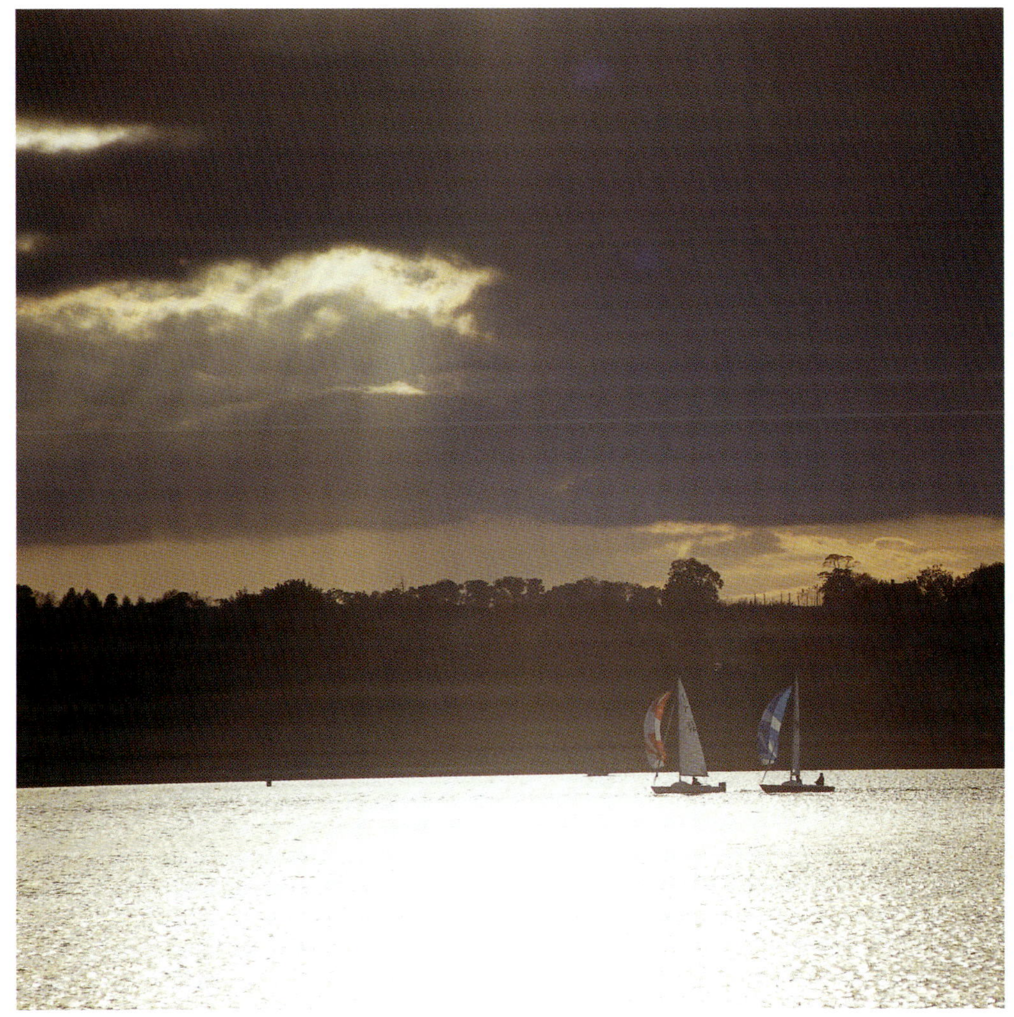

Sailing into the light.

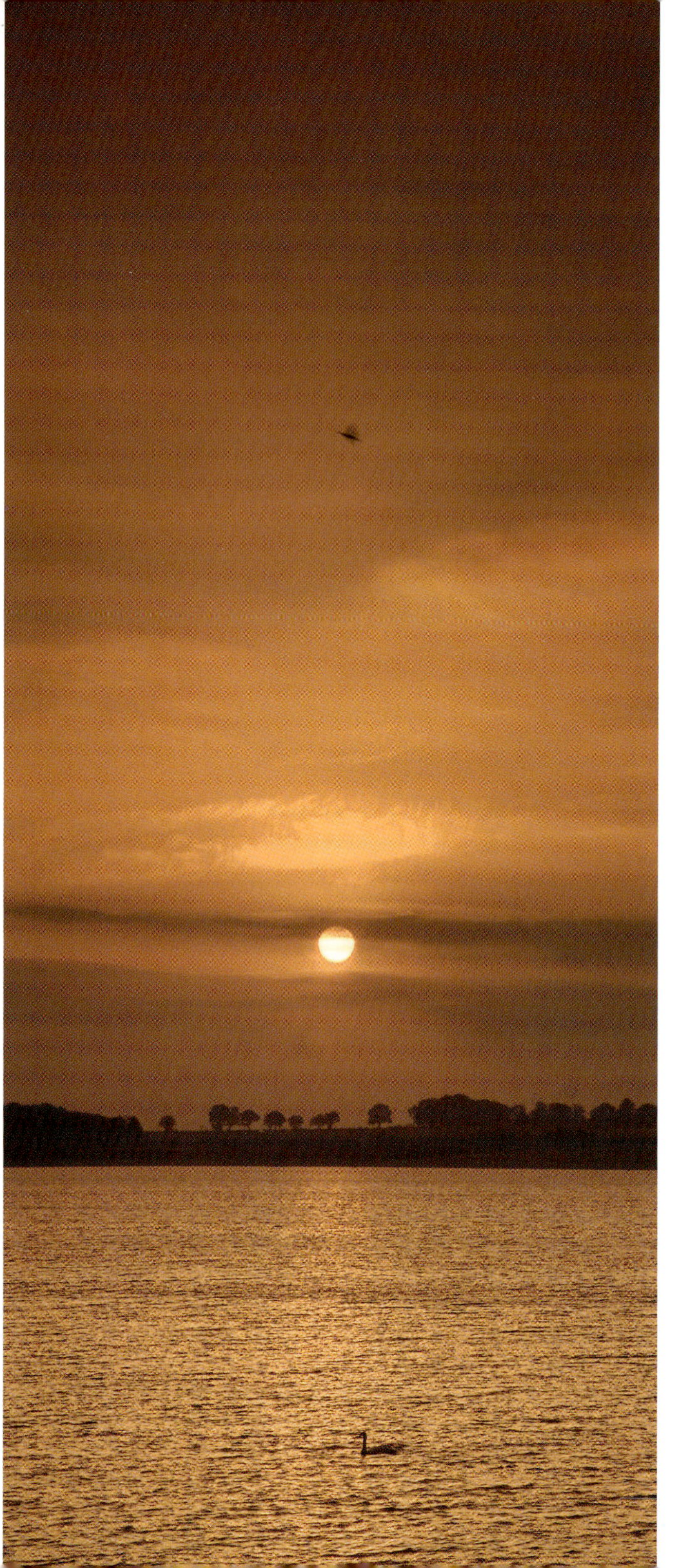

A fluke, fun shot out of a
series, which has been cropped
to emphasize the coincidence.

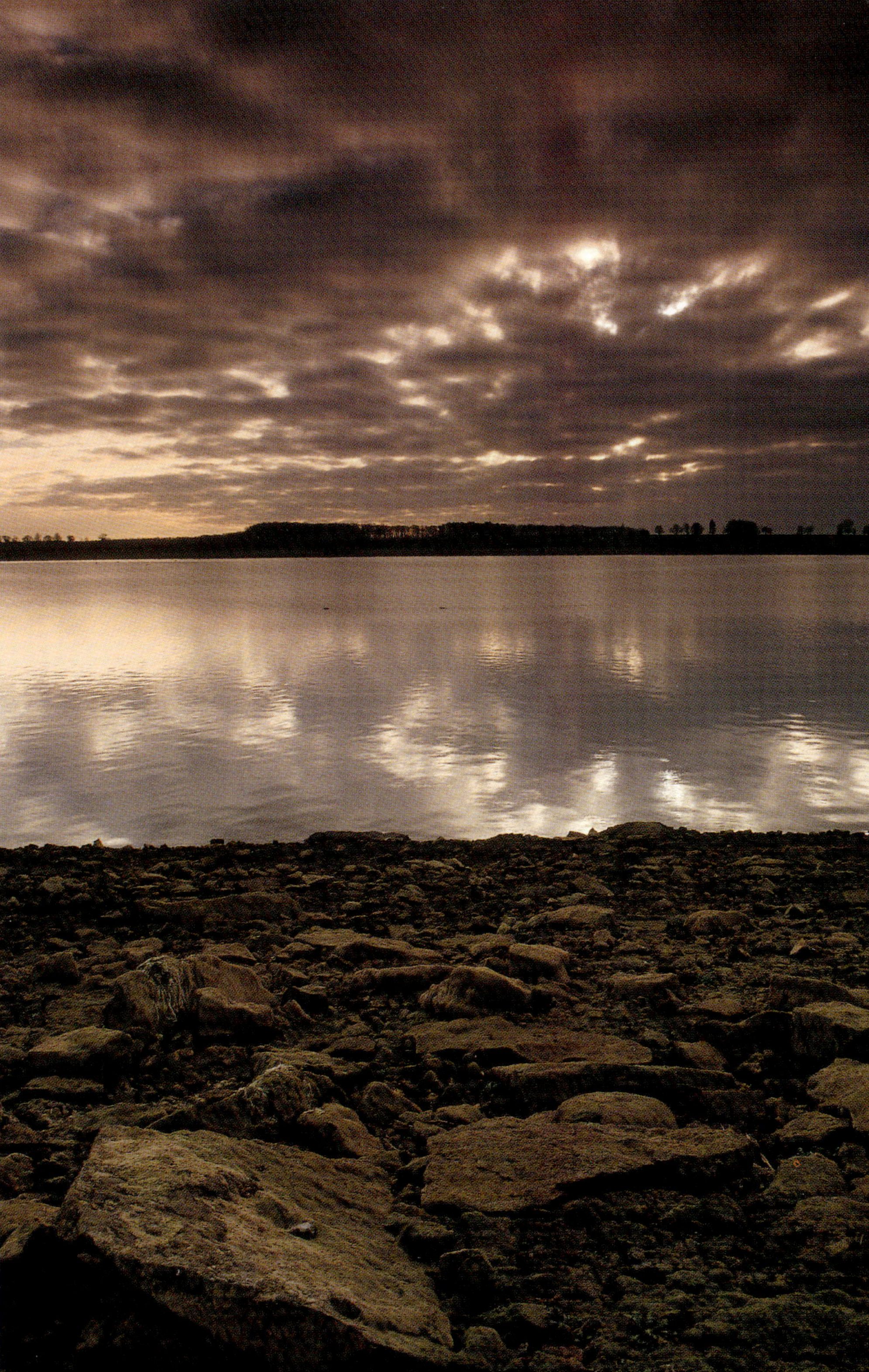

Looking south from
Syke's Spinney, towards
a low winter sun.

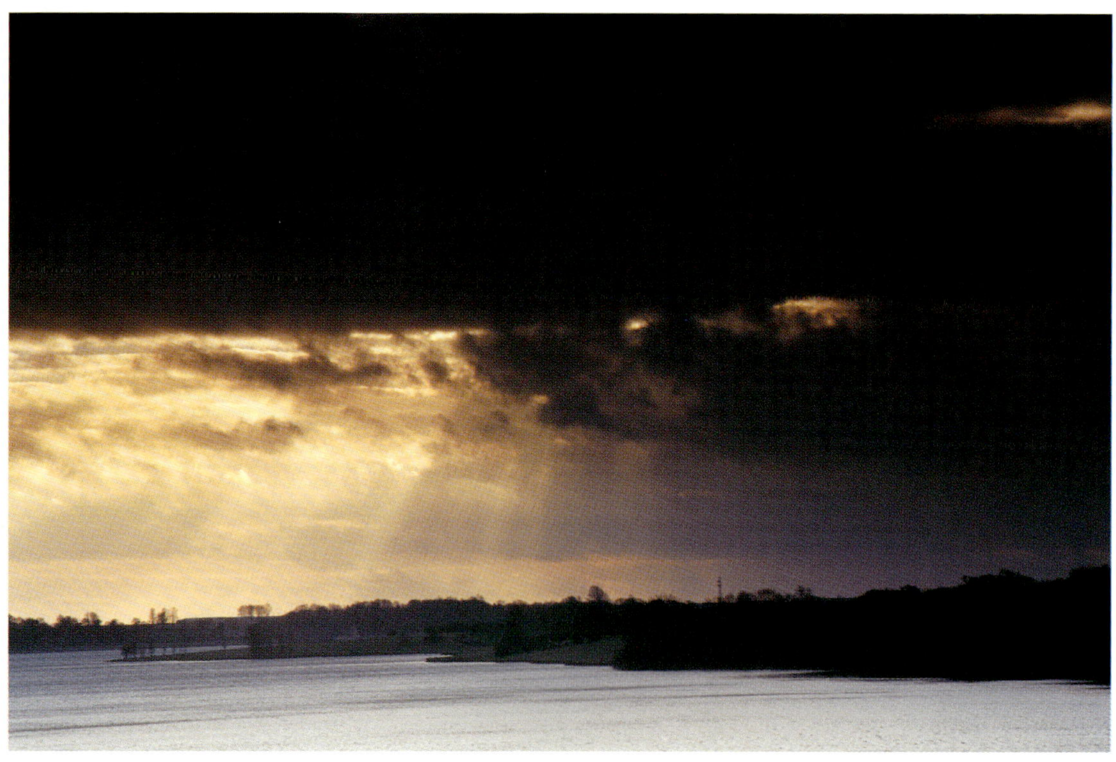

These were the last rays of the rising sun, before it was obscured
by the dense black clouds for the rest of the day.

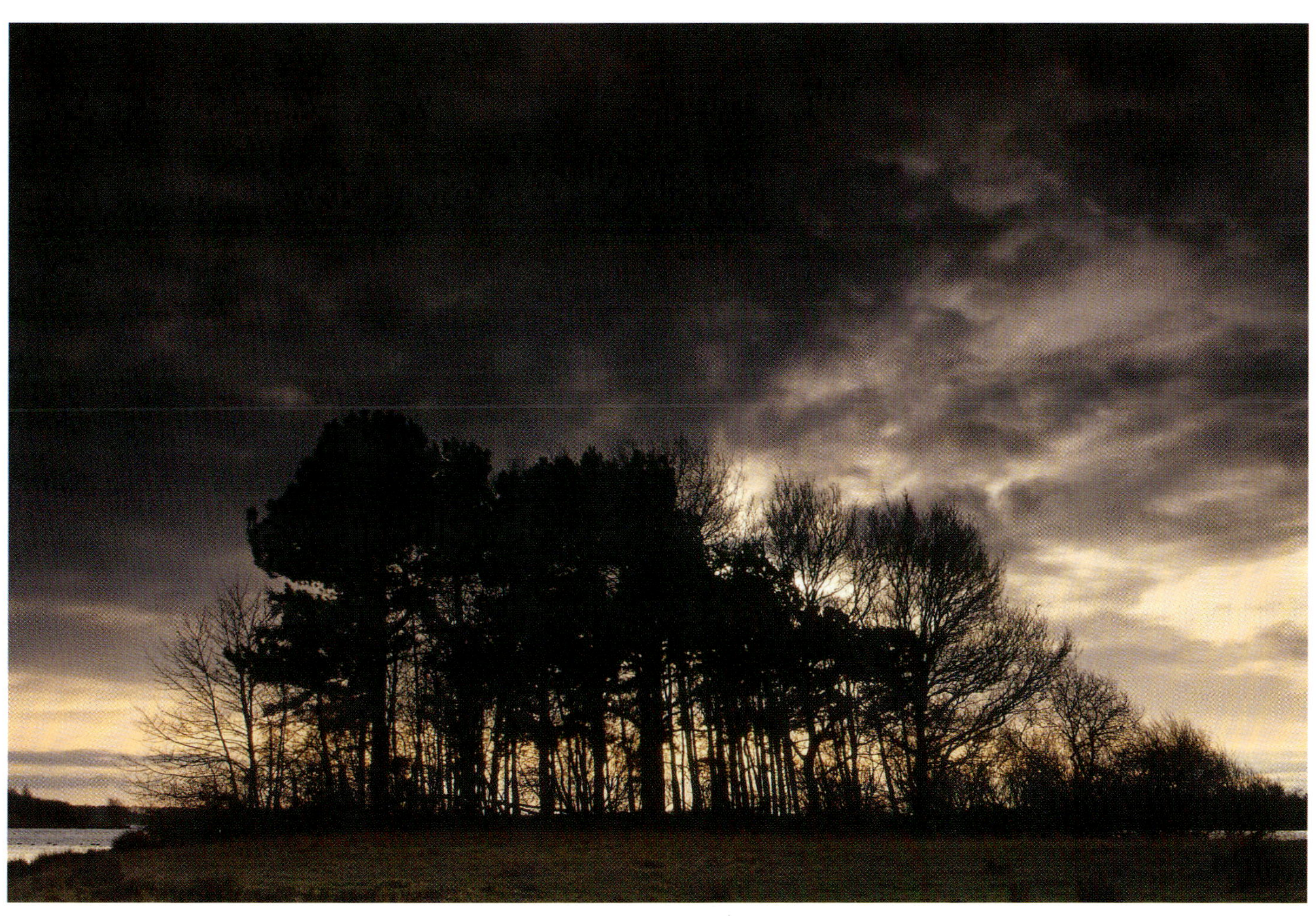

The trees at the end of Barnsdale Creek are silhouetted against a dramatic post-dawn sky.

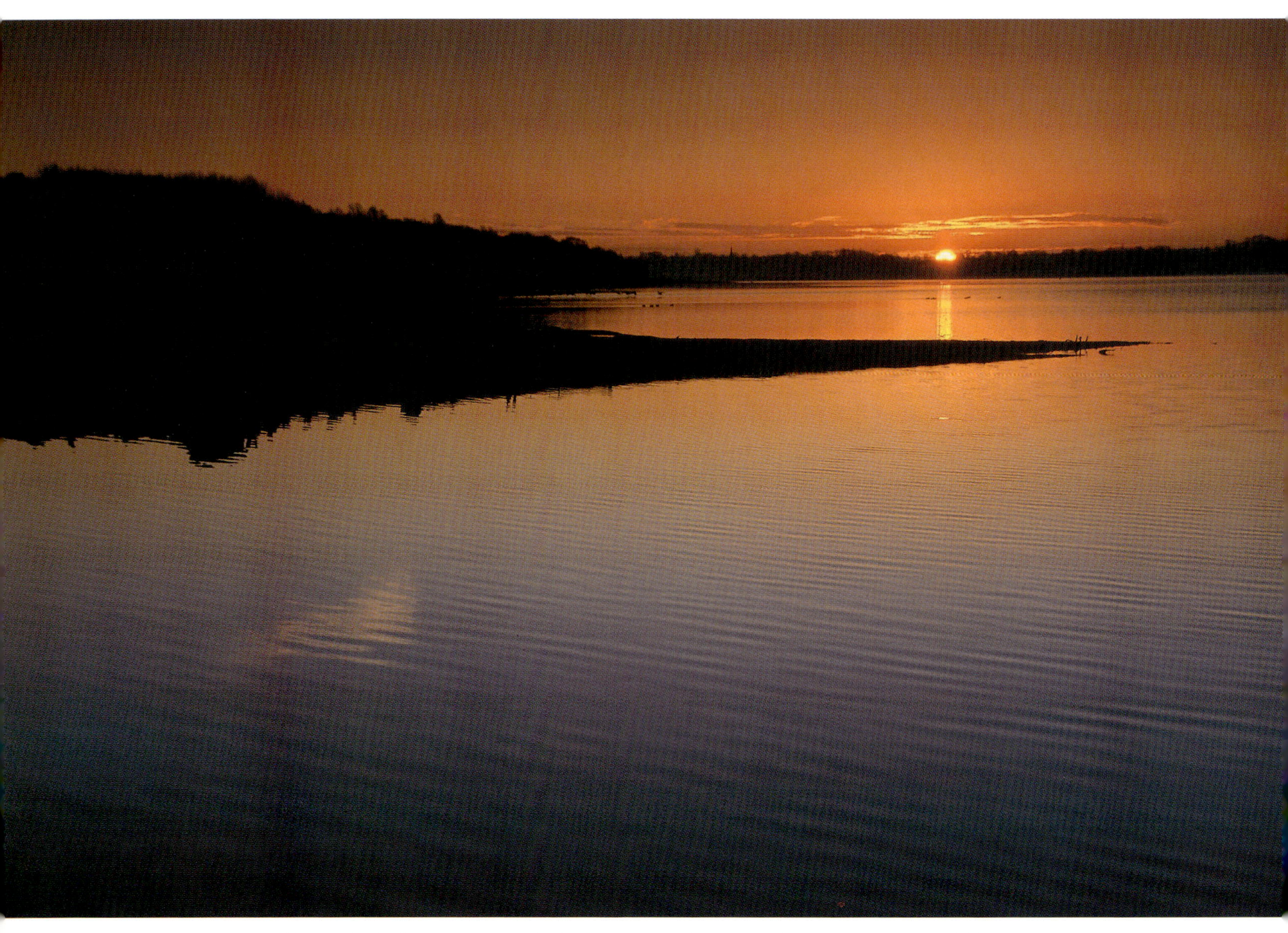

The gentle ripples on the water in the foreground, give the whole scene a very peaceful feeling.

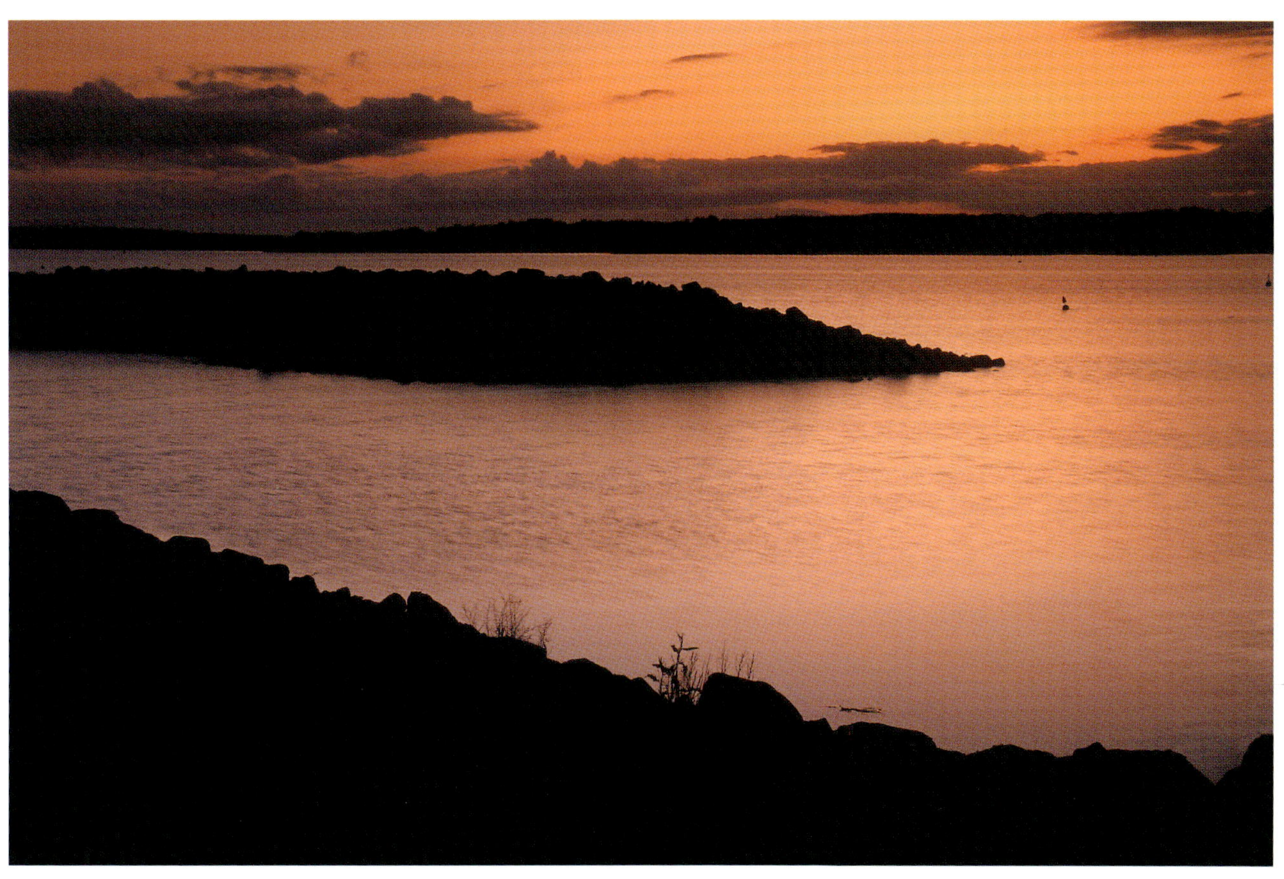

Late evening at the dam.

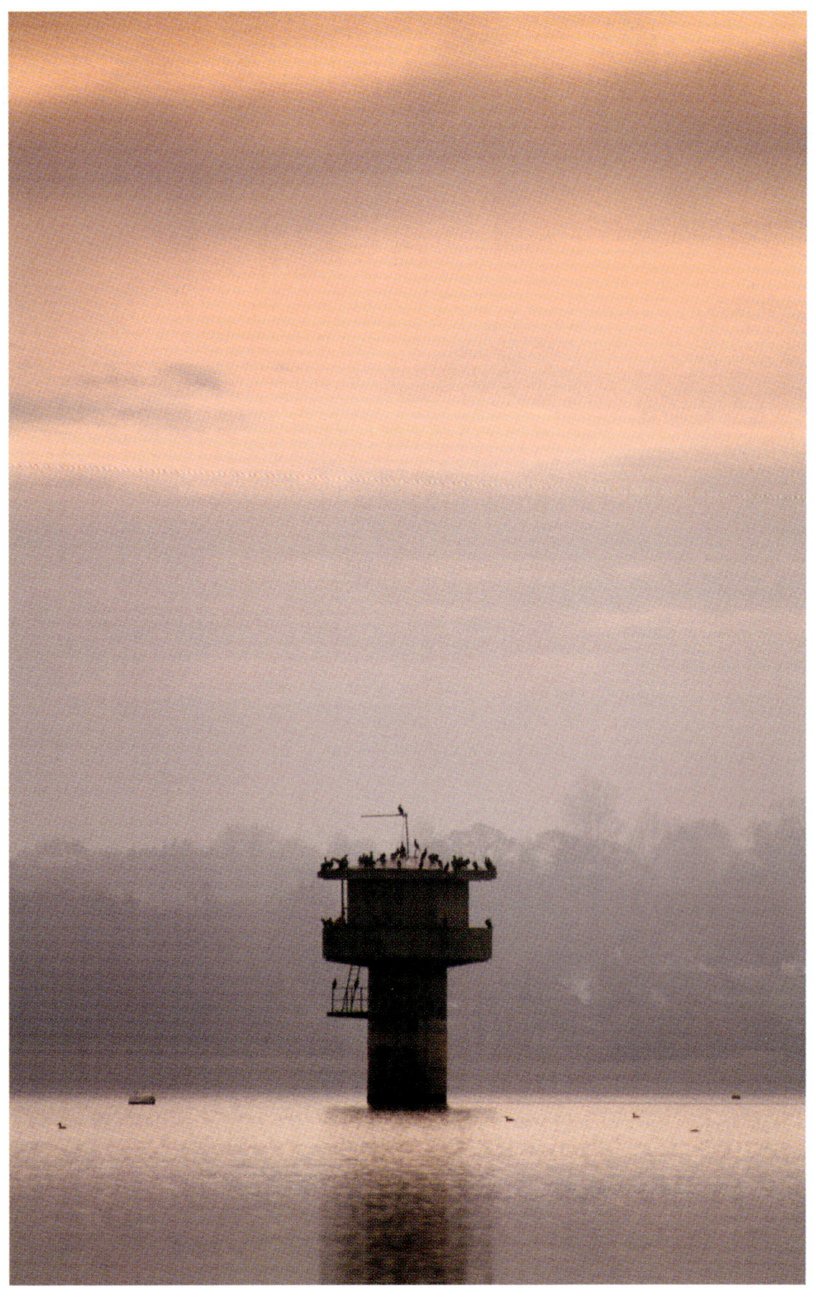

Rutland Water's largest birds' nest.

Total calm.

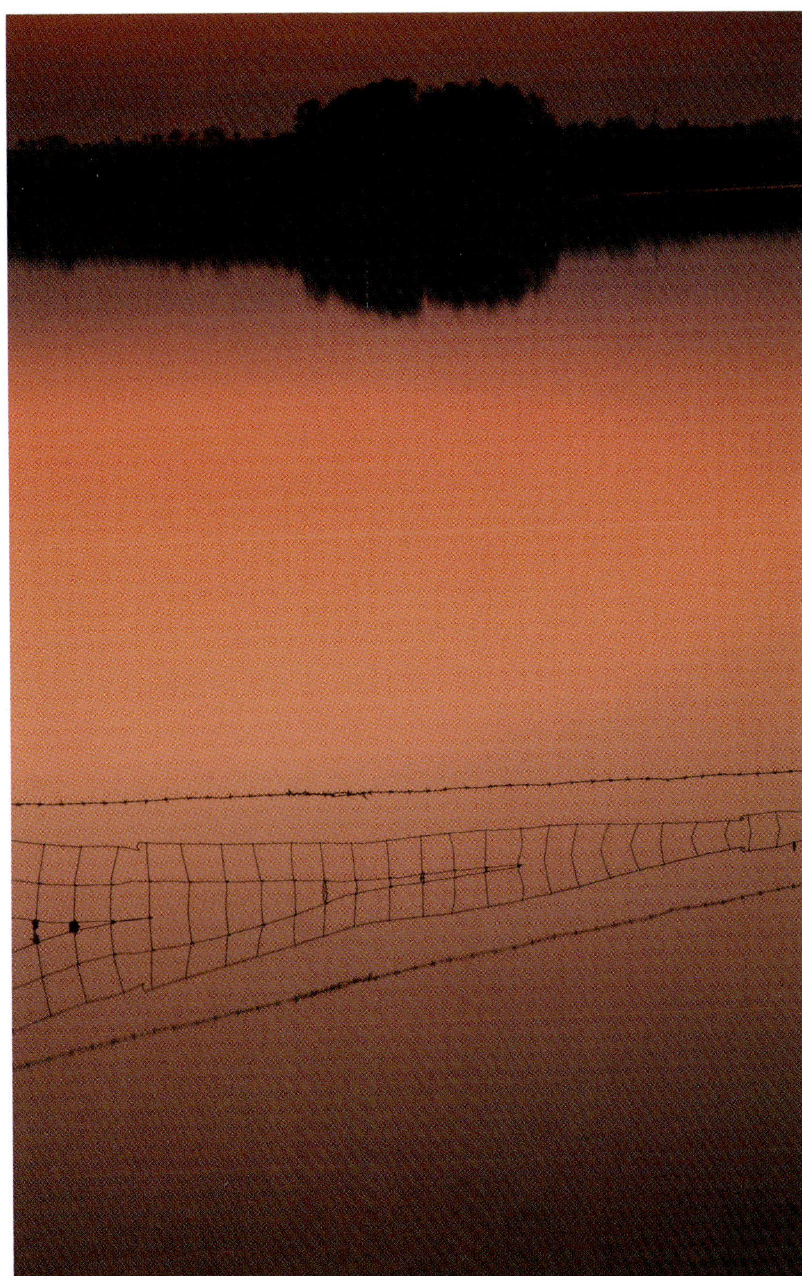

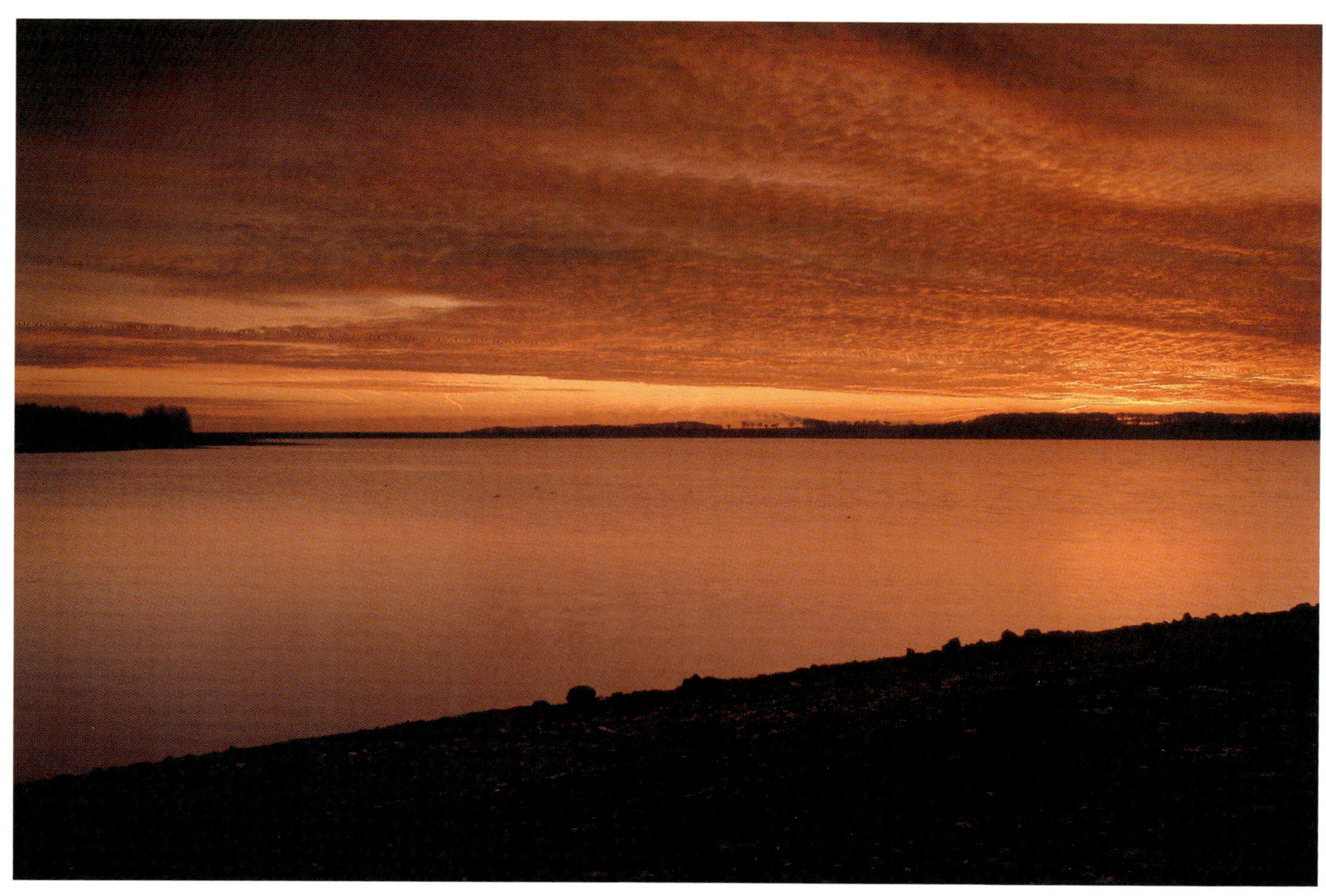

Within three minutes this incredible sky had all but disappeared…

Later, on the
same day, there was
another brief but
stunning sky.

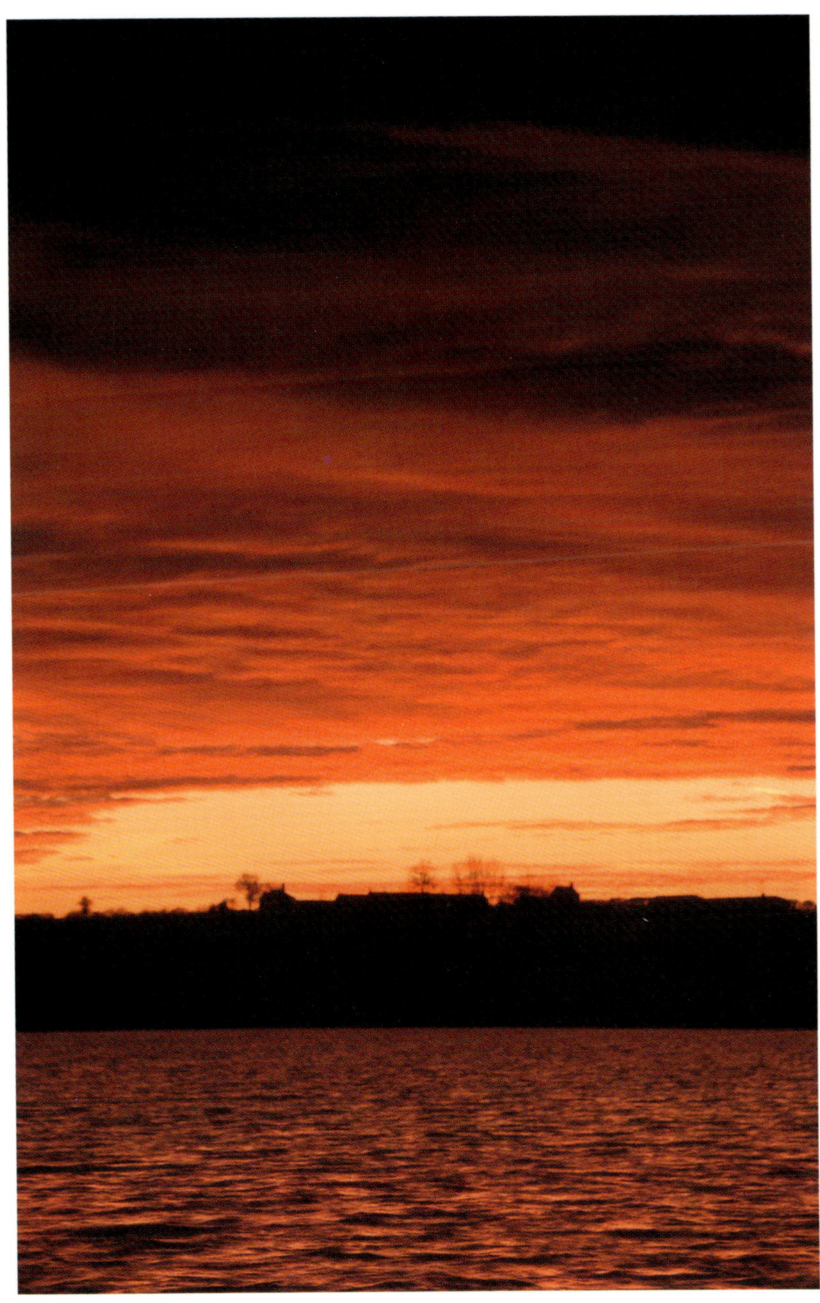

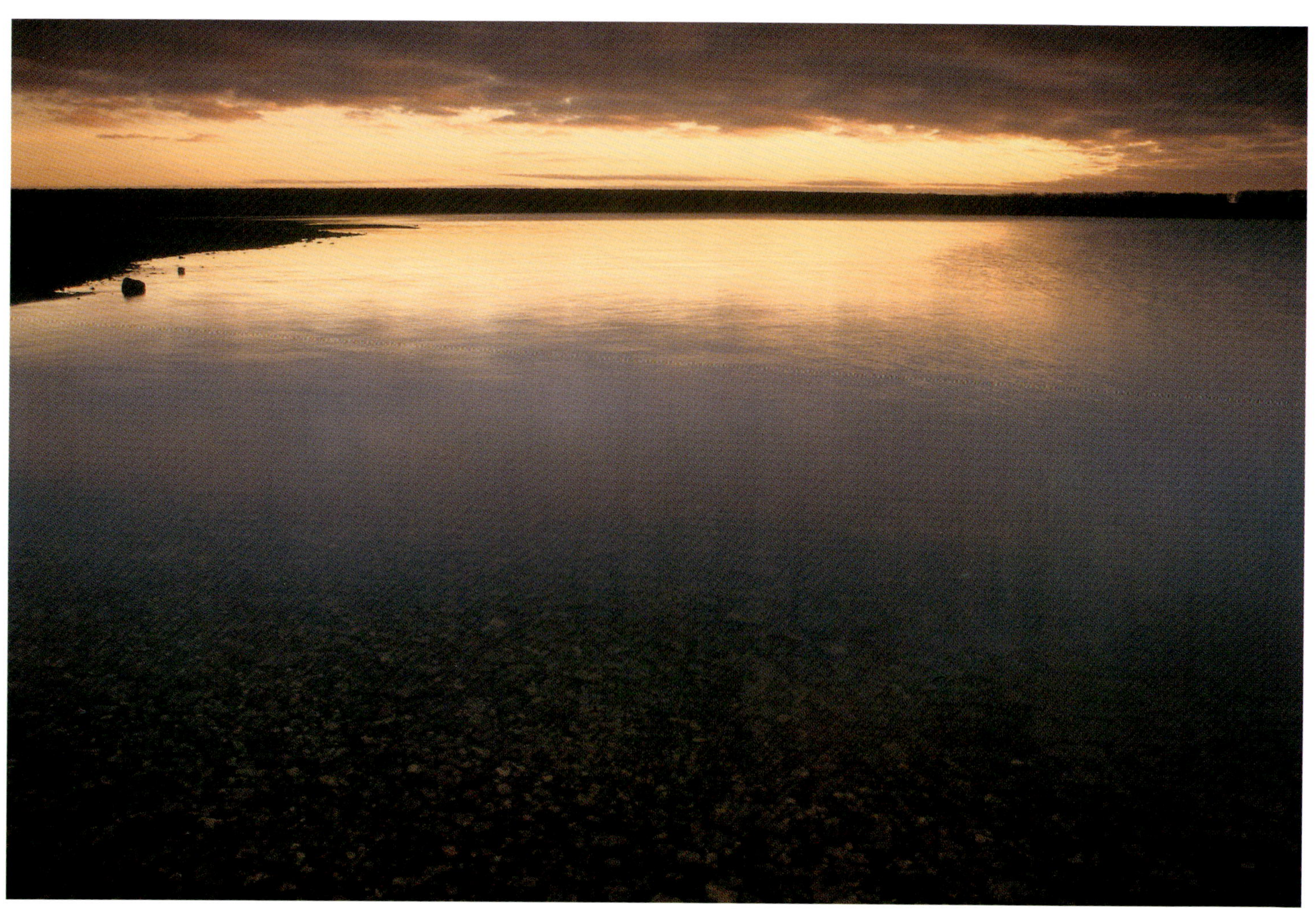

Standing on a spit of land exposed by the low water level gives the impression of being
in the middle of the Water, looking directly at the dam.

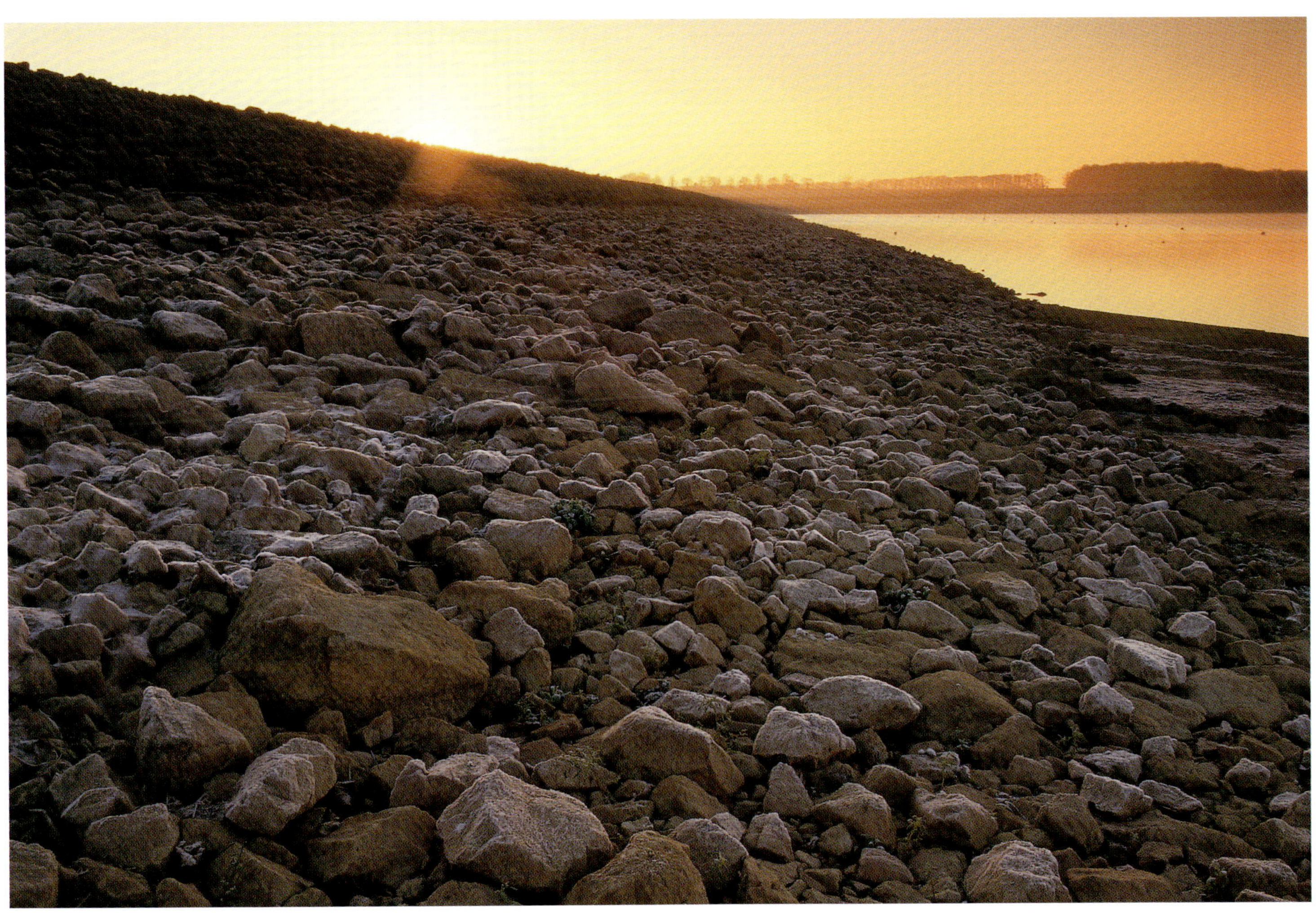

At water levels this low, the extent of the dam is quite imposing.

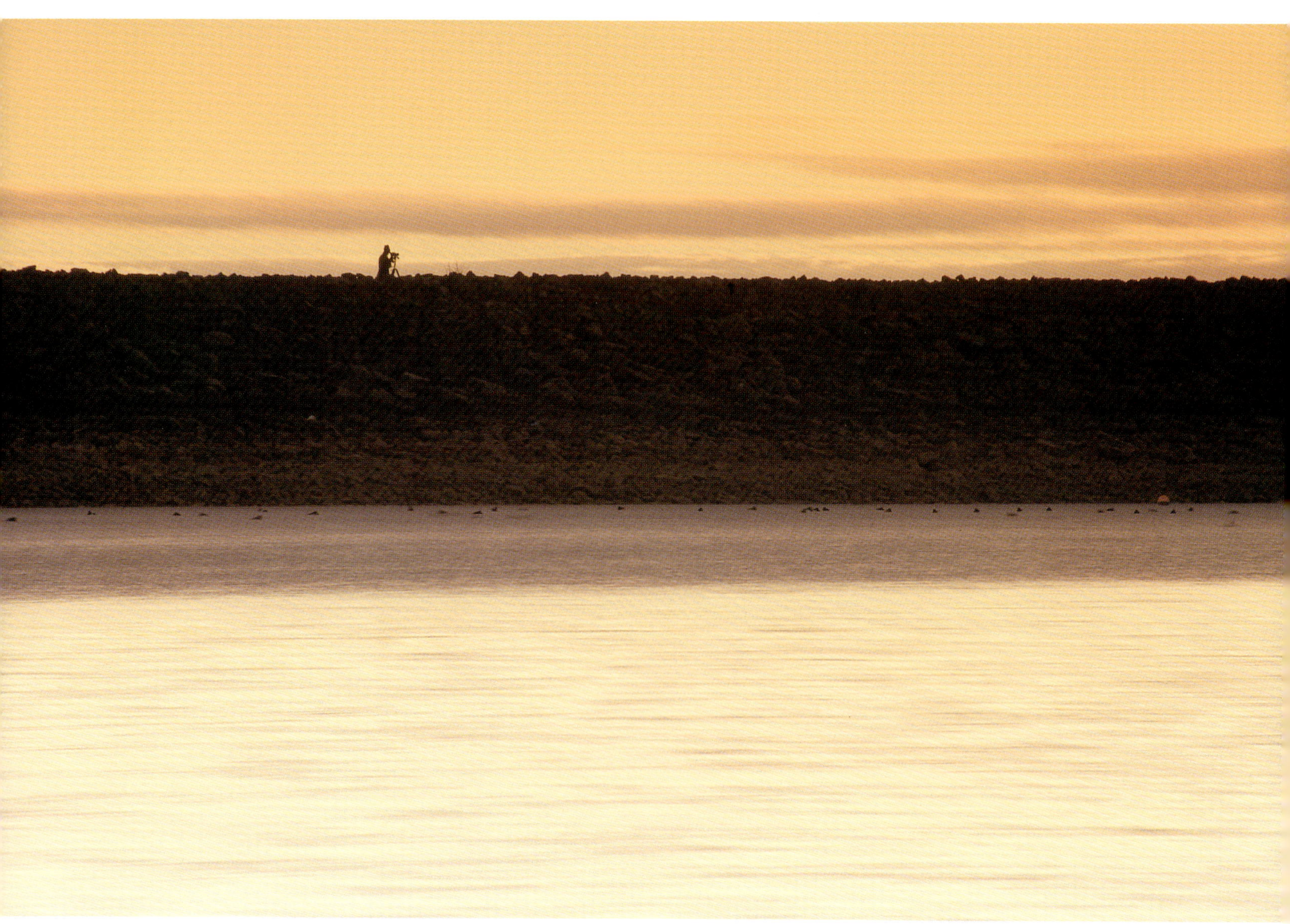

Birdwatching at dawn.

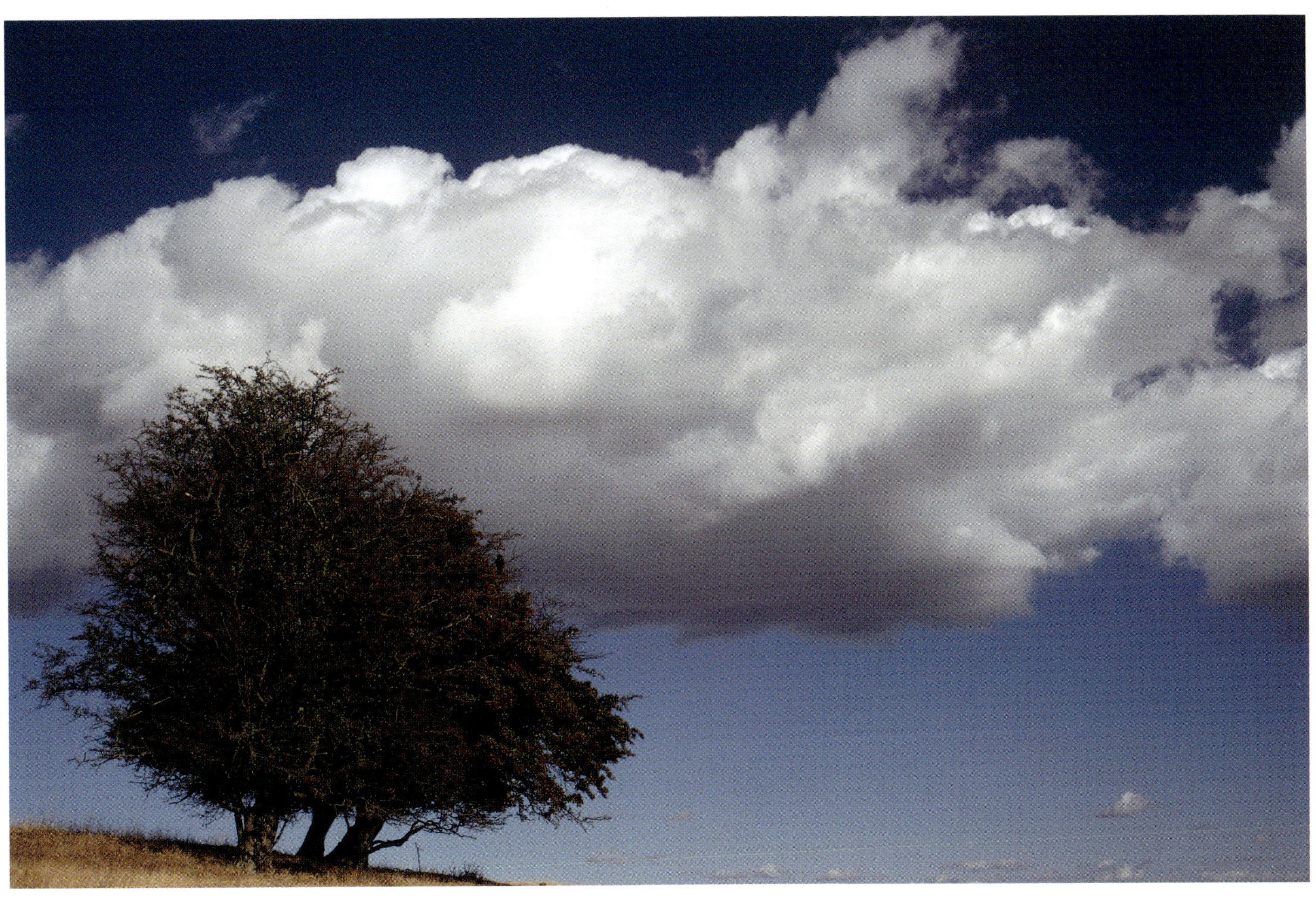

The lone rook adds the final detail to these isolated trees.

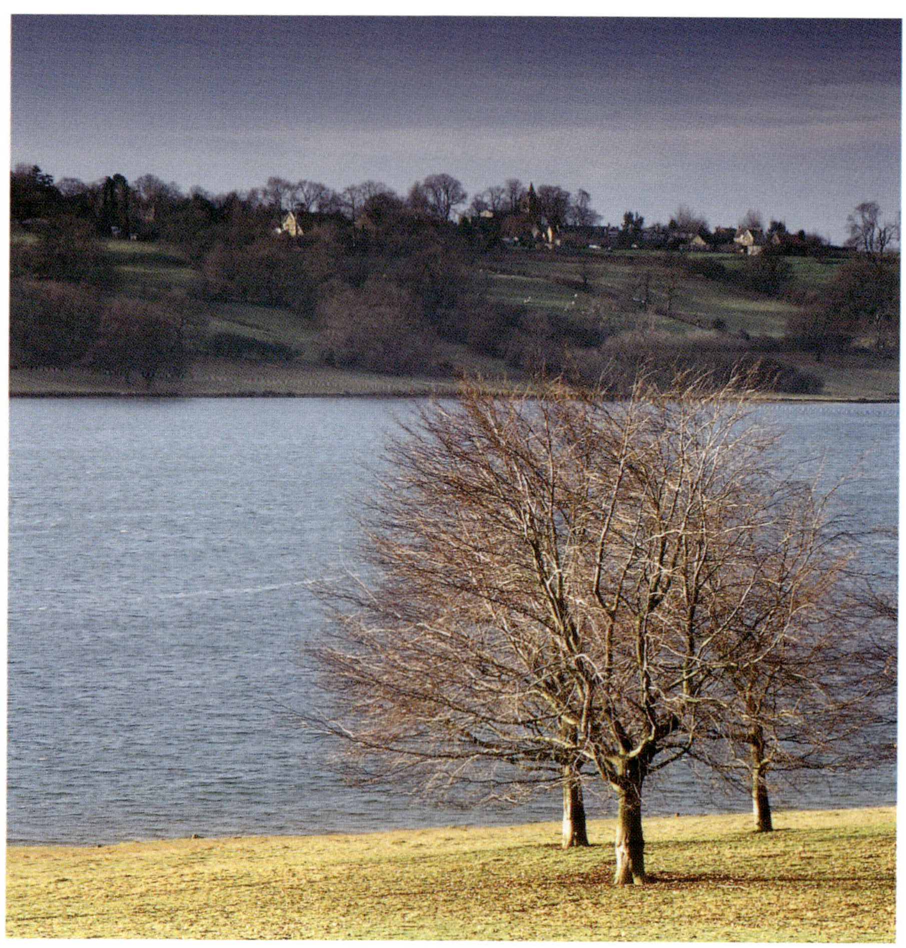

The early morning sun lights up the houses in Hambleton village.

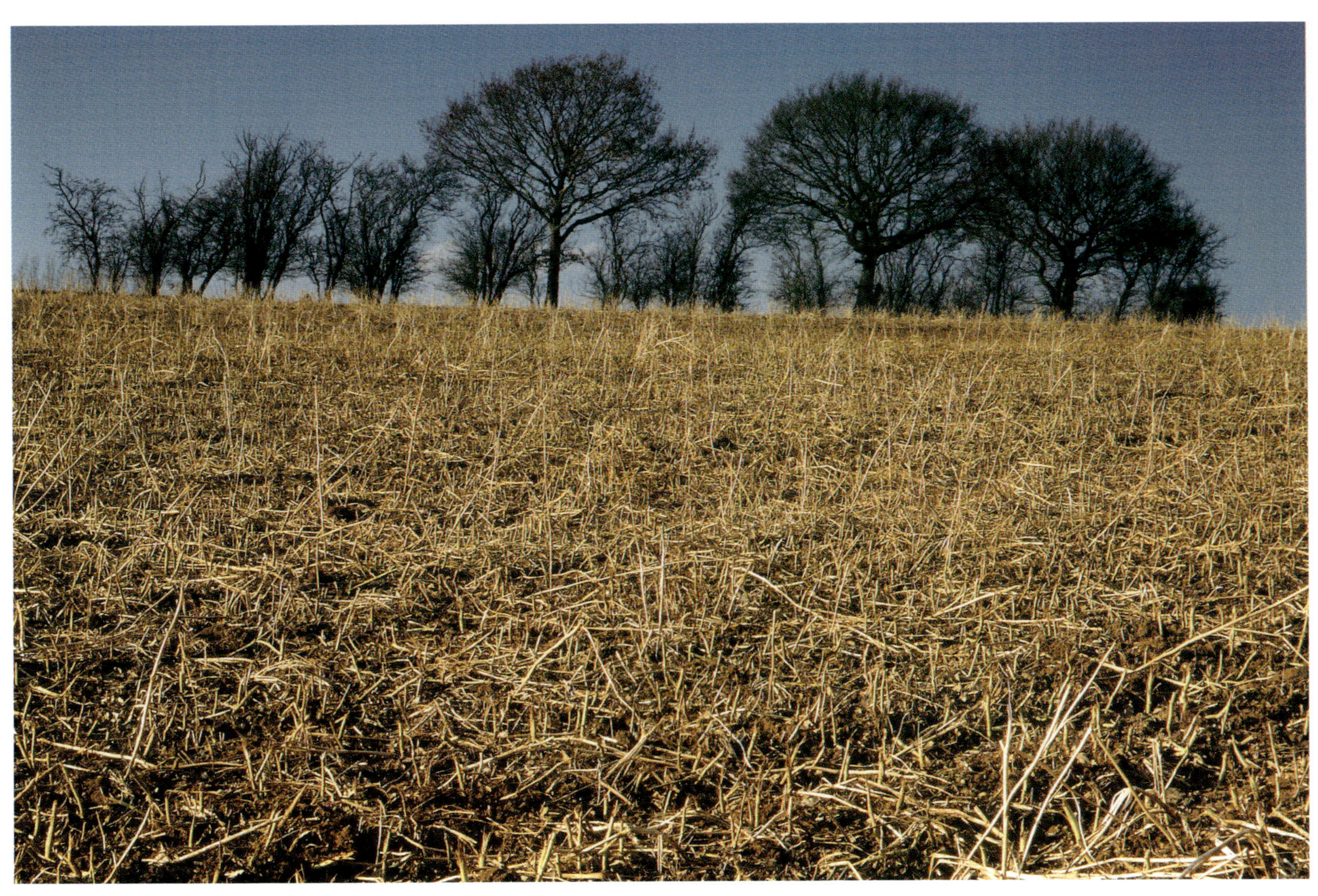

February.

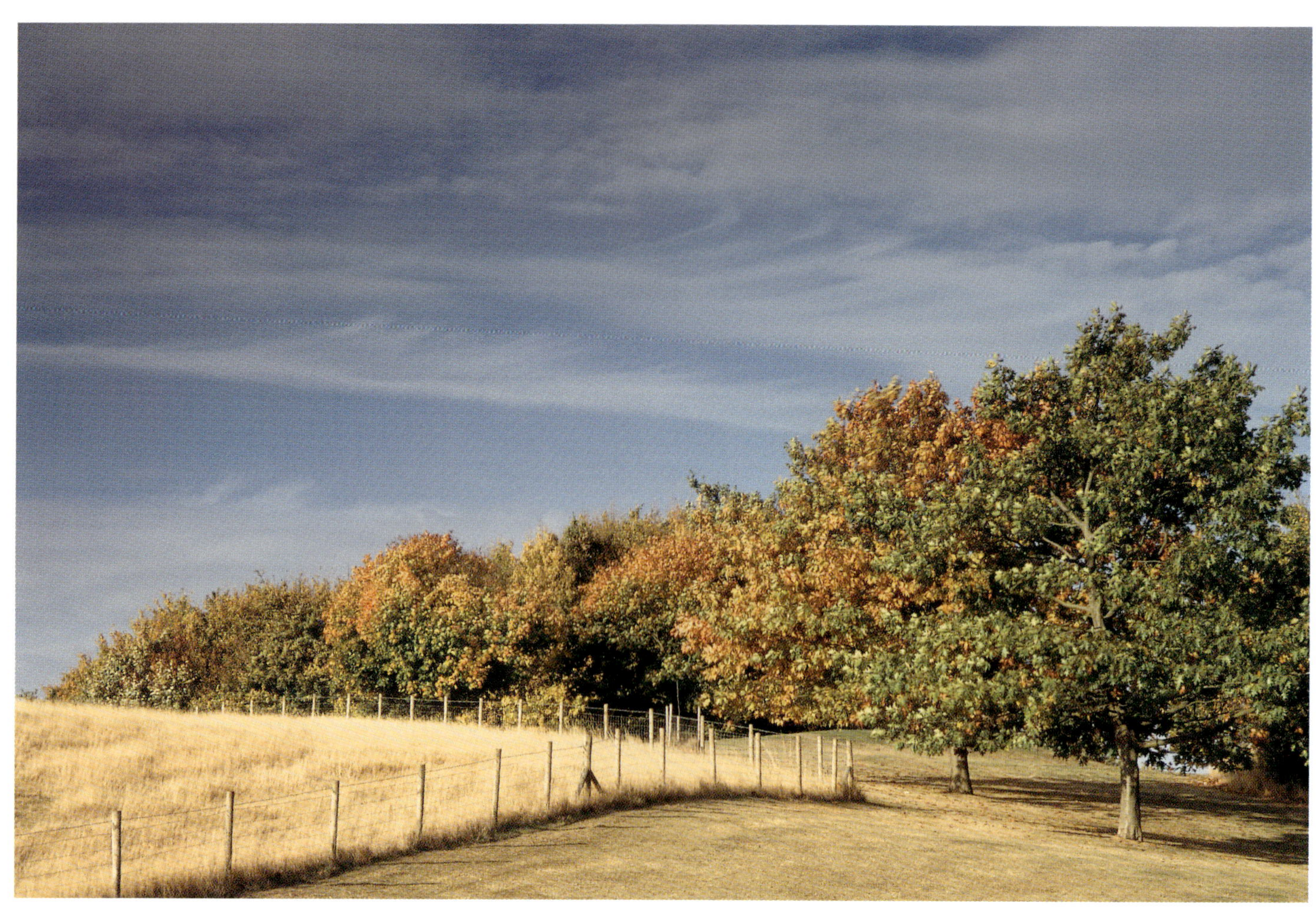

Barnsdale in October.

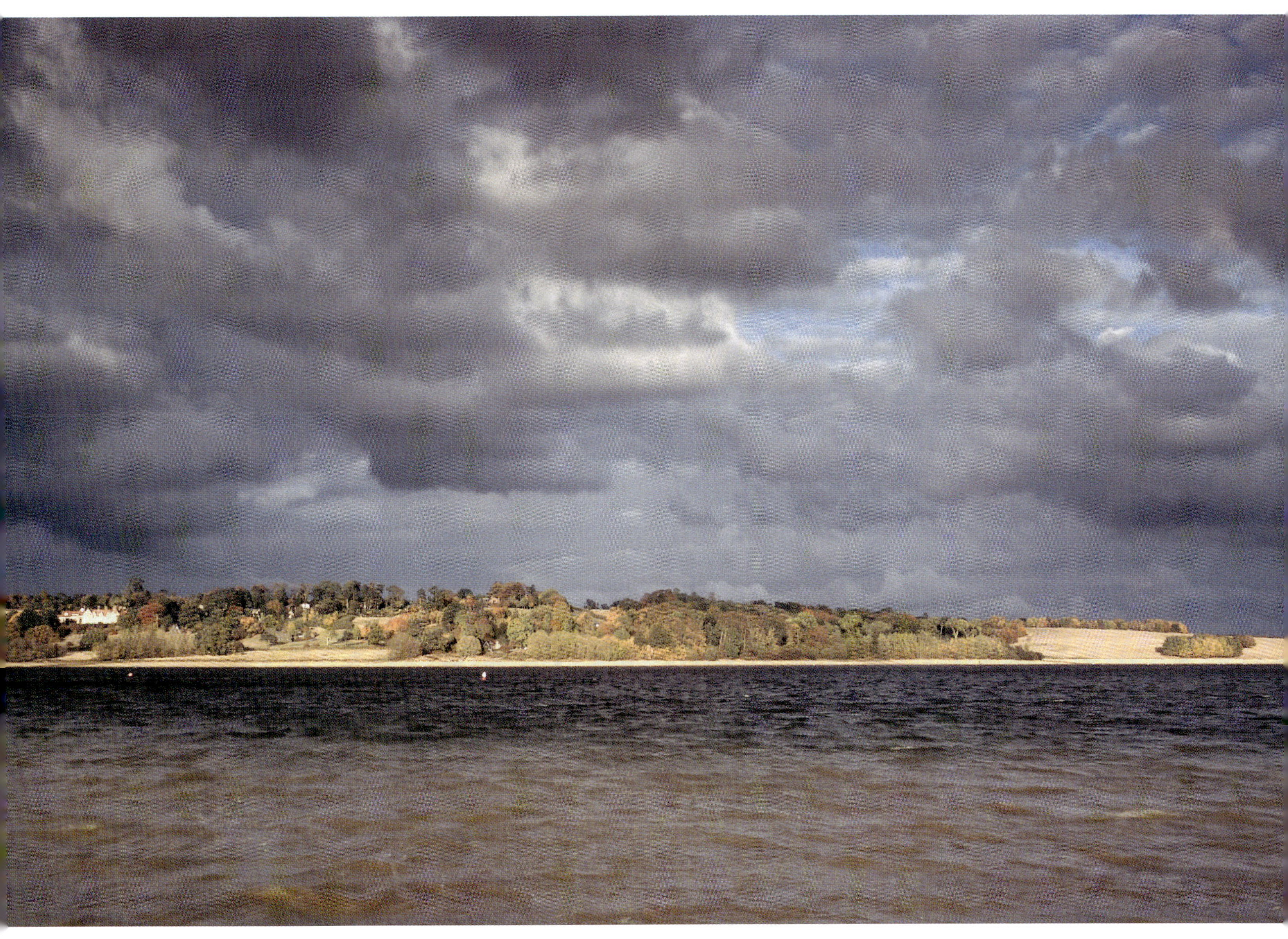

Sometimes, if the wait is long enough, the sun will break through the clouds in exactly the right place.

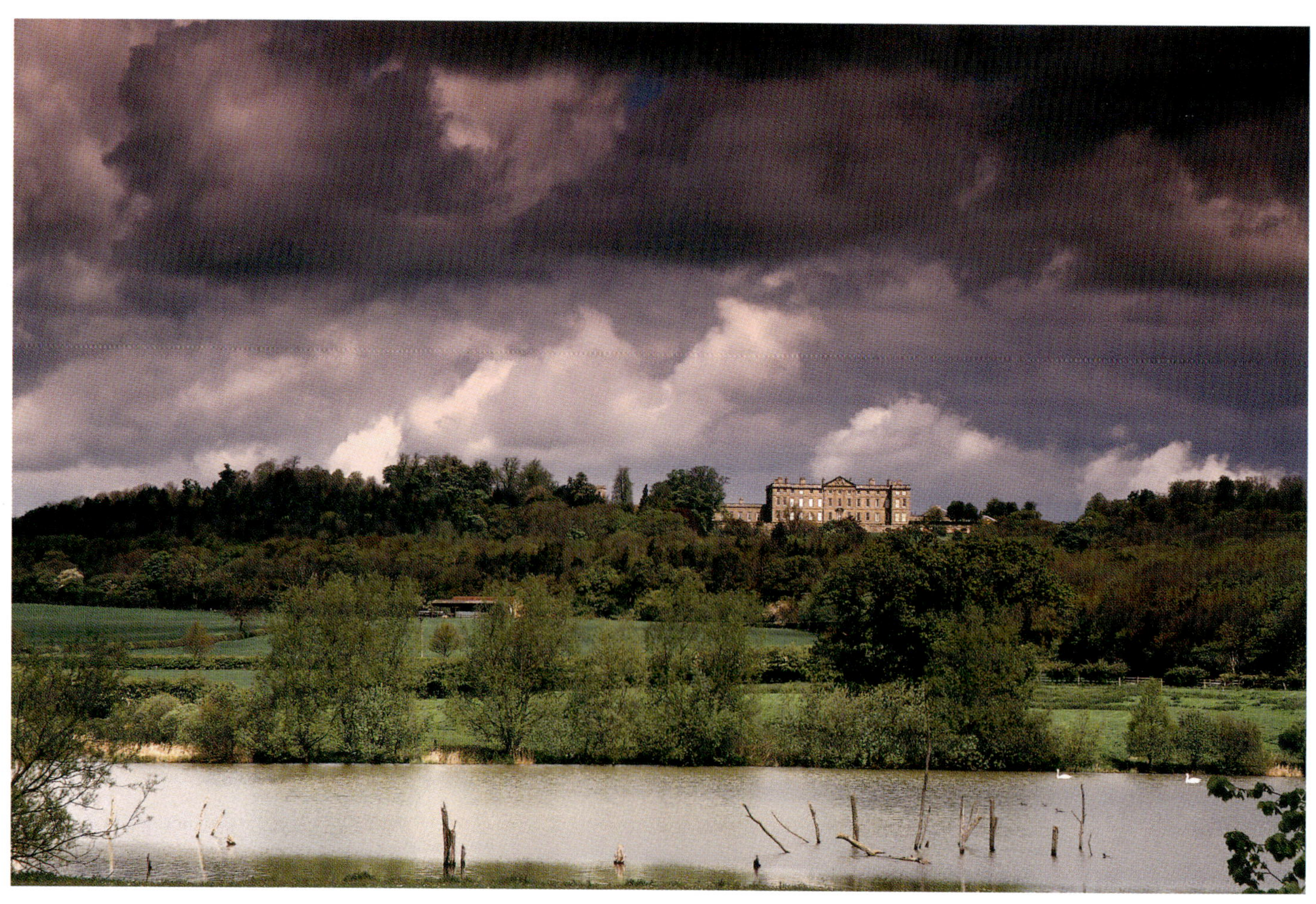

The clouds were moving so quickly, it was not too long a wait before the patches of sunlight lit up Burley House.

Even on a bright sunny day it is very shaded inside Barnsdale Arboretum, The foreground patch of light identifies the start of the path through the trees.

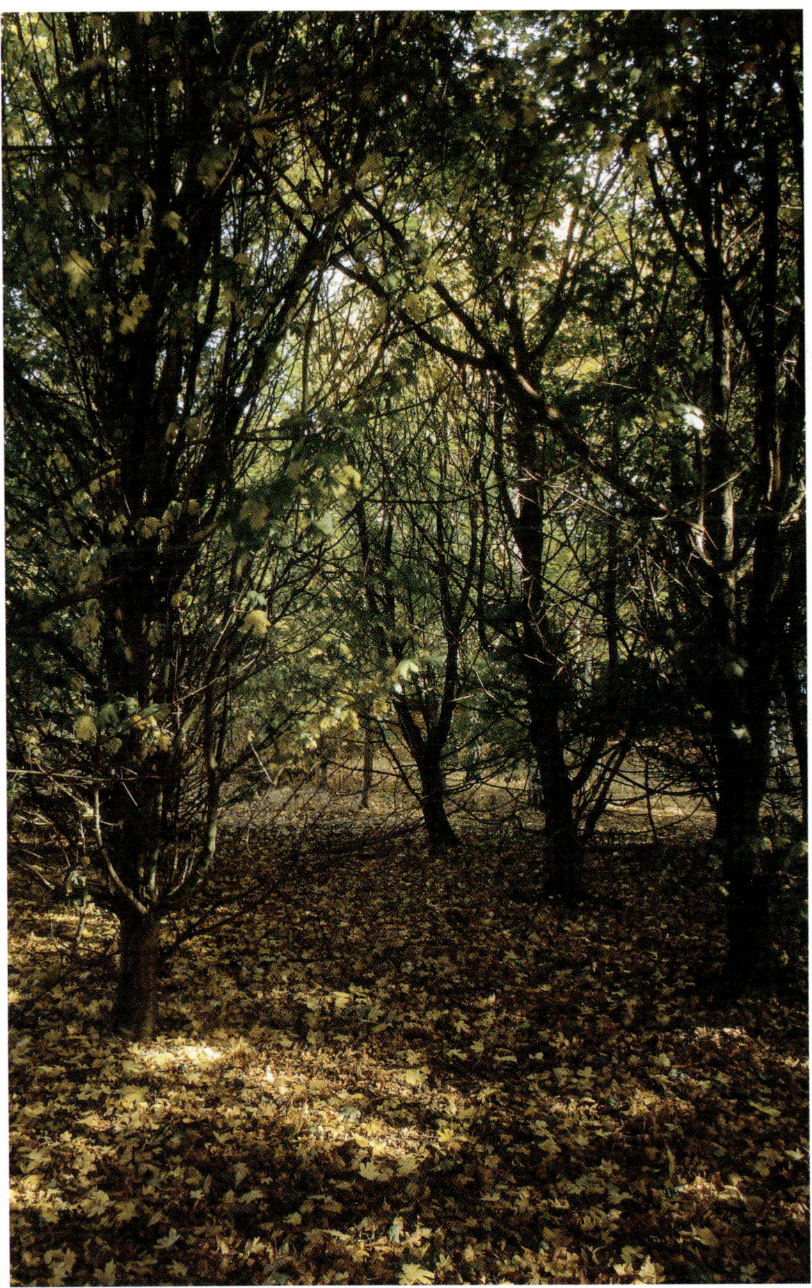

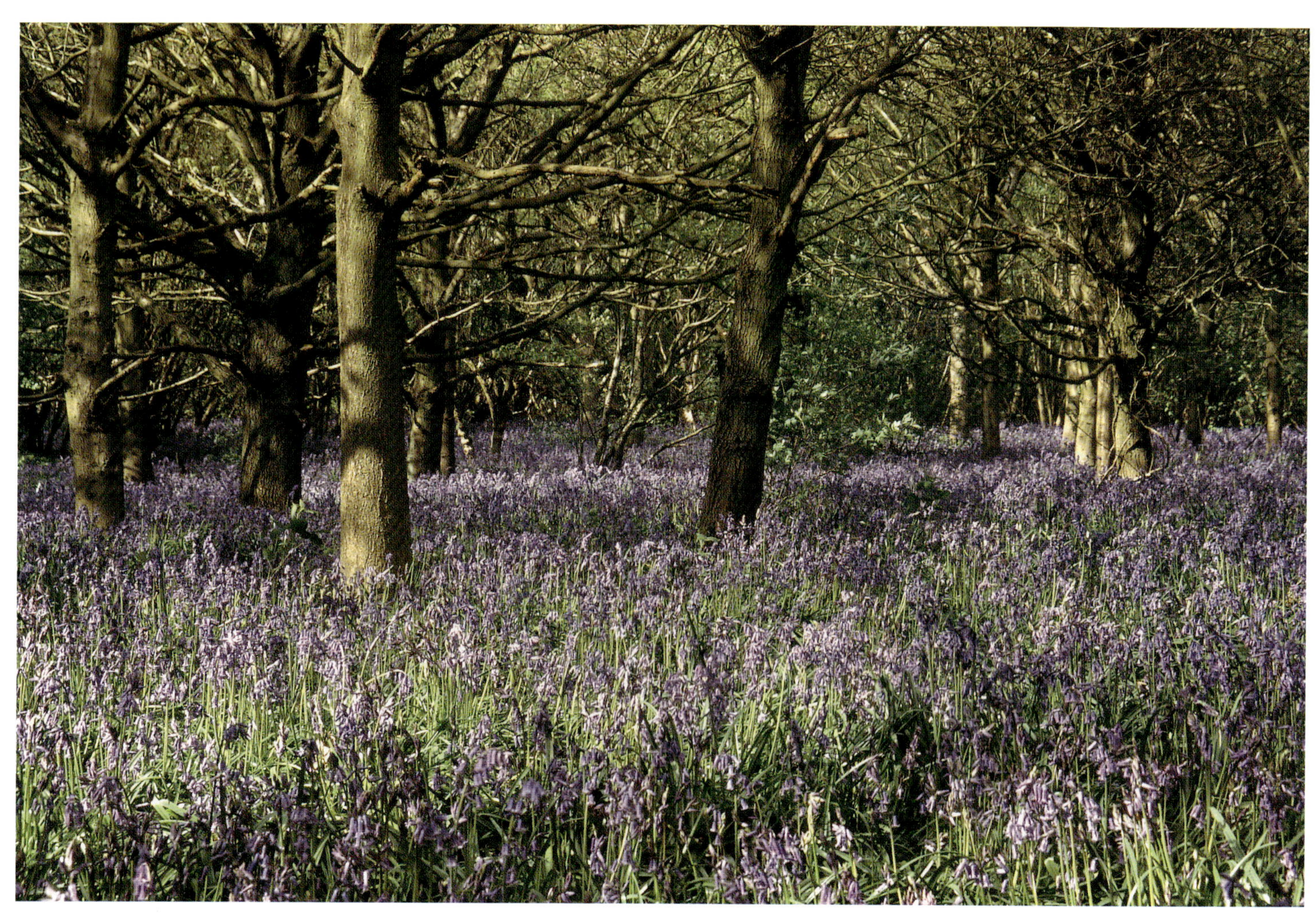

Bluebell wood.

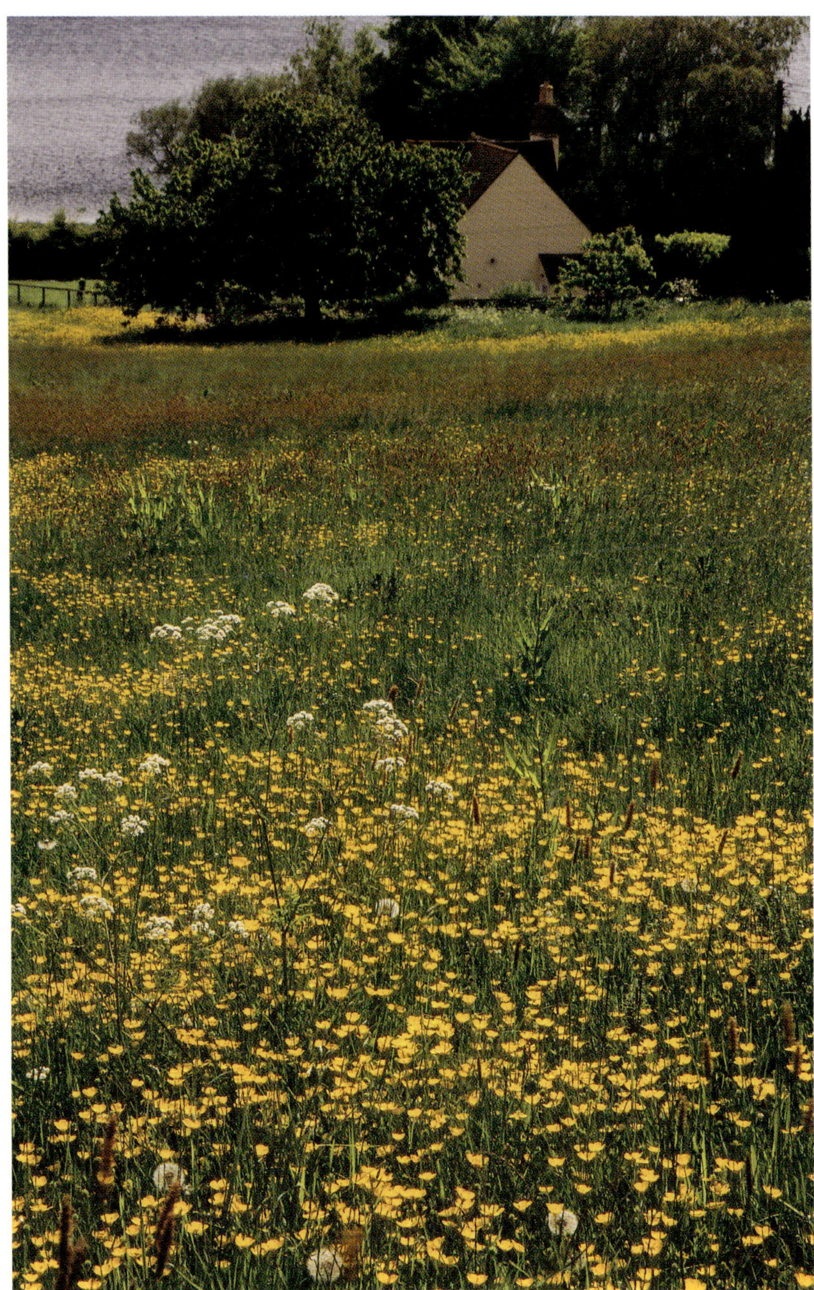

Old Hall Cottages,
Hambleton –
where I used to live.

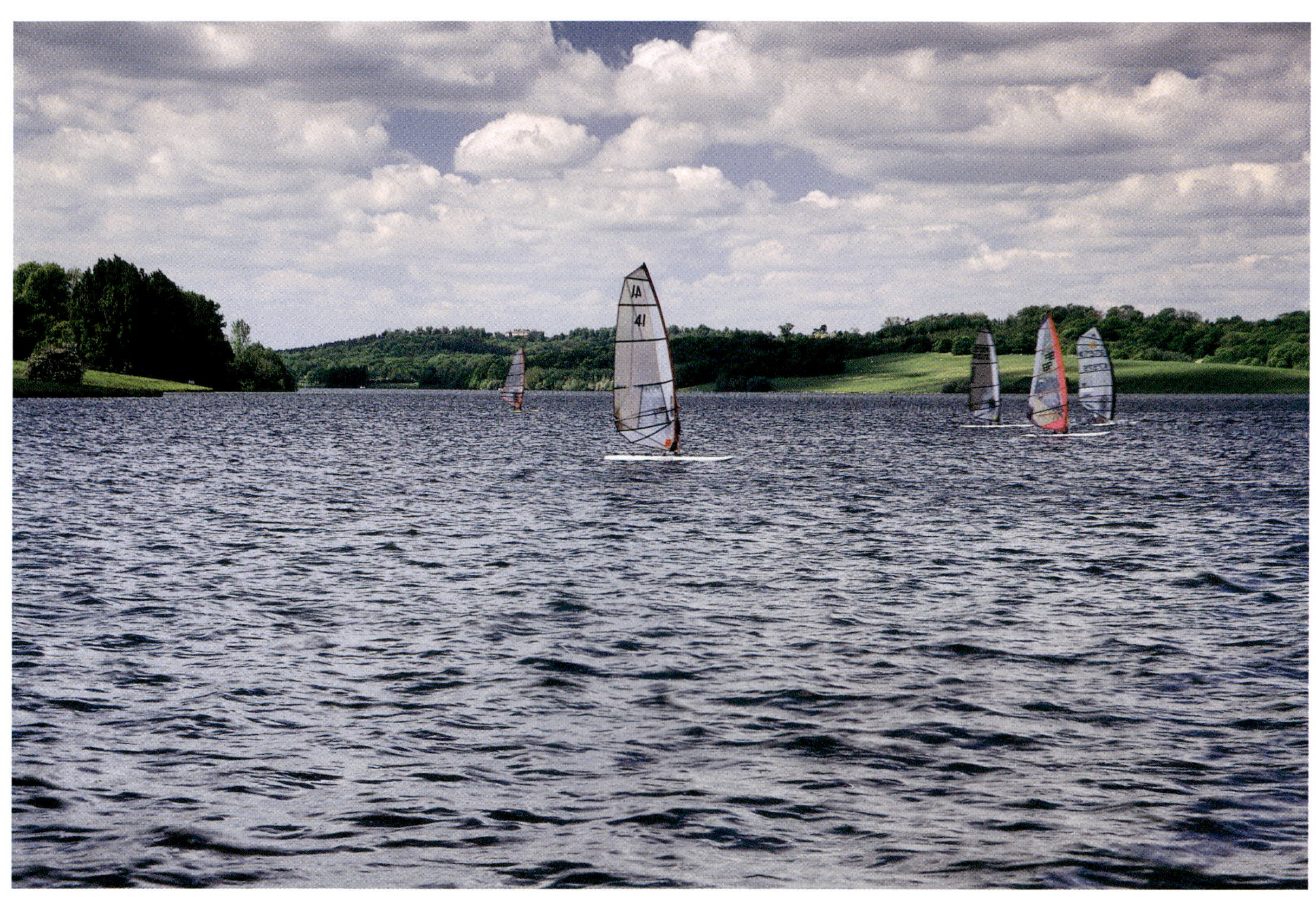

A perfect day for the National Windsurfing Championships.

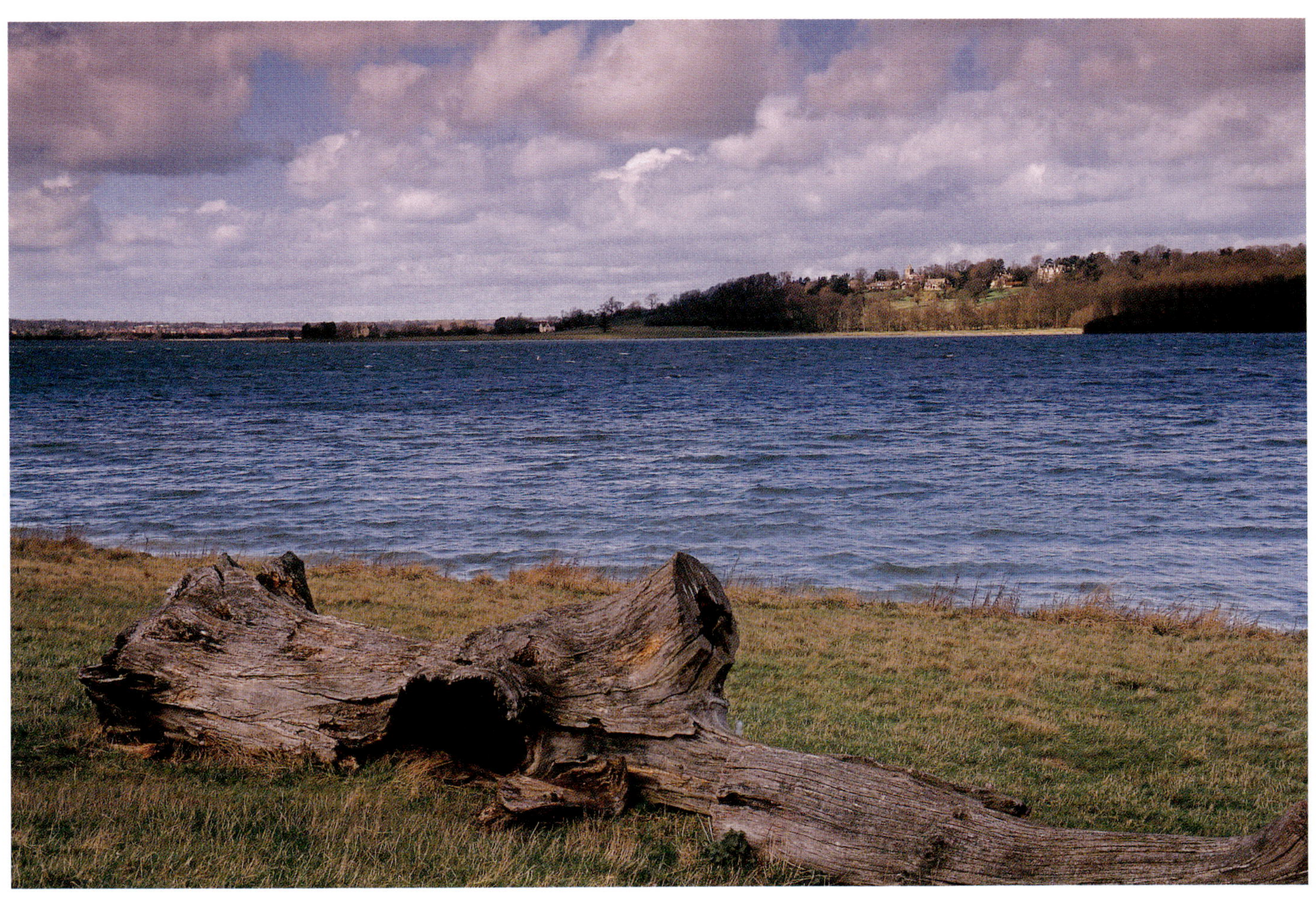

The clouds and the sun combine to highlight Upper Hambleton.

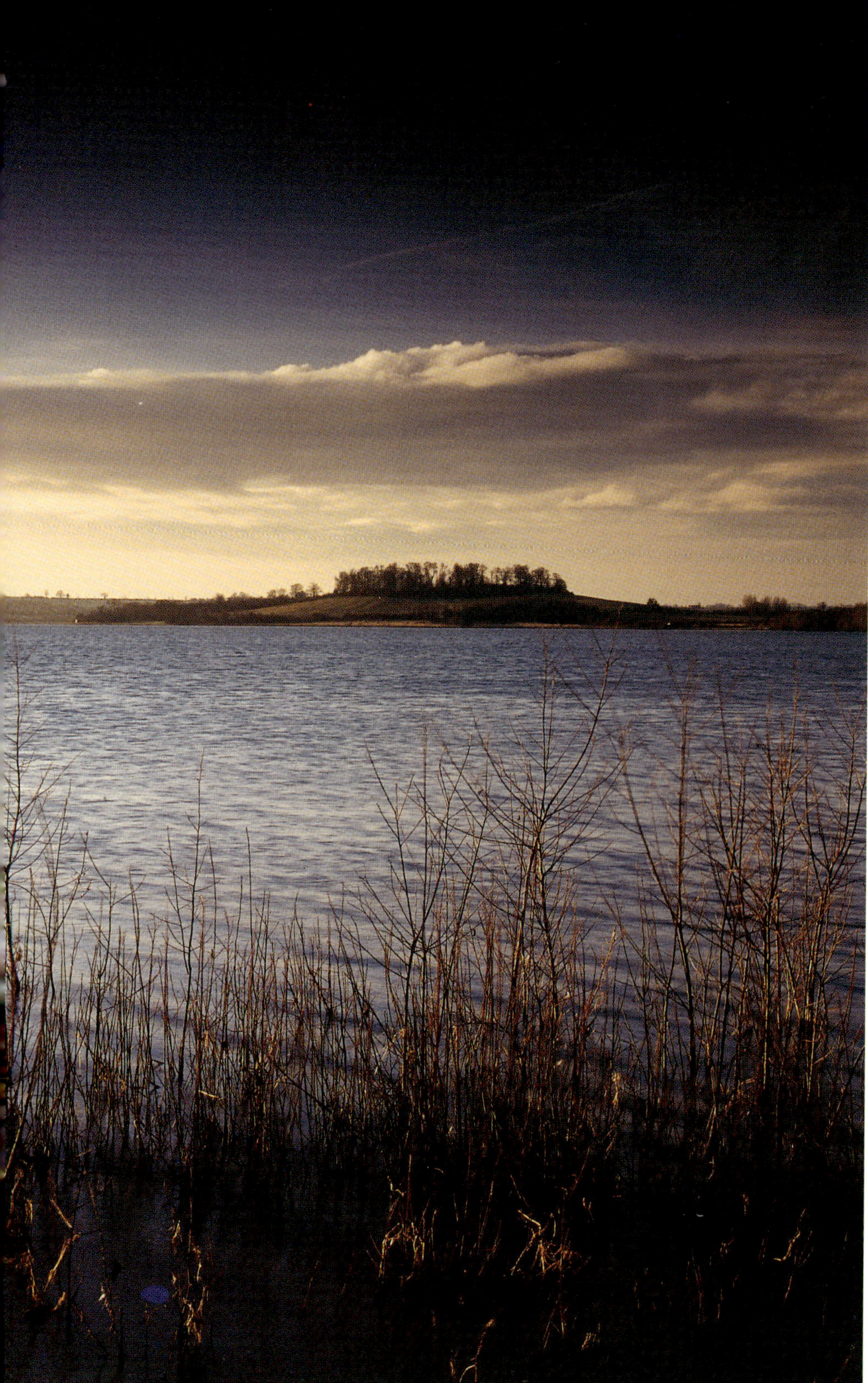

A bright winter's sun rising to the
left, adds emphasis to the deep
blues of the sky and water.

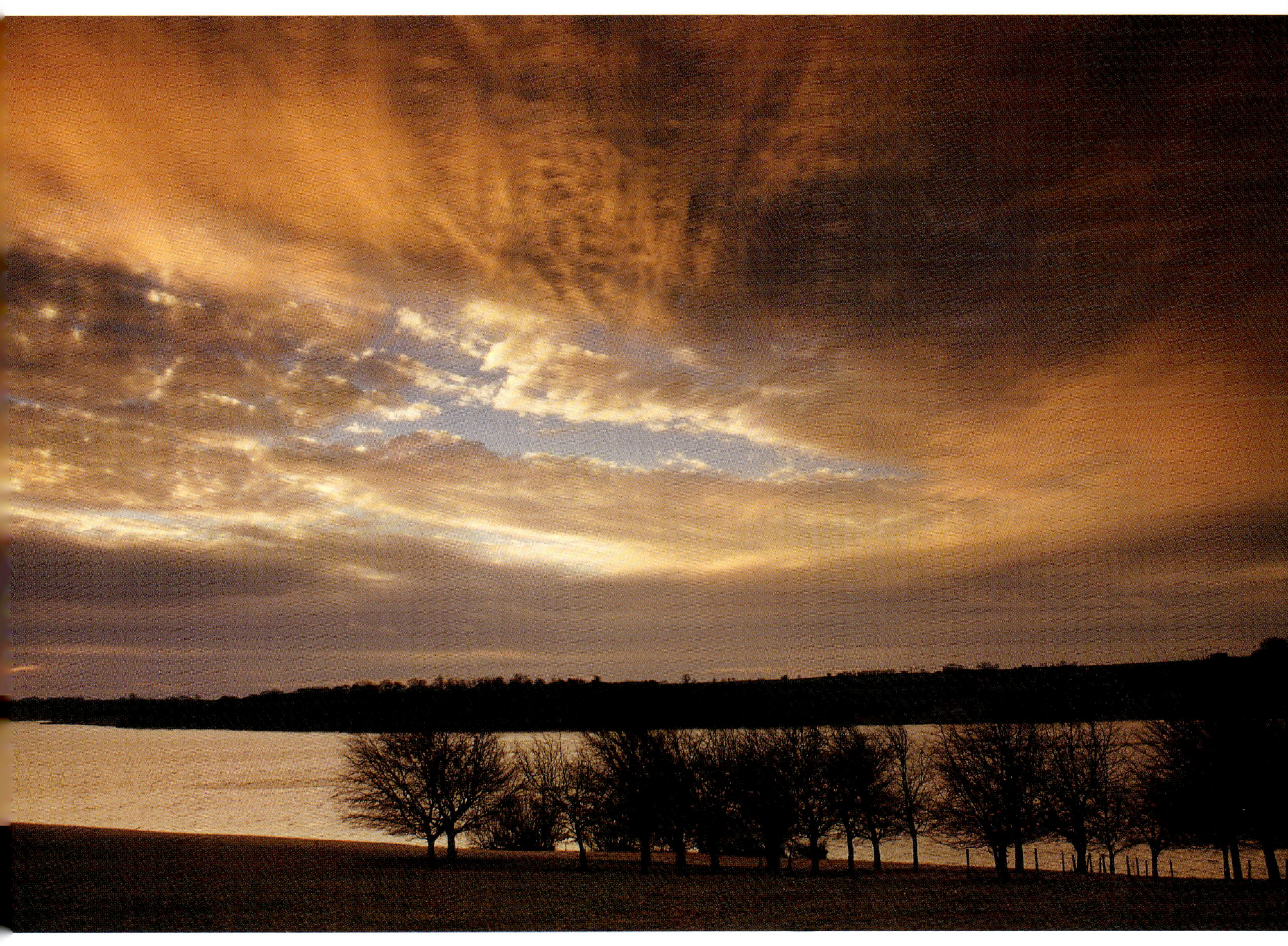

Sunrise at Barnsdale.

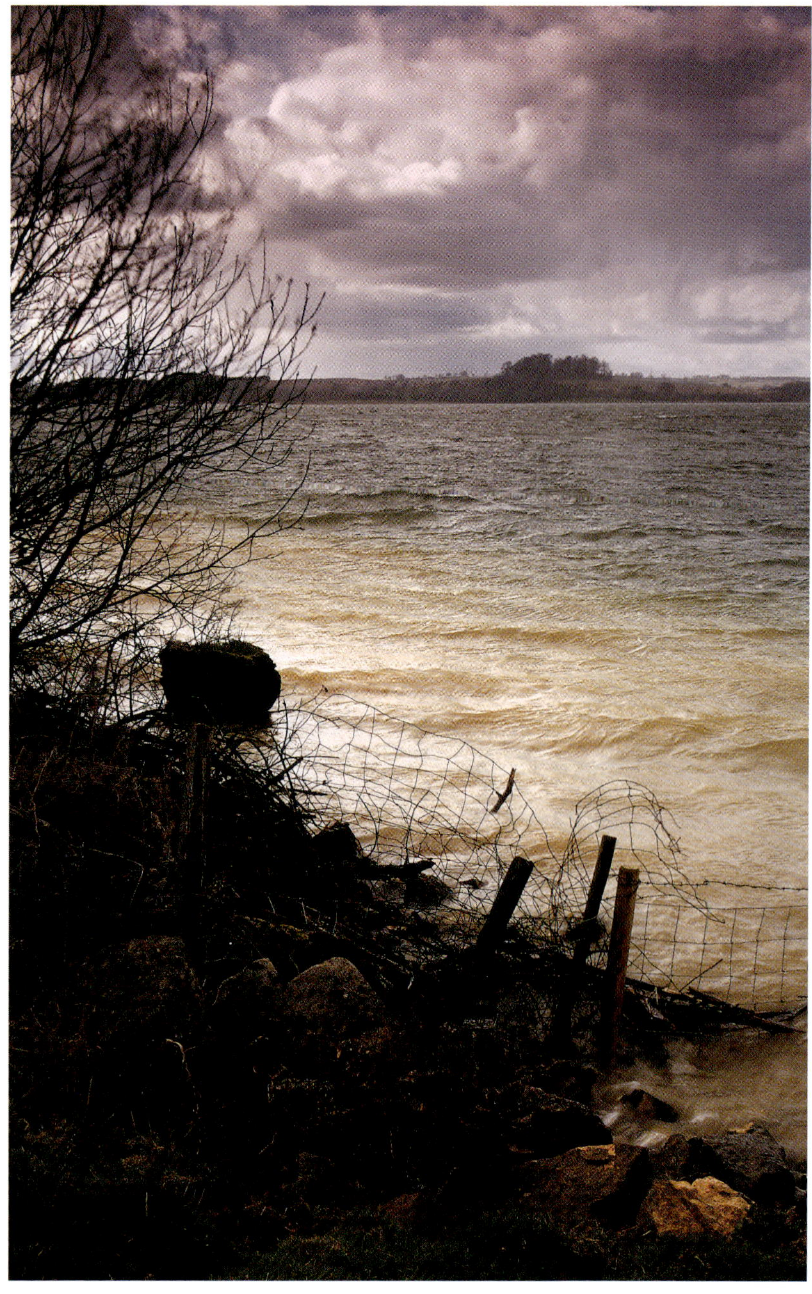

There was just time to take this scene
and pack up the camera before the
approaching storm did its worst…

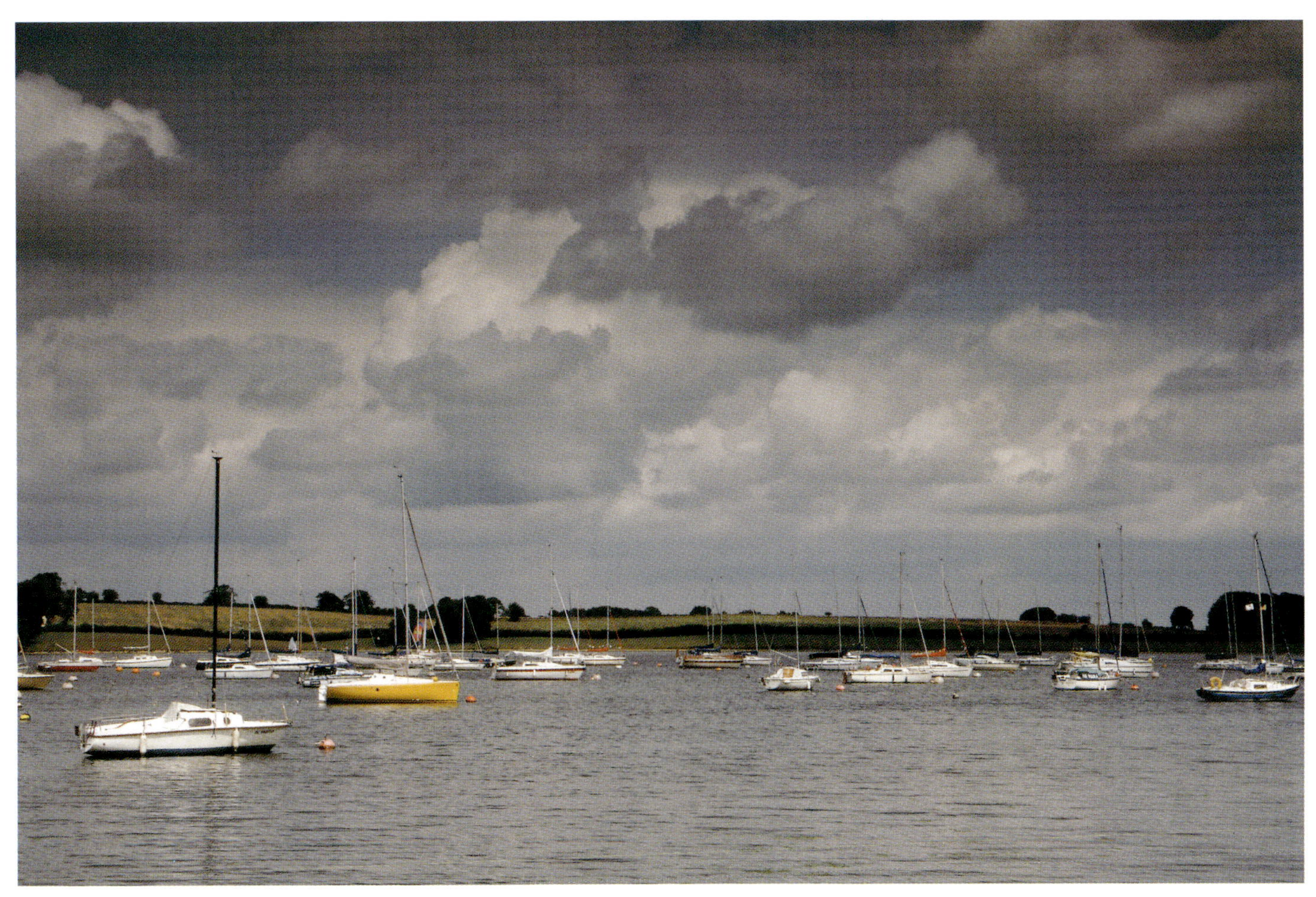

Moored boats at Rutland Water Sailing Club on a summer's day.

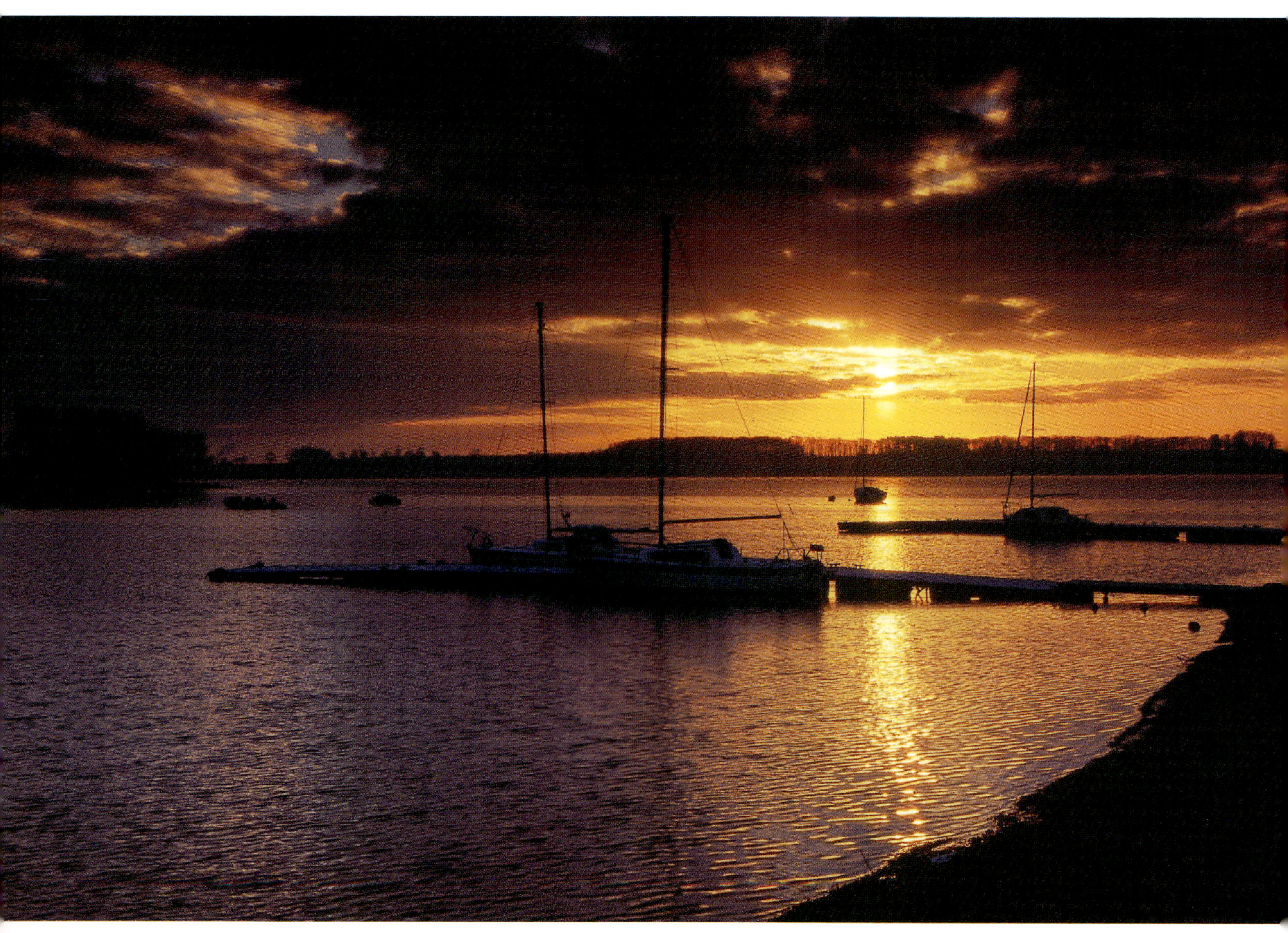

The start of a January day at Whitwell Sailing Club.

The tiny lights of Barnsdale Hall Hotel –
dwarfed by a dark and imposing sky.

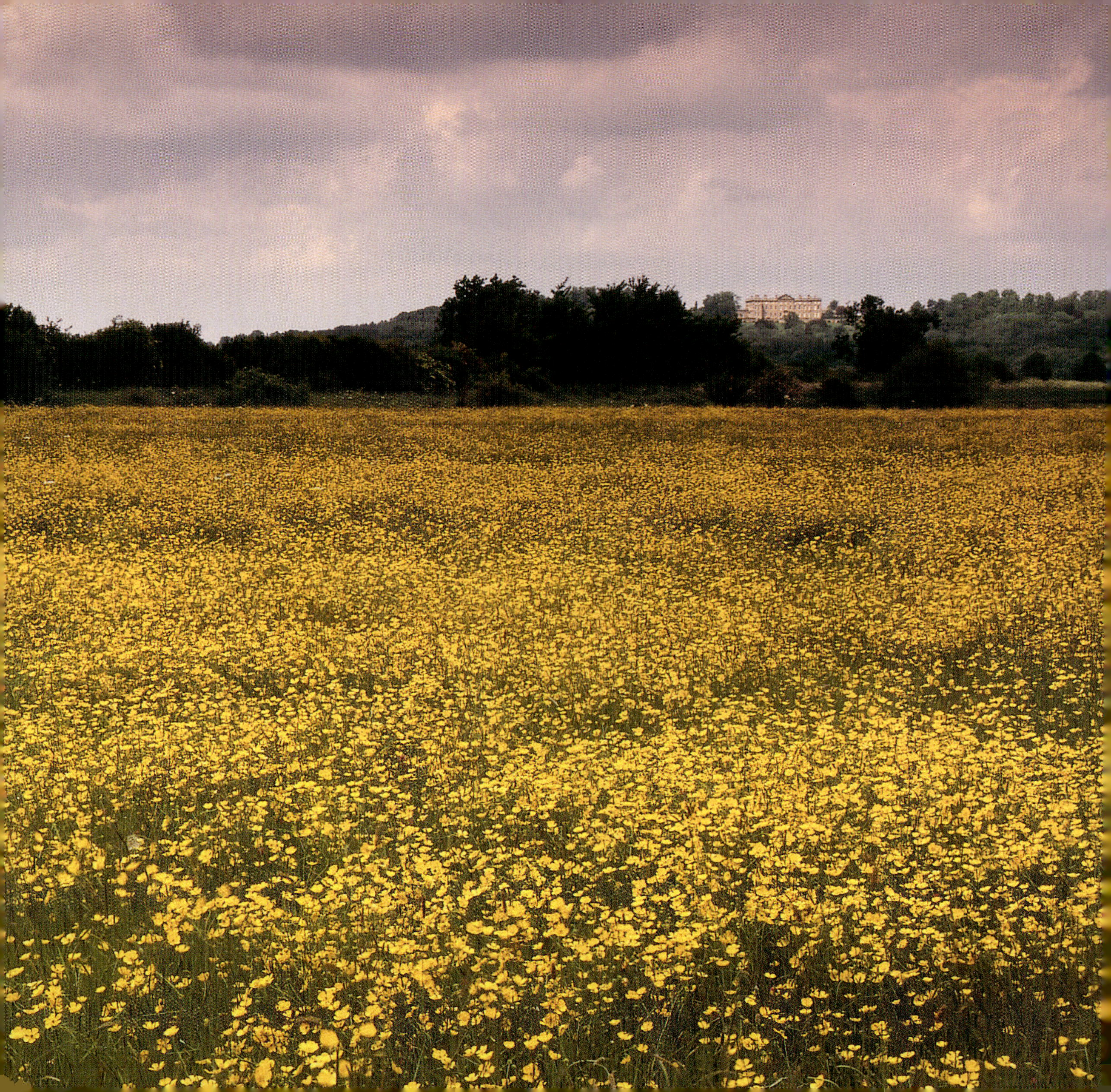

A place to sit in Barnsdale Wood,
overlooking the Water.

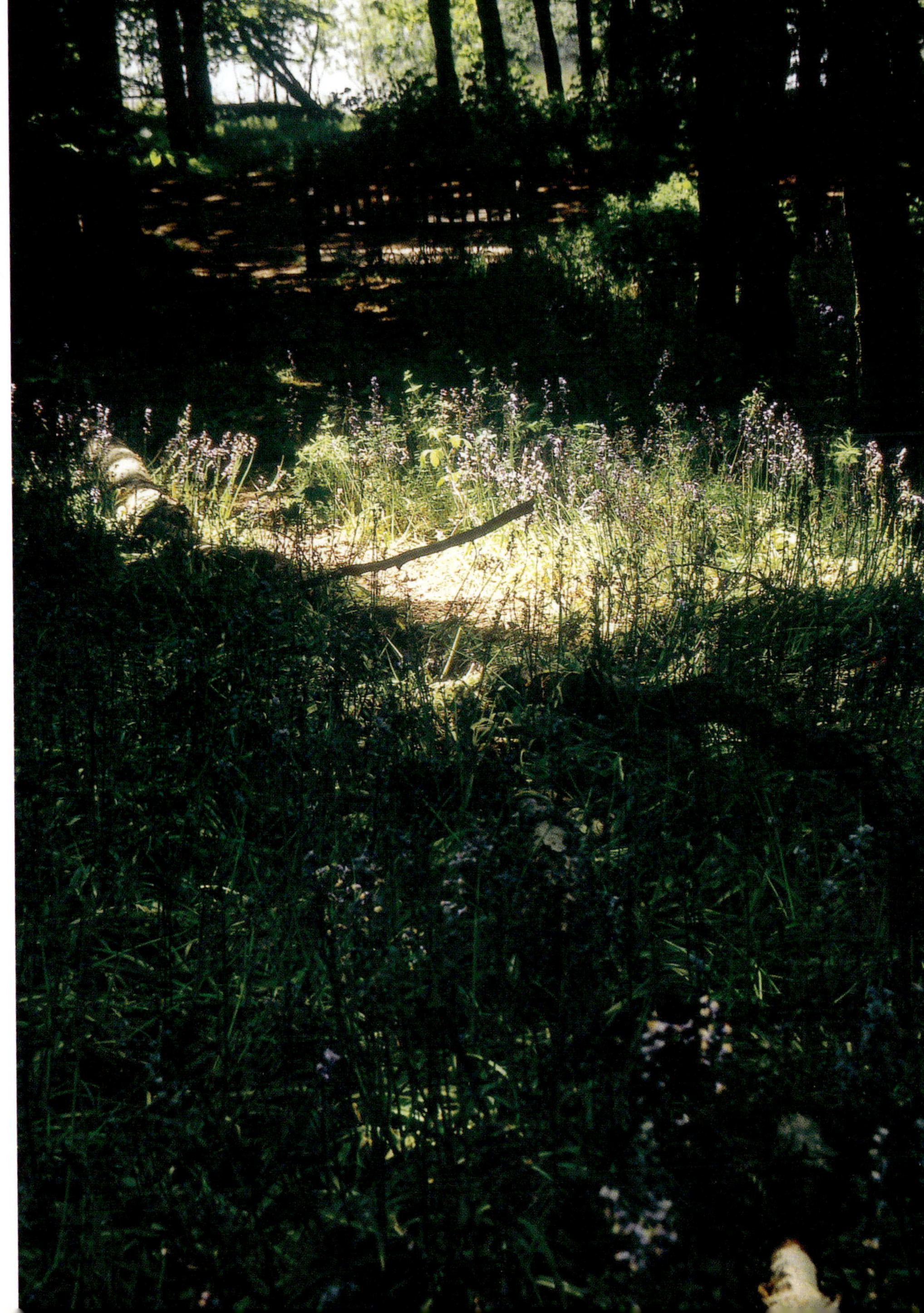

Opposite page: The meadows at
Egleton Nature Reserve.

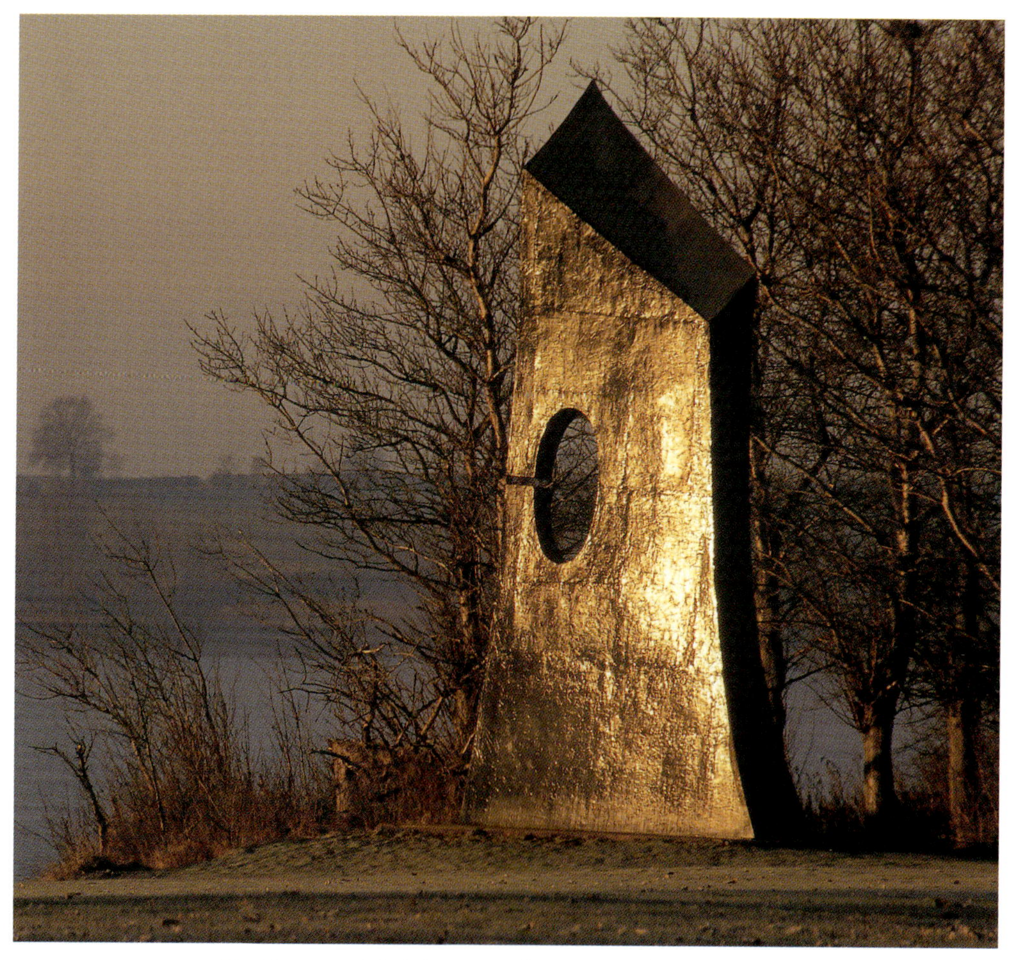

The Tower at Syke's Lane, caught in the early morning light.

The water levels are so low that it is possible
to see the foundations of a house demolished
and submerged some 25 years previously, and
the top of Brown's Hill, also normally
hidden underwater.

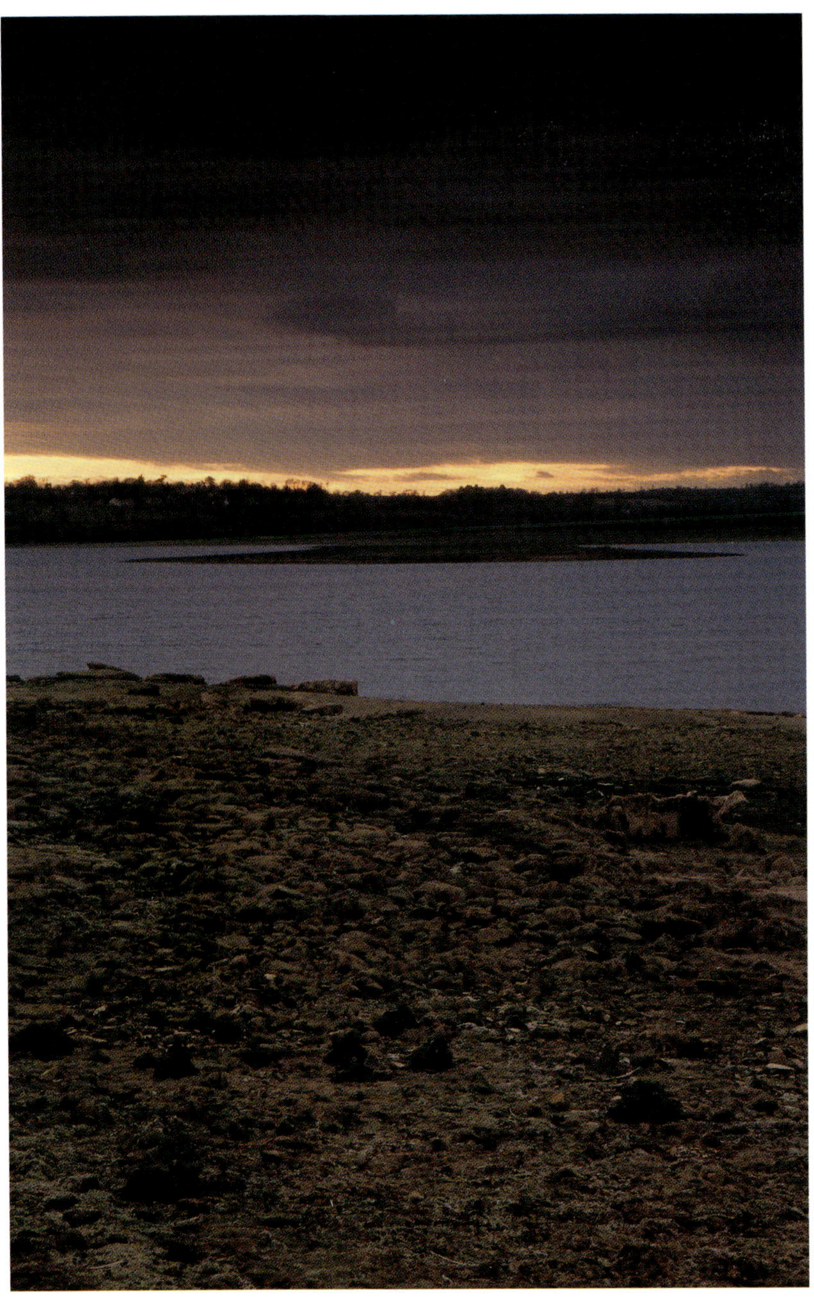

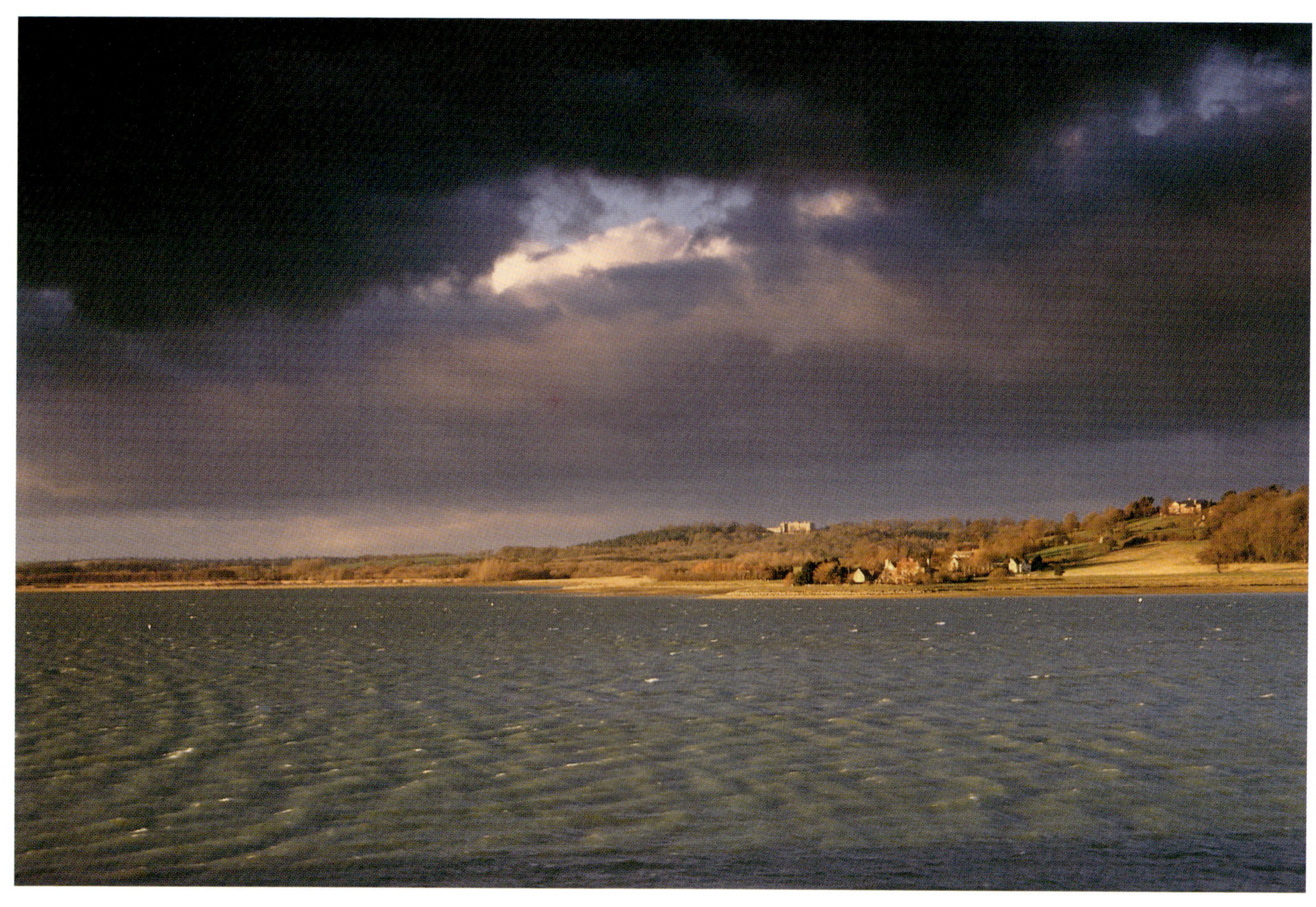

Chasing the light.

Looking away from the setting sun there is still colour in the sky, with the low moon adding the final detail.

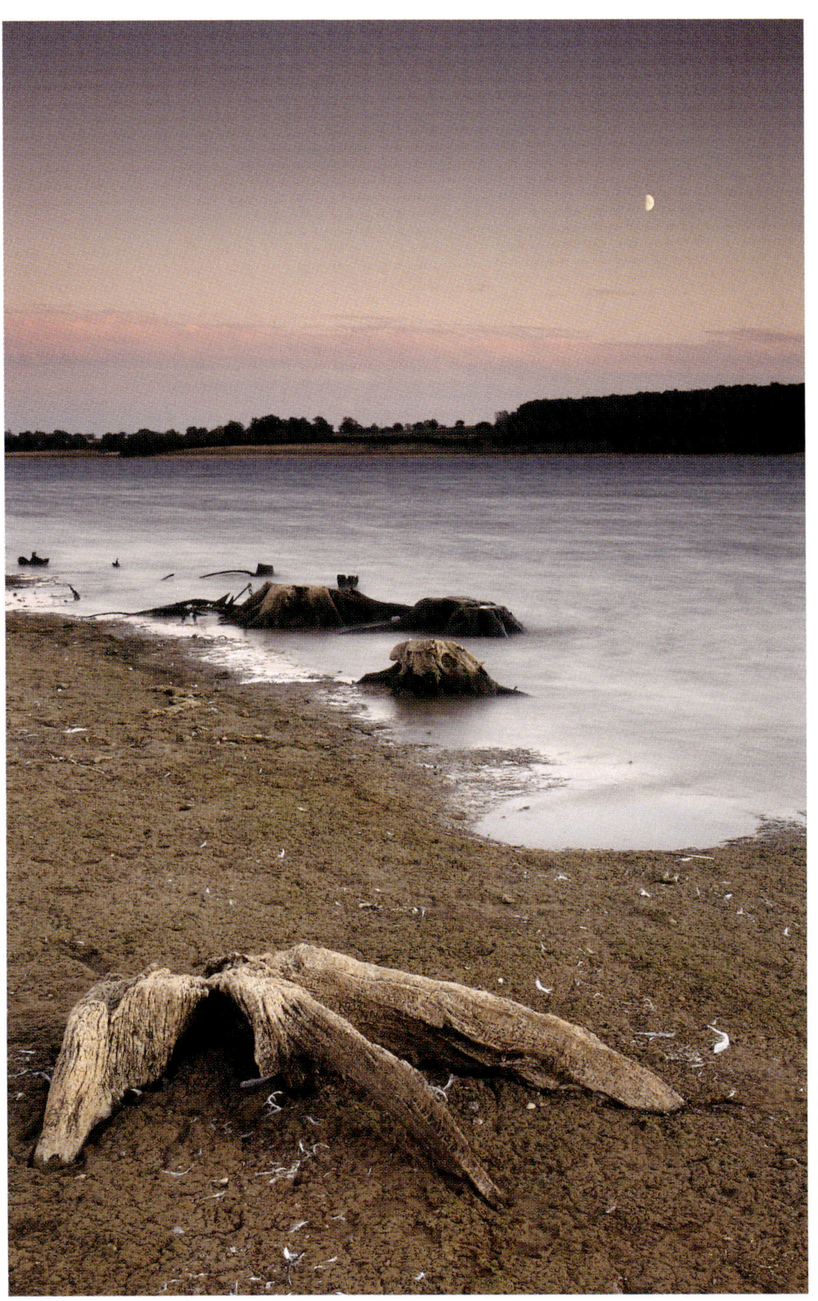

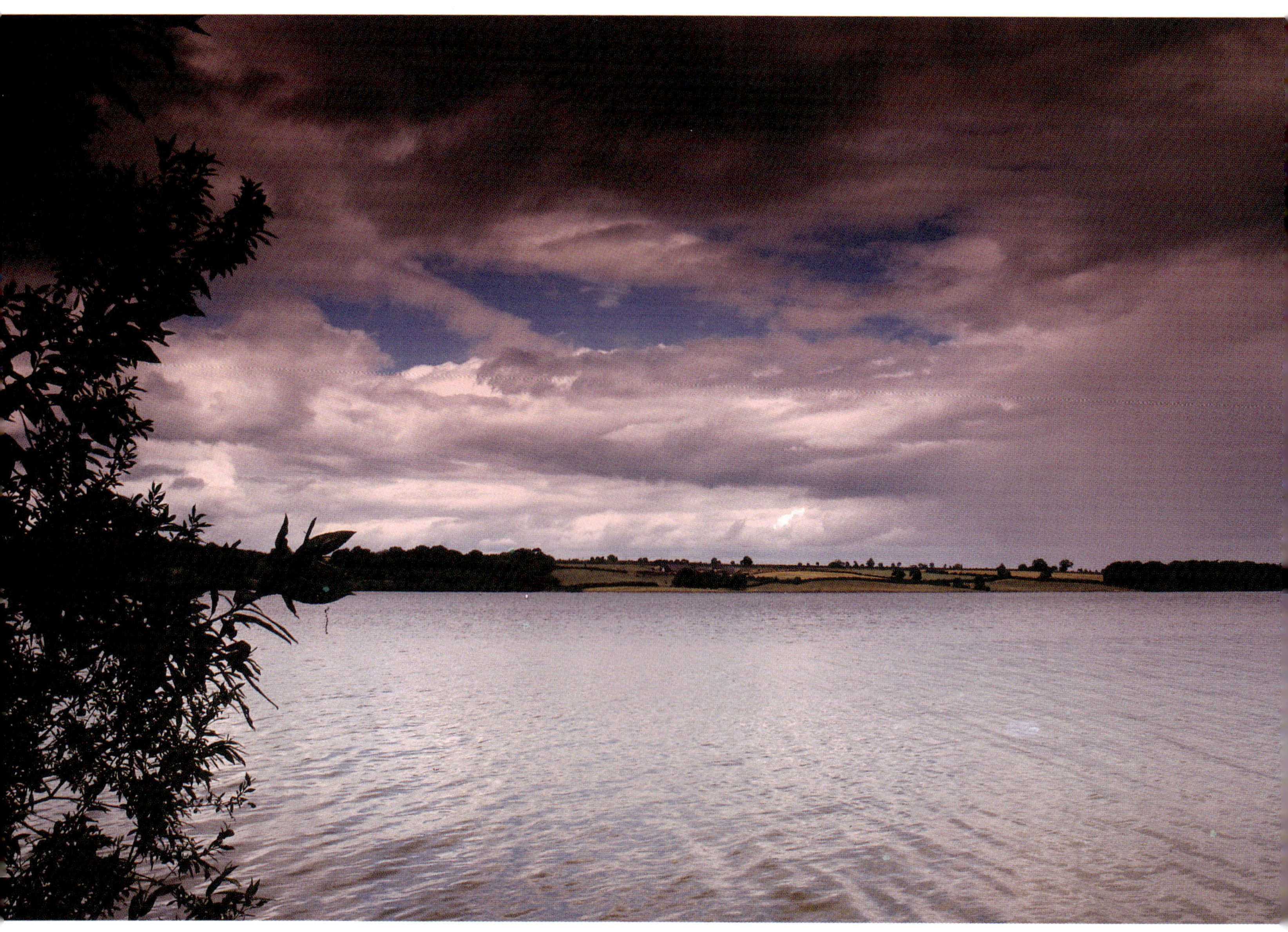

The peninsula looking very small and vulnerable, sandwiched between acres of water and a vast sky.

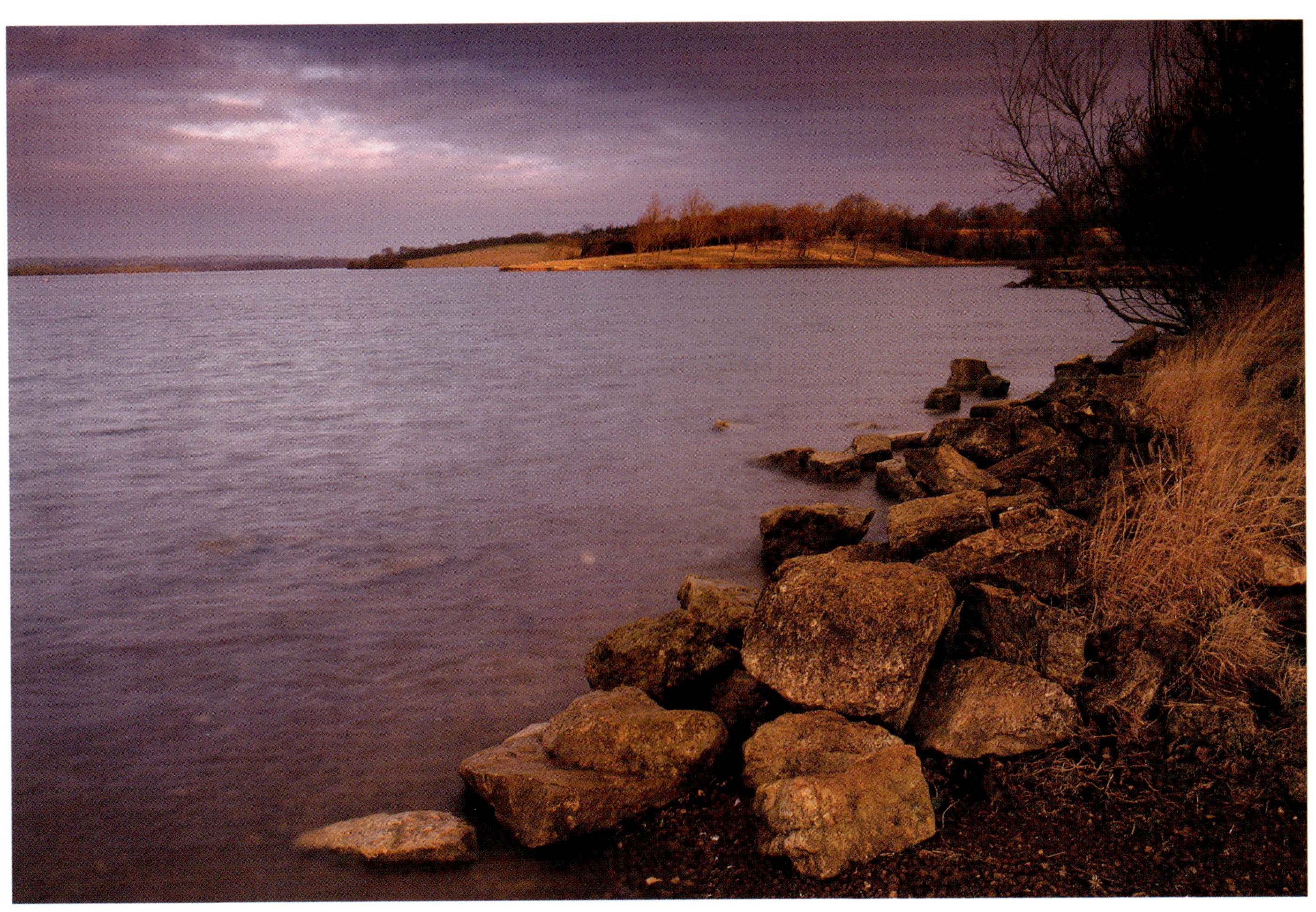

The light from a strong early morning sun brings a warm glow to the foreground rocks and distant shoreline.

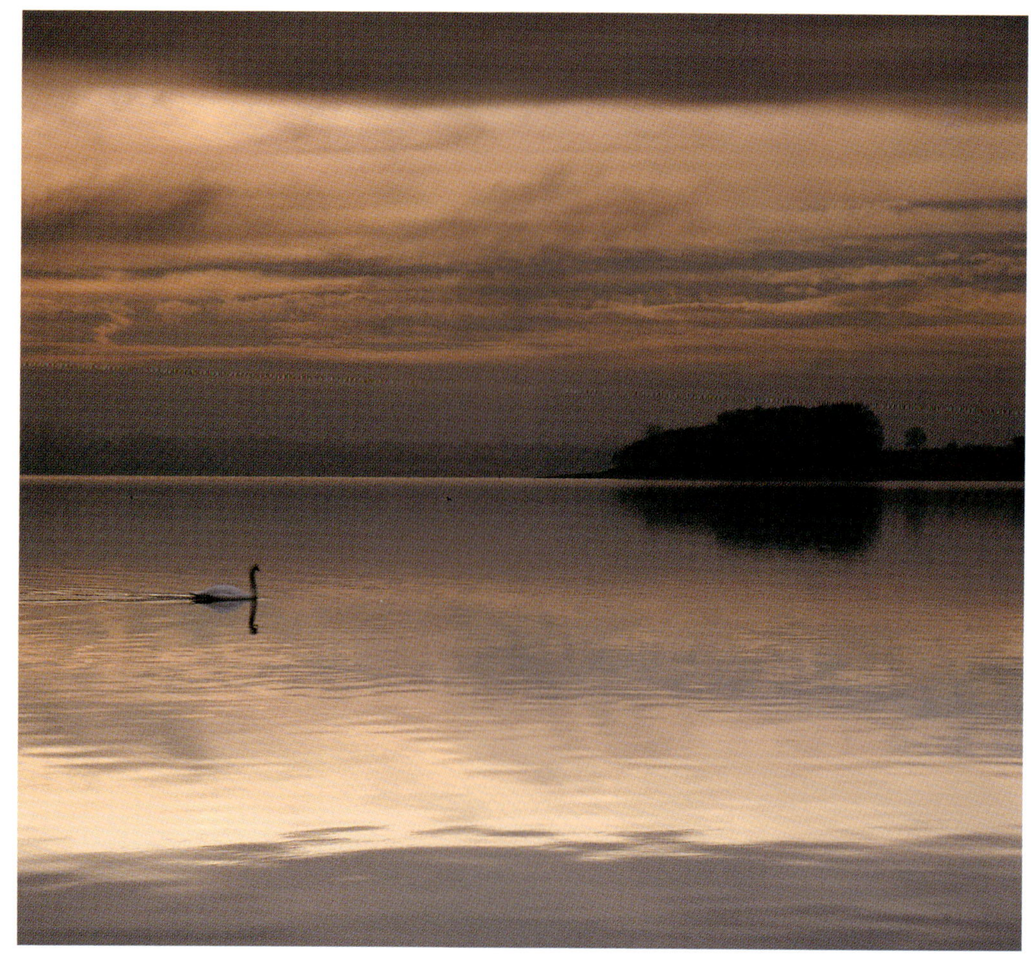

Sometimes, a swan will appear at just the right moment.

In this light, Barnsdale Creek could be somewhere in the Everglades.

On a very foggy November morning,
all but the closest detail is hidden.

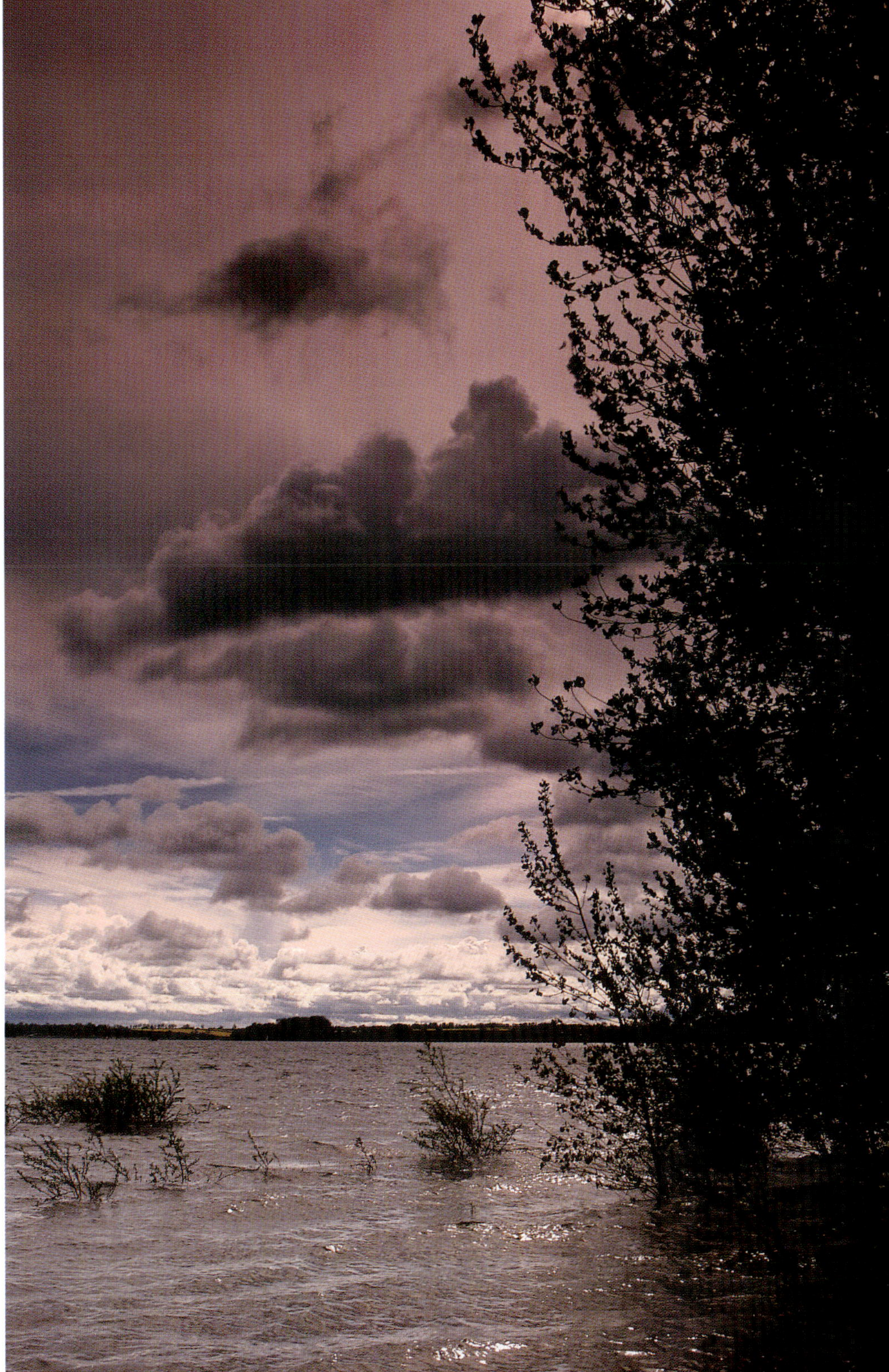

The disappearing cloudscape creates
a tremendous feeling of distance.

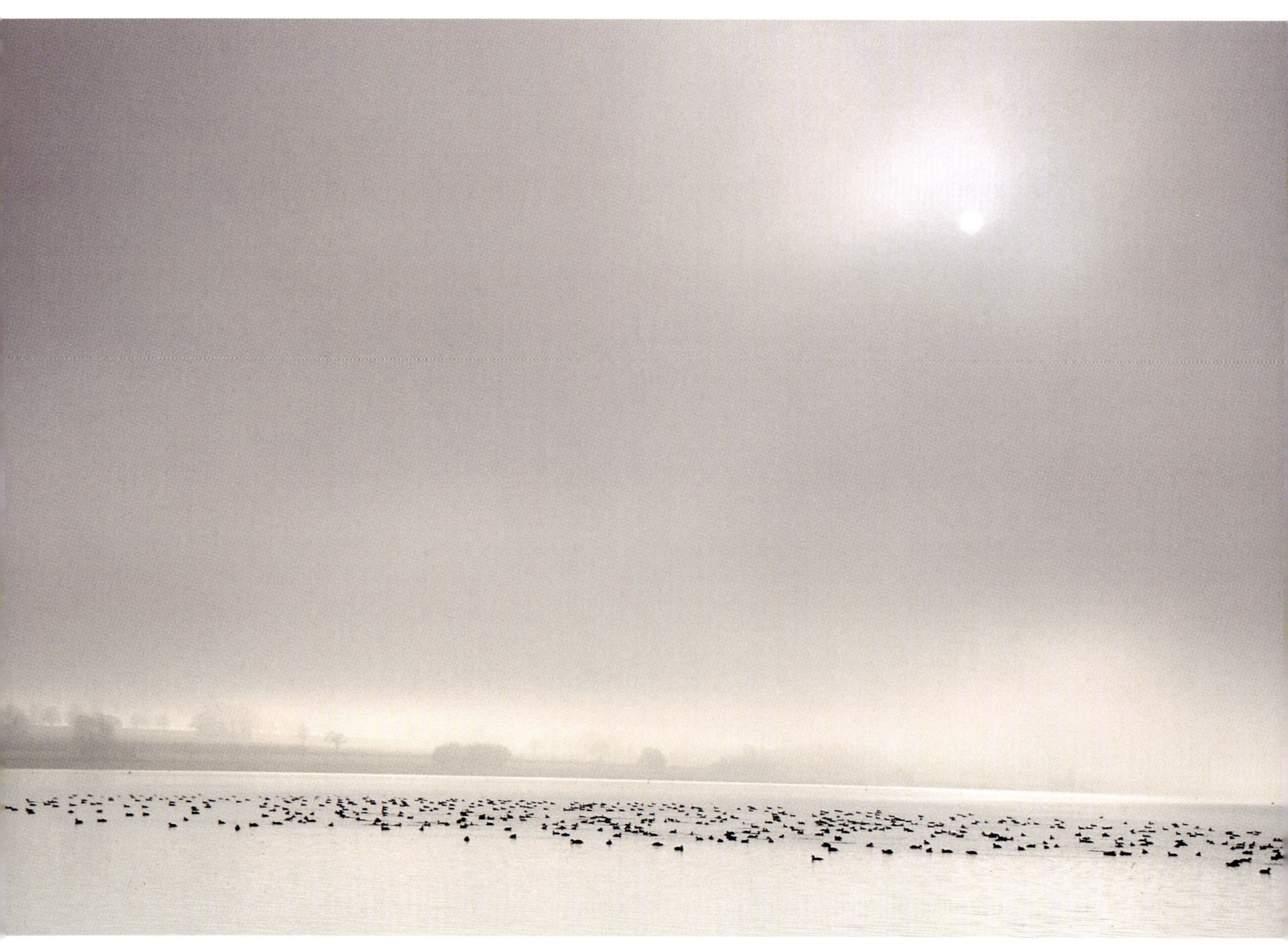

The midday sun has just enough strength through the fog to create highlights on the water.

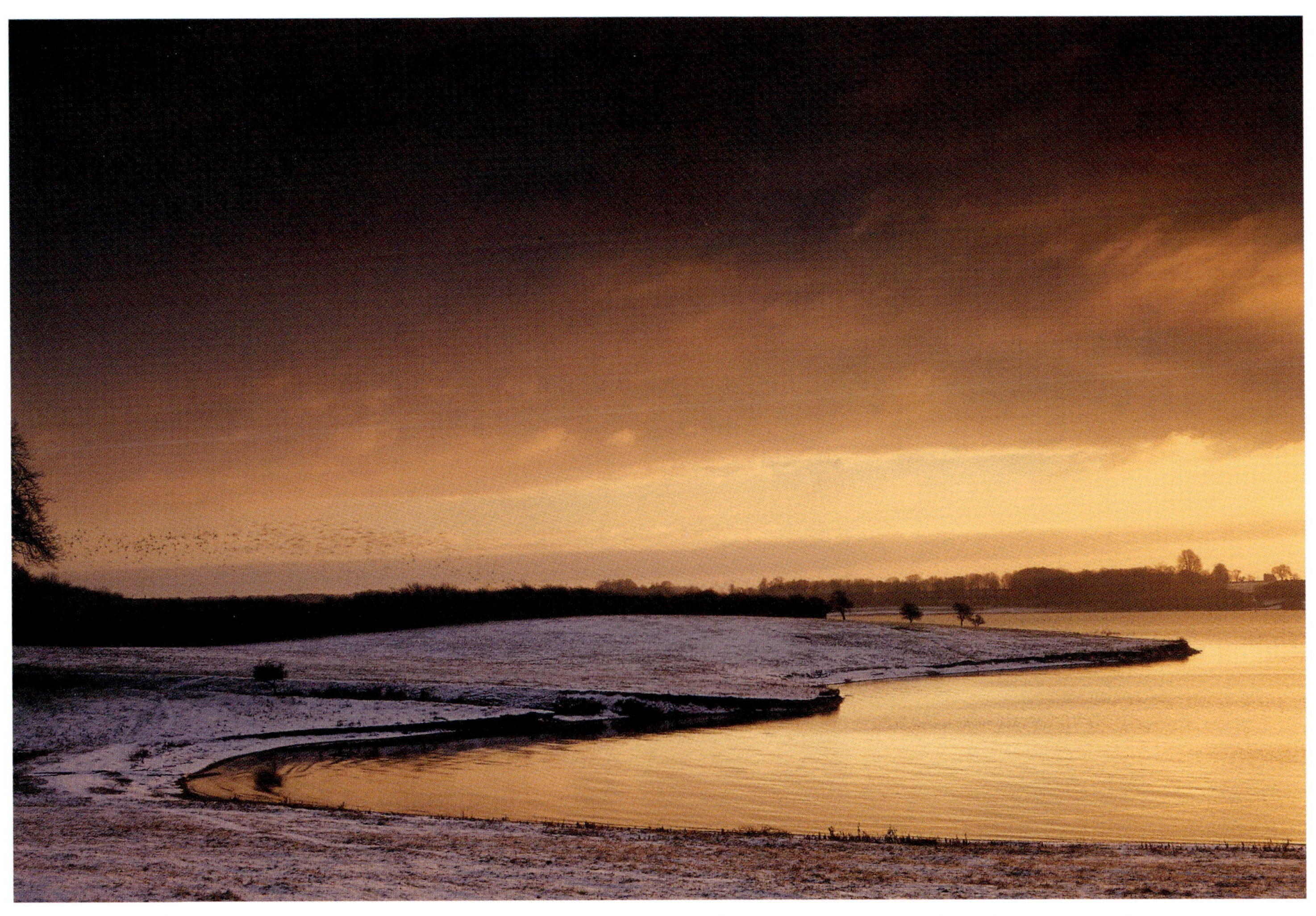

My son's favourite and his choice for the back cover – even the flock of birds flew into exactly the right area of the cloud pattern.

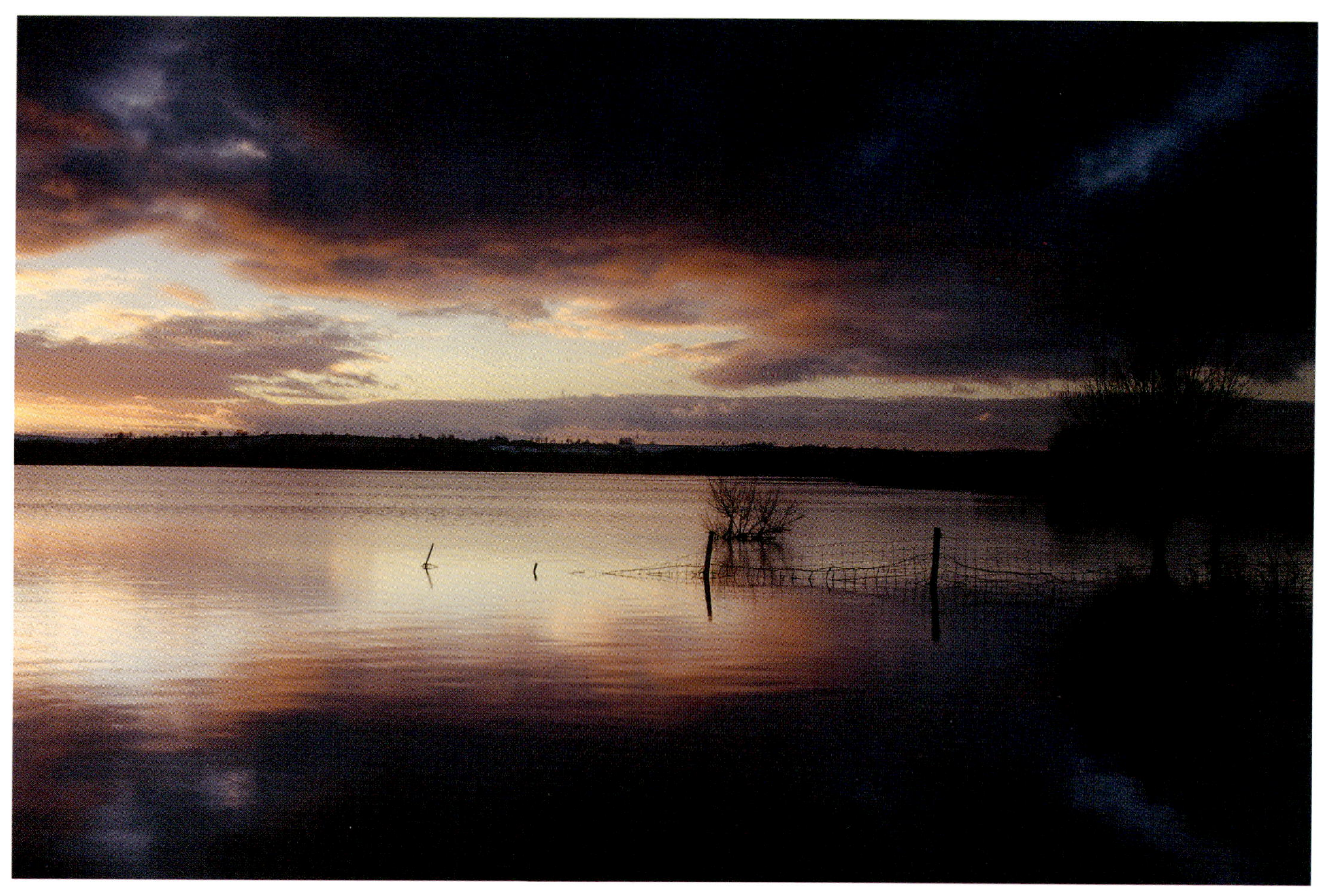

In a secluded spot in a corner of the peninsula, this late January afternoon was completely peaceful.

It is very rare to see the water as 'wild' as this, given Rutland Water's sheltered location.

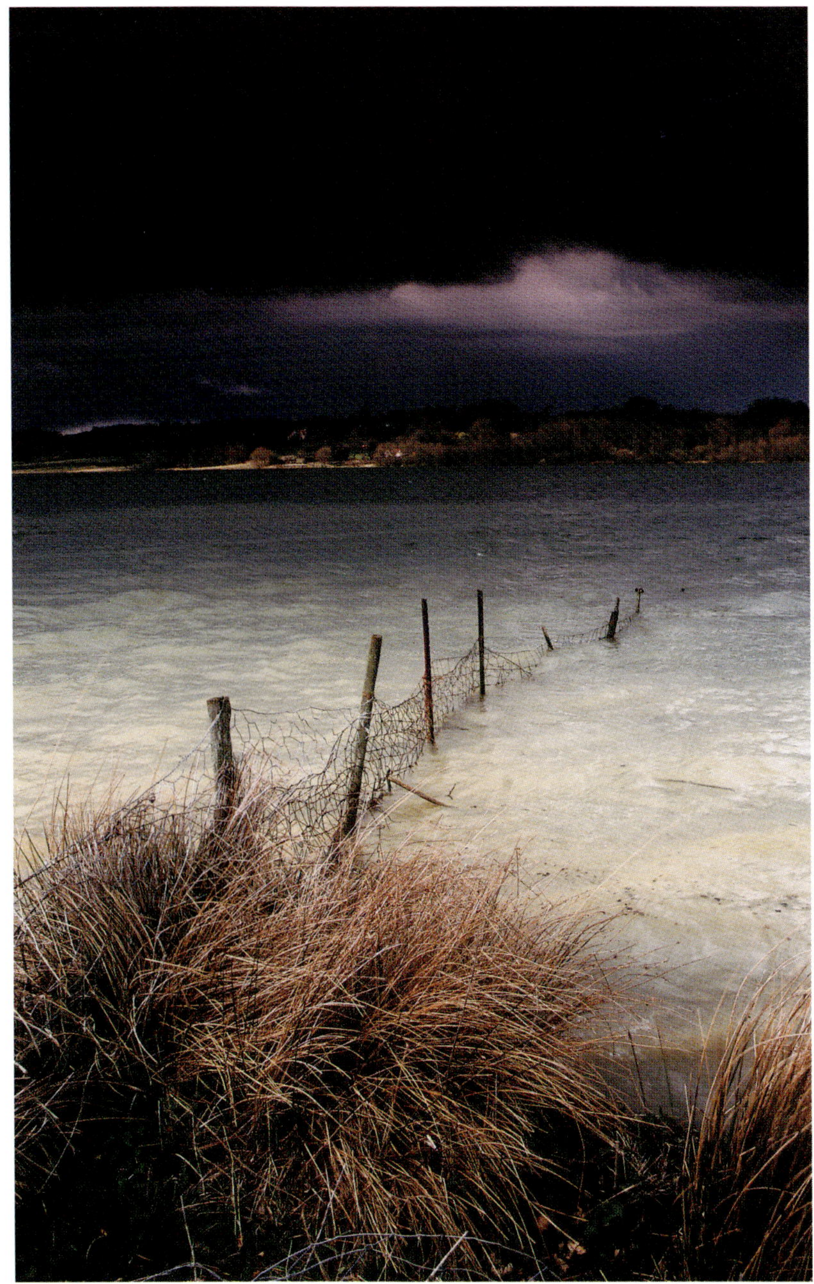

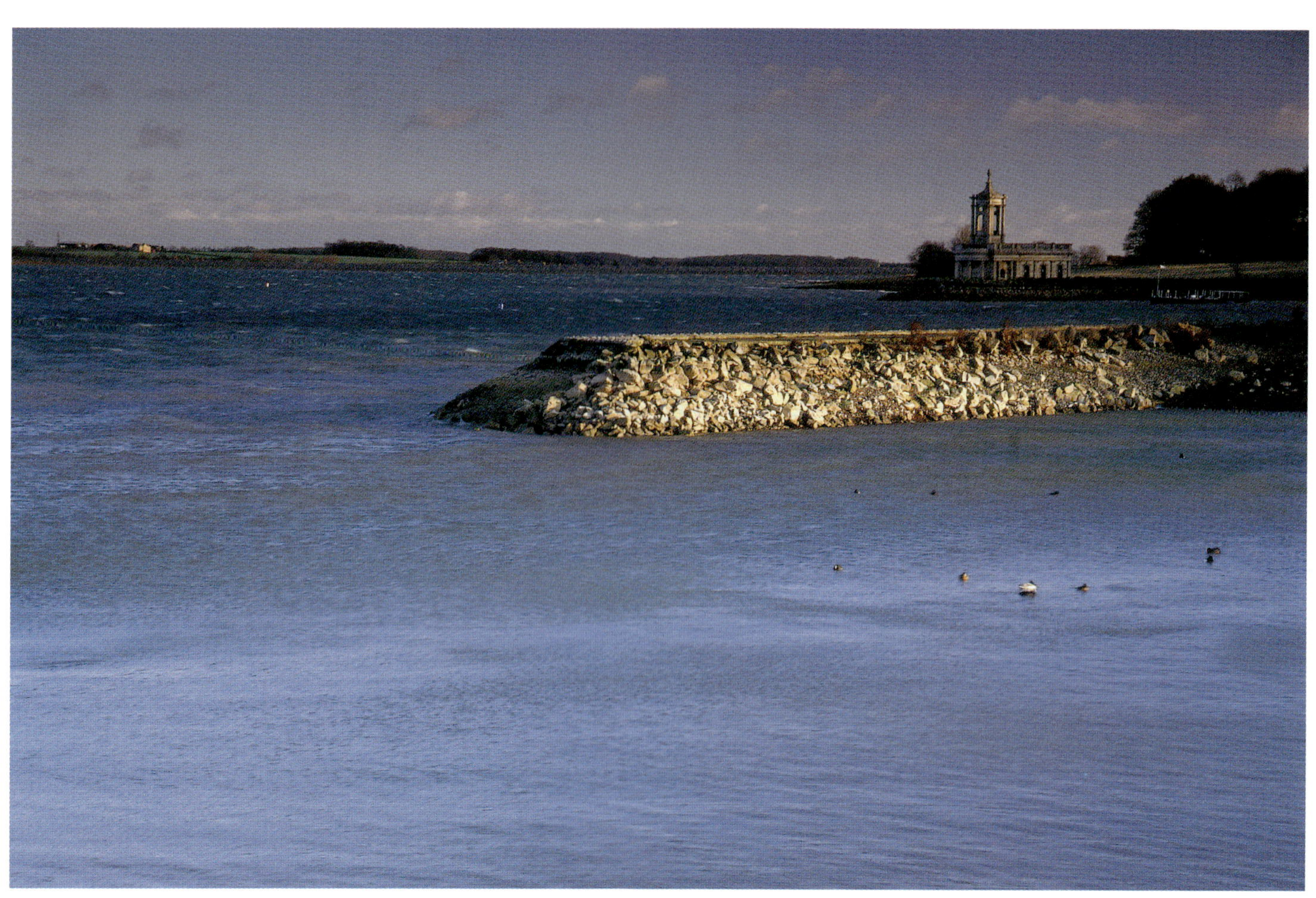

Morning sunlight catches the harbour wall at Edith Weston and Normanton Church tower.

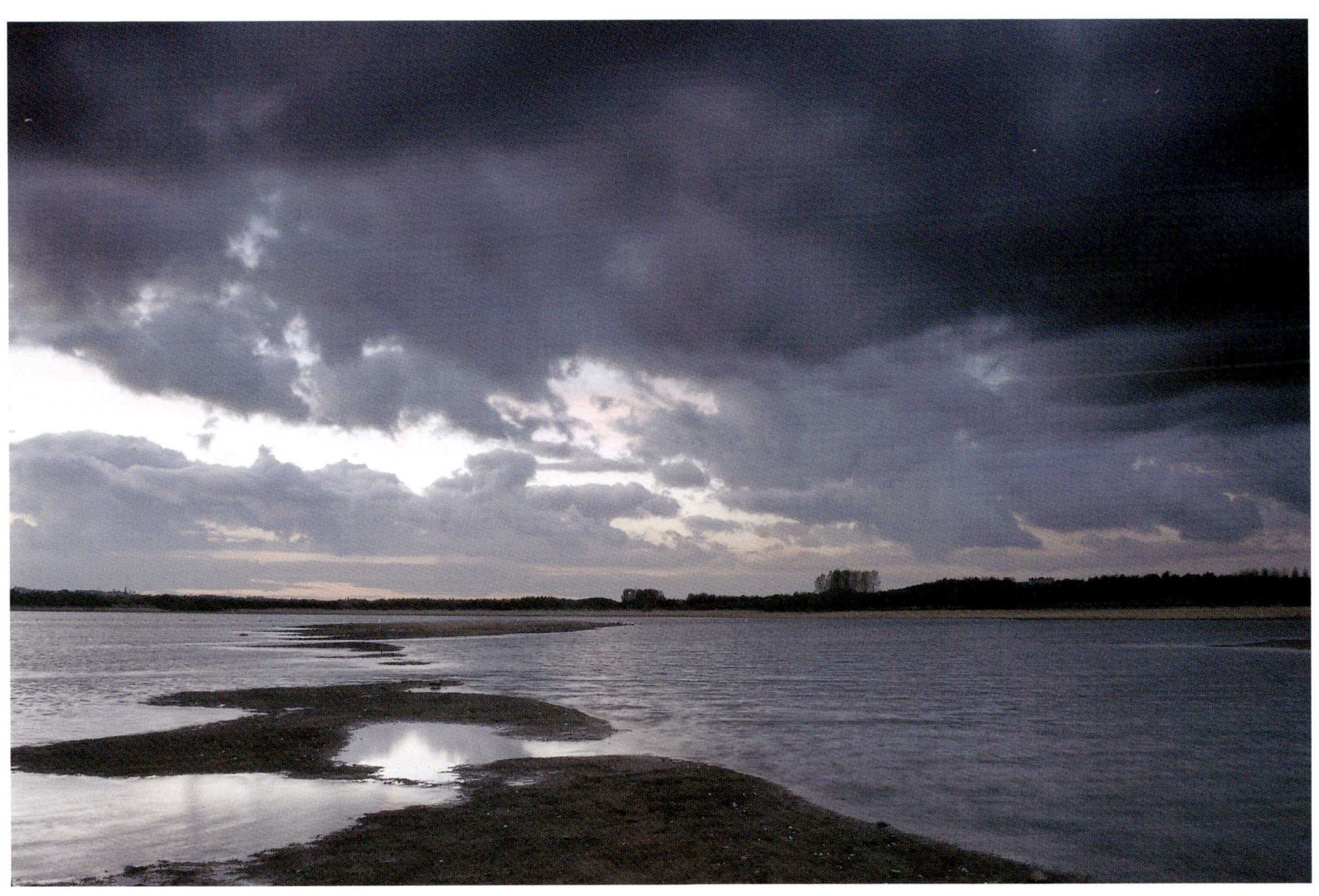

At low water levels, the countors of the 'old' landscape are revealed.

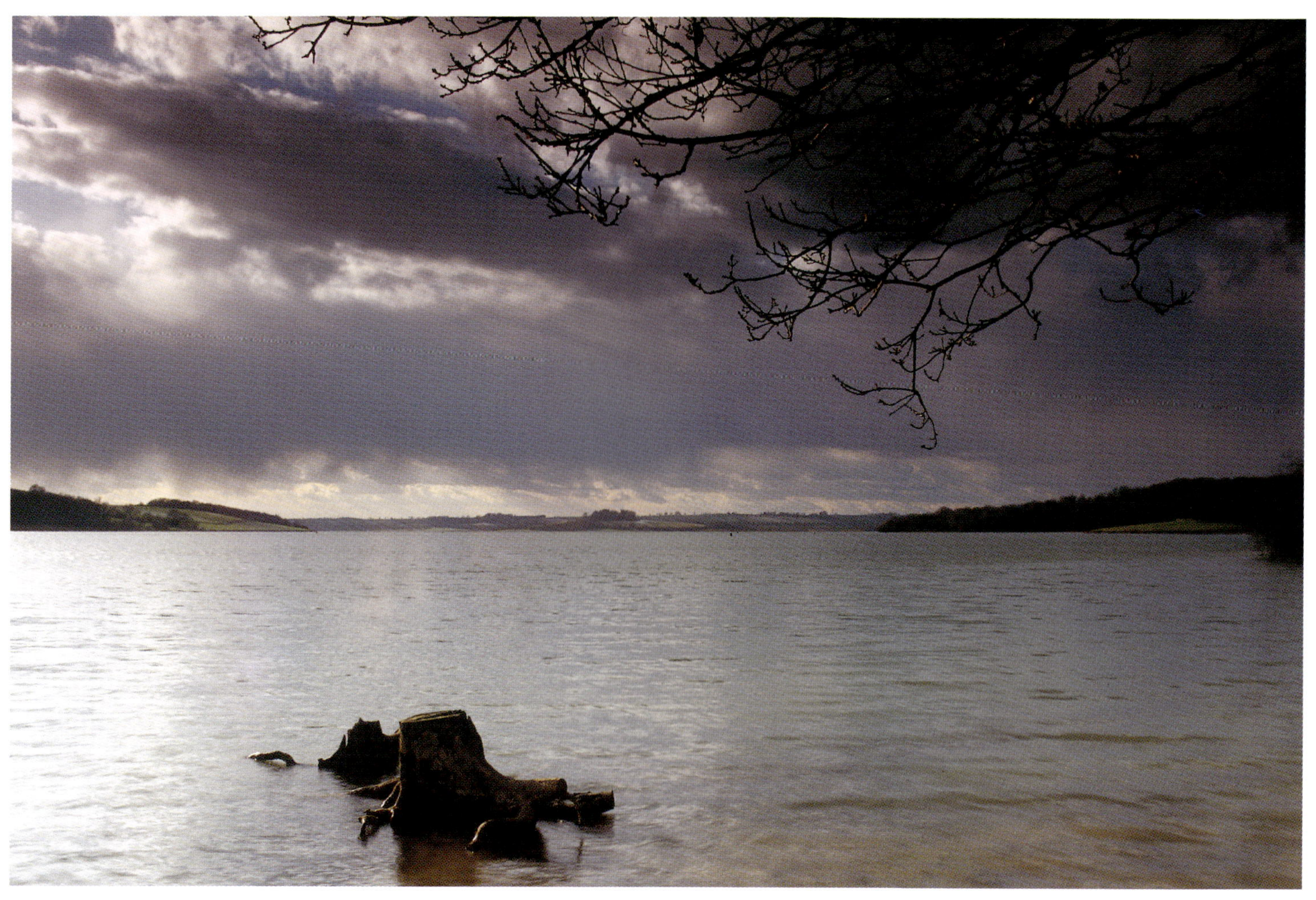

Taken from a spot only accessible at very low water levels, the 'landfall' is four miles distant.

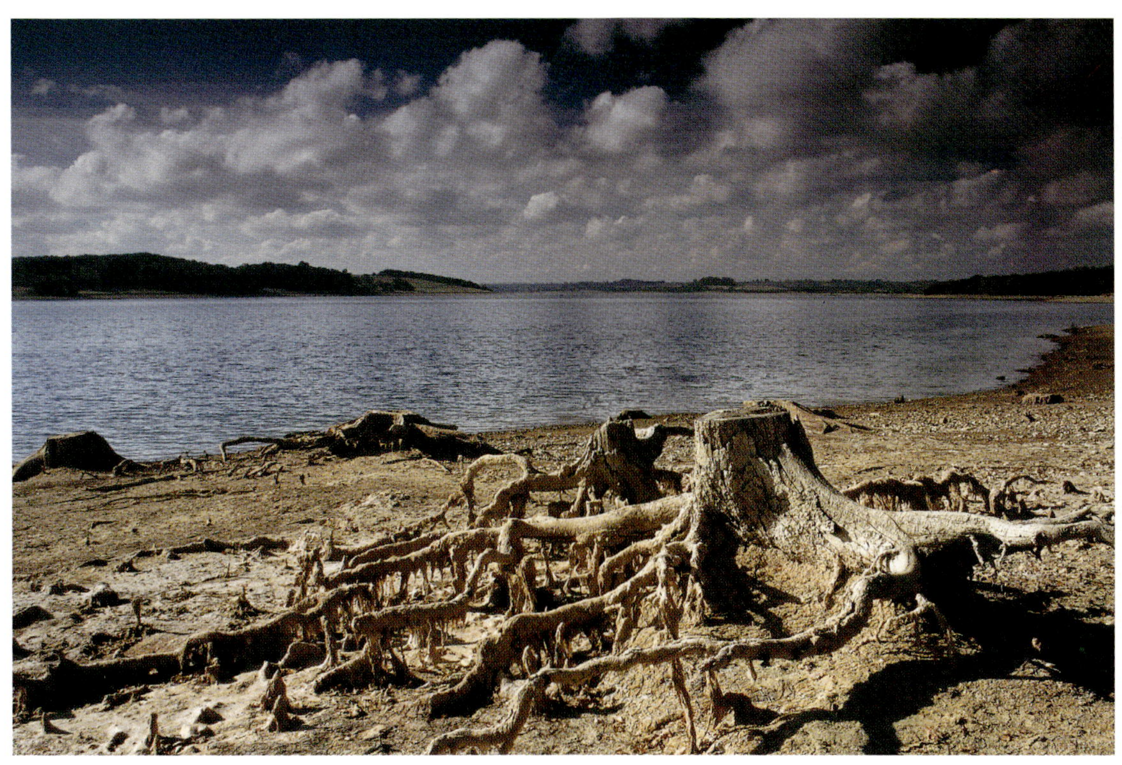

Having spent so long underwater the tree stumps, when revealed,
bring an almost prehistoric air to the landscape.

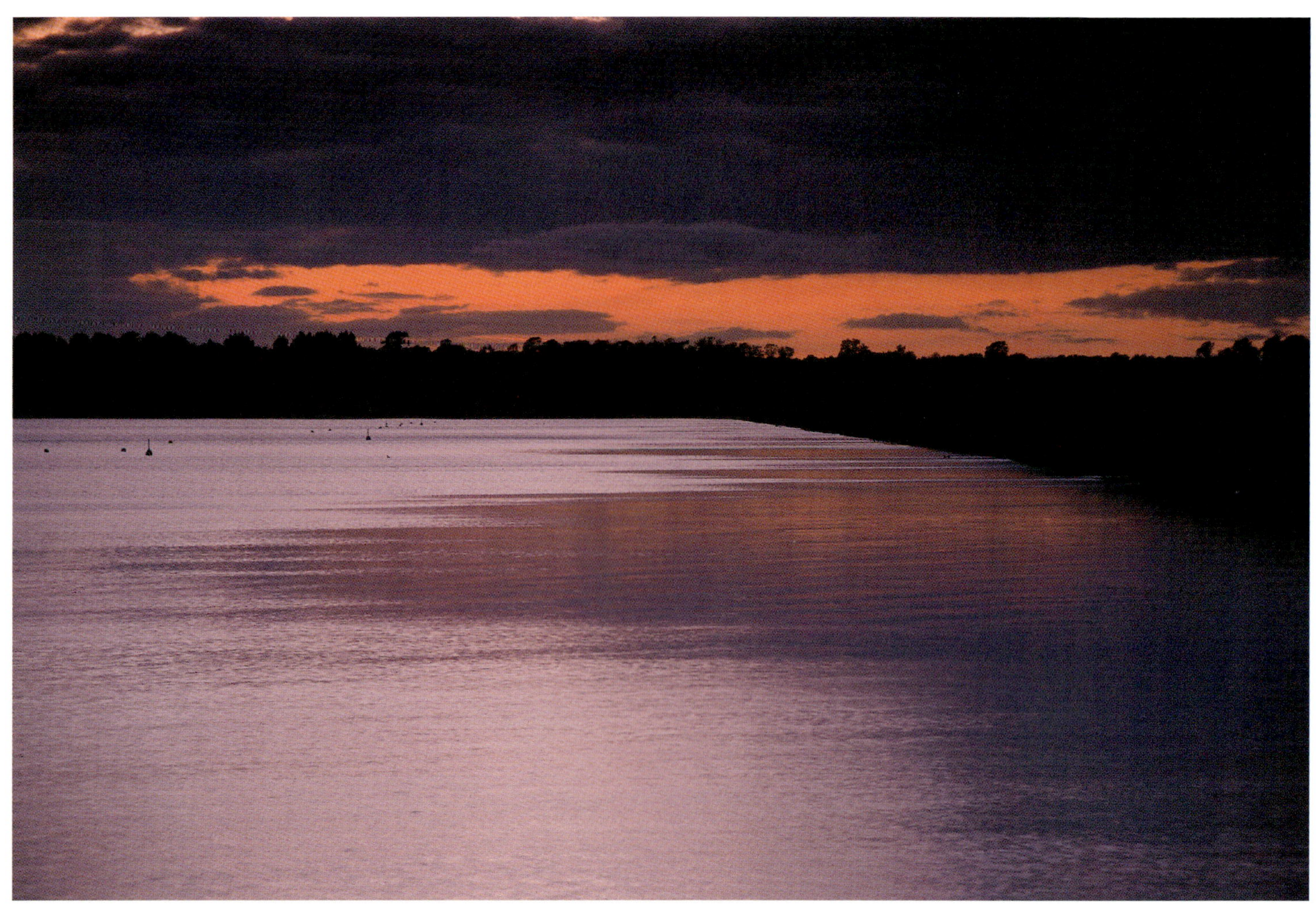

On some evenings, the colour in the sky is not just in the direction of the sunset – this is looking north along the length of the dam.

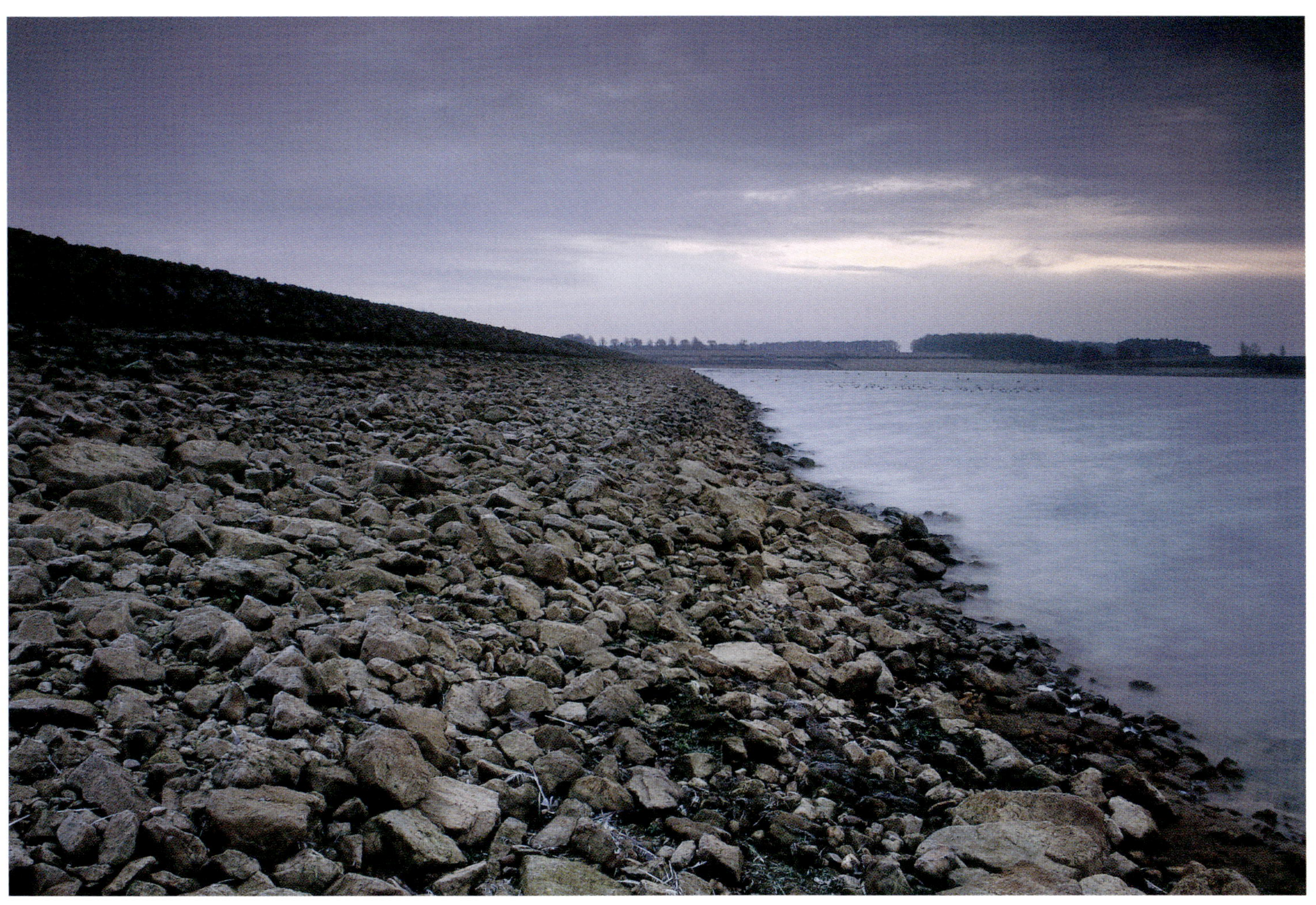

On a cloudy and overcast morning, a very slow exposure has added an ethereal effect to the slowly-moving water.

Lax Hill – an alternative view.

Shades of blue.

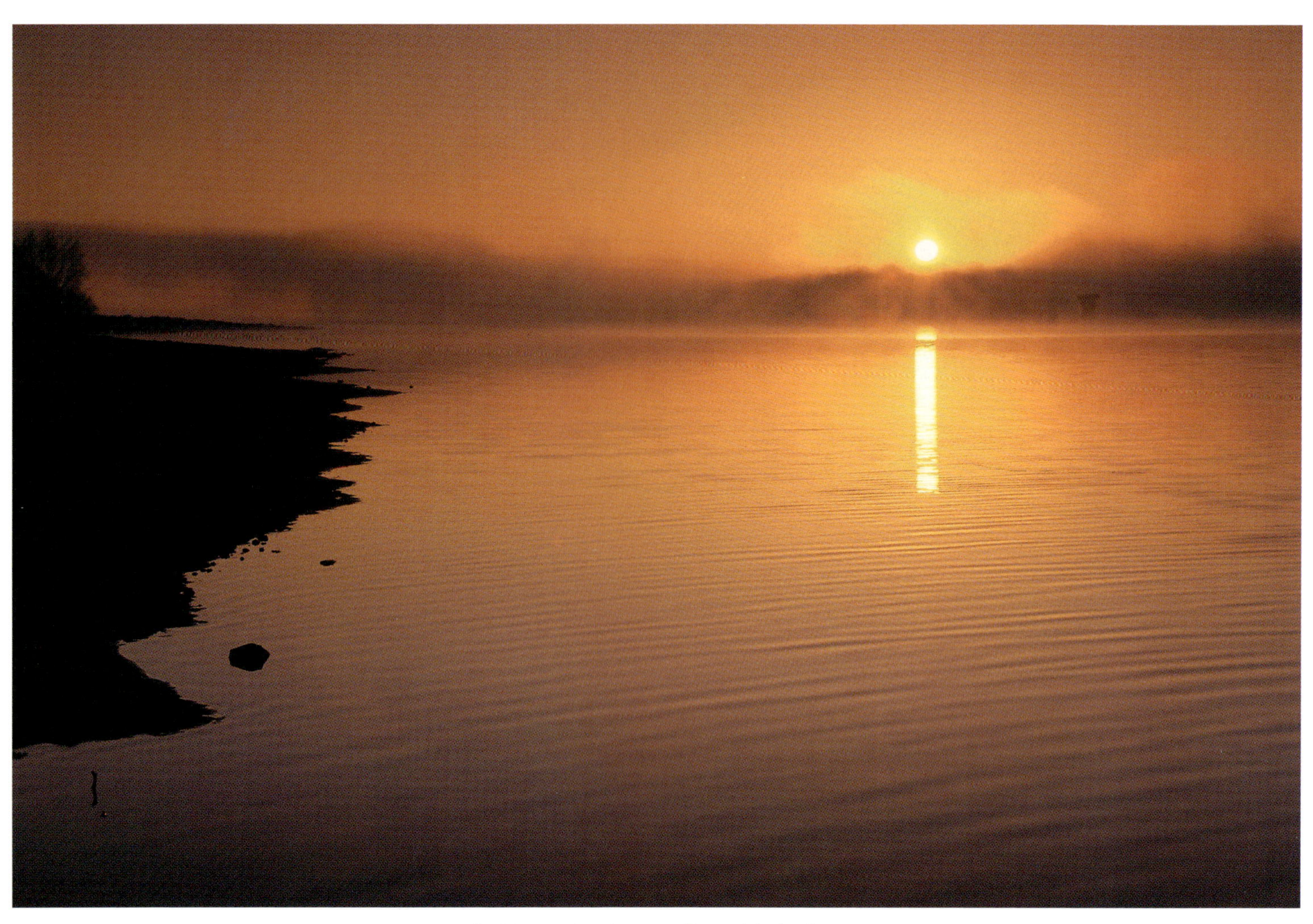

A rising early mist, near Barnsdale Lodge.

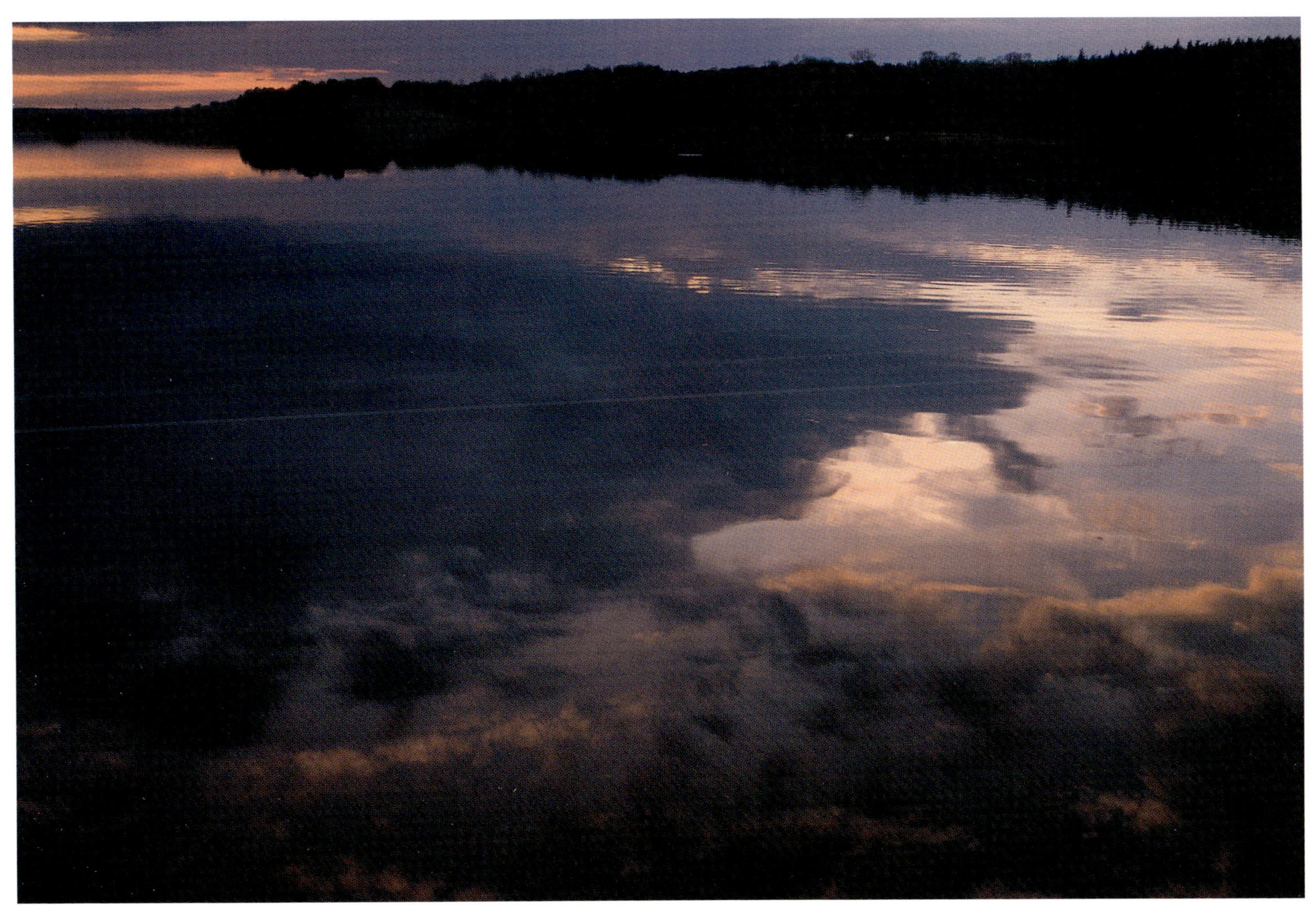

Reflections.

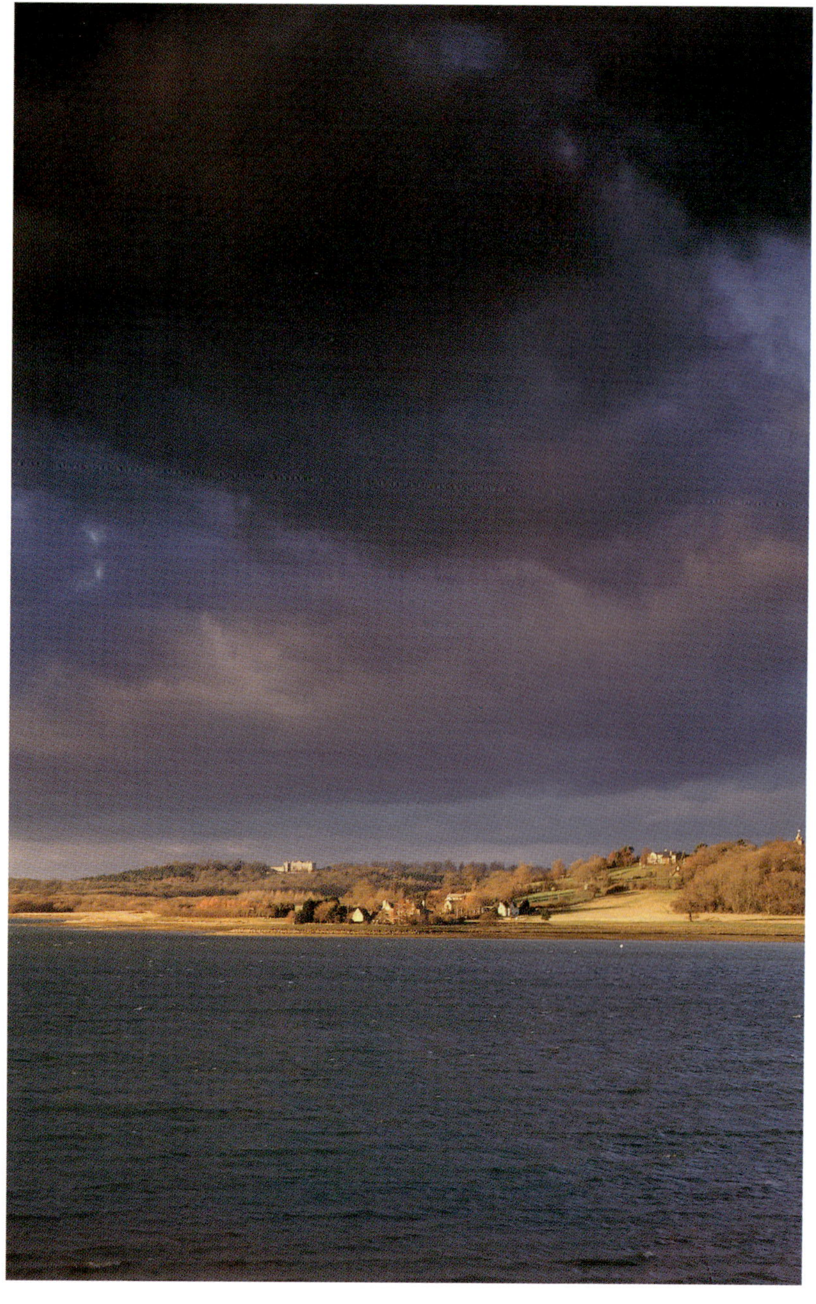

Nature's stagelighting
of the peninsula.

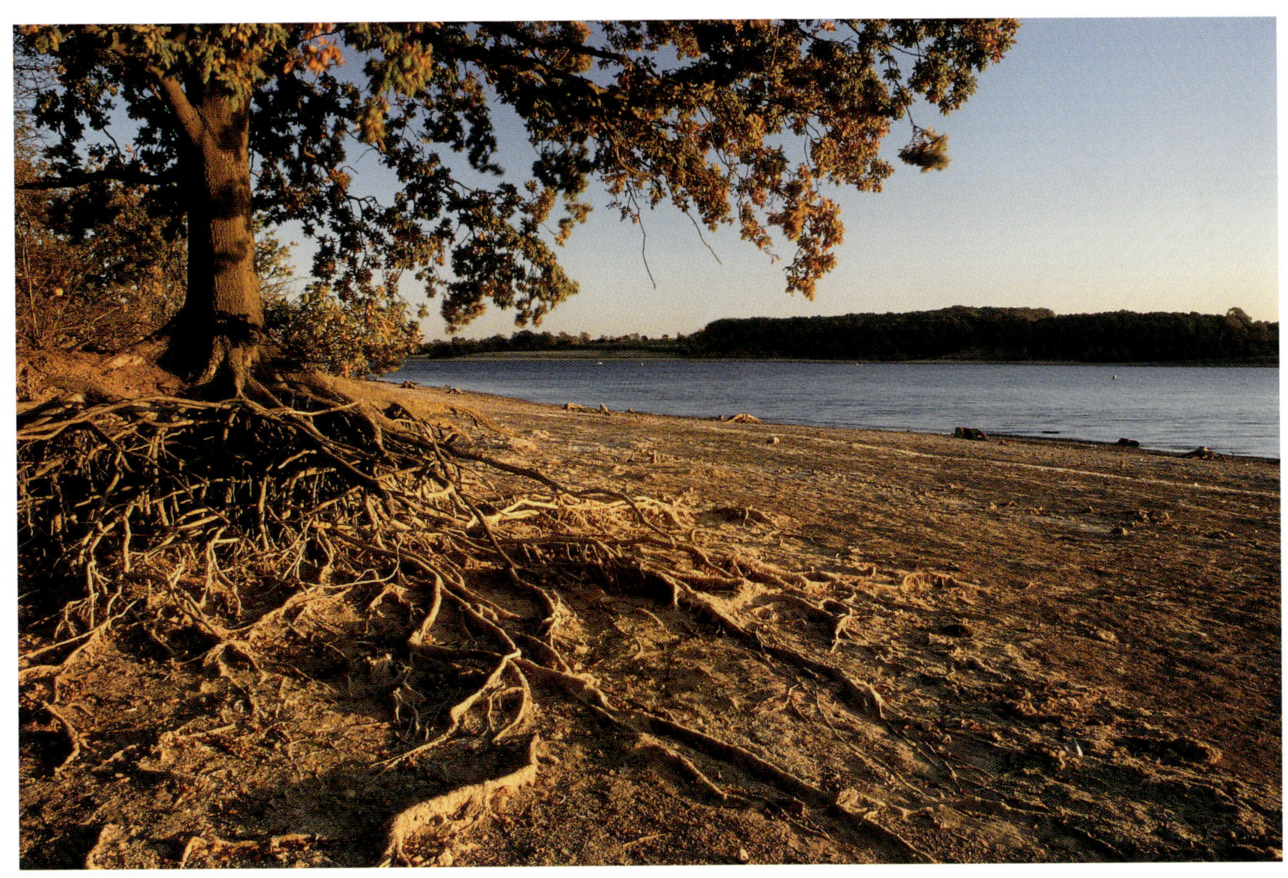

Below the normal shoreline at Hambleton Wood.

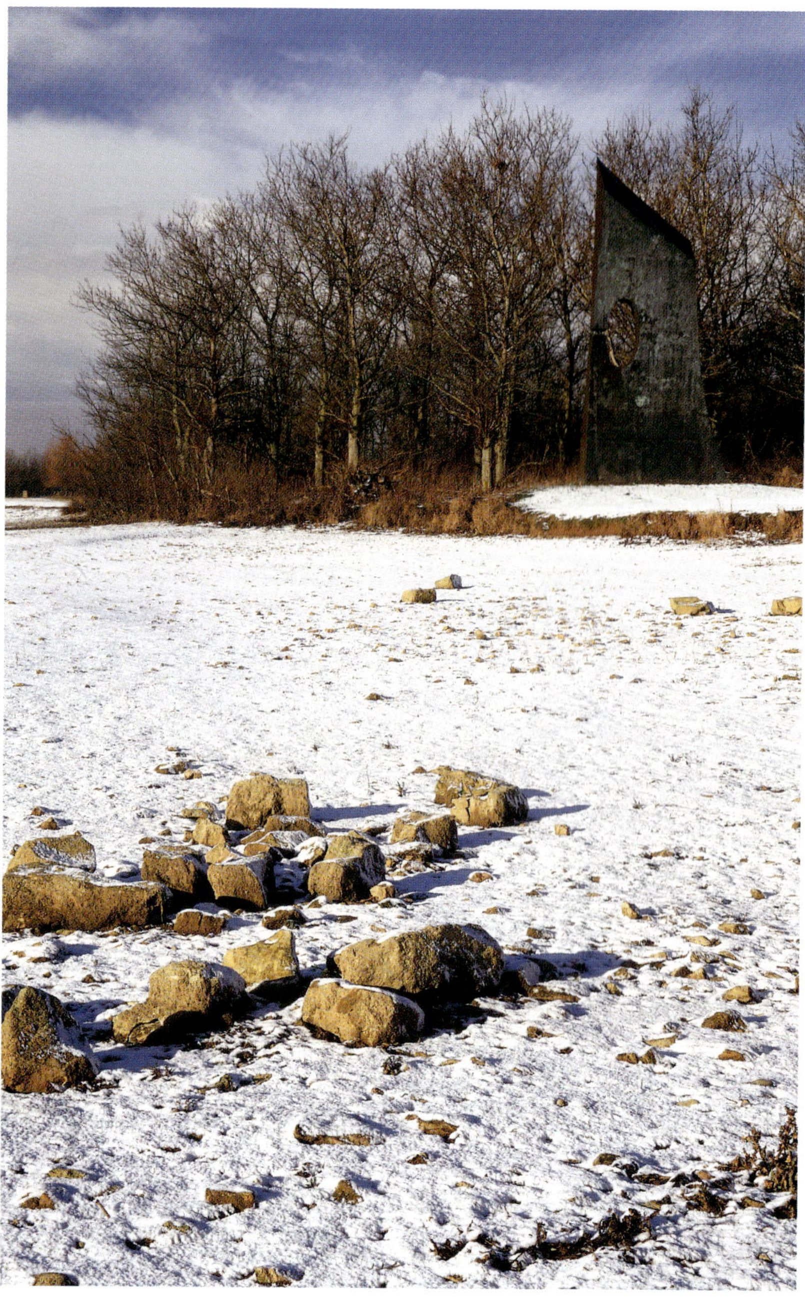

According to the artist:
'neither a figure nor an object…'

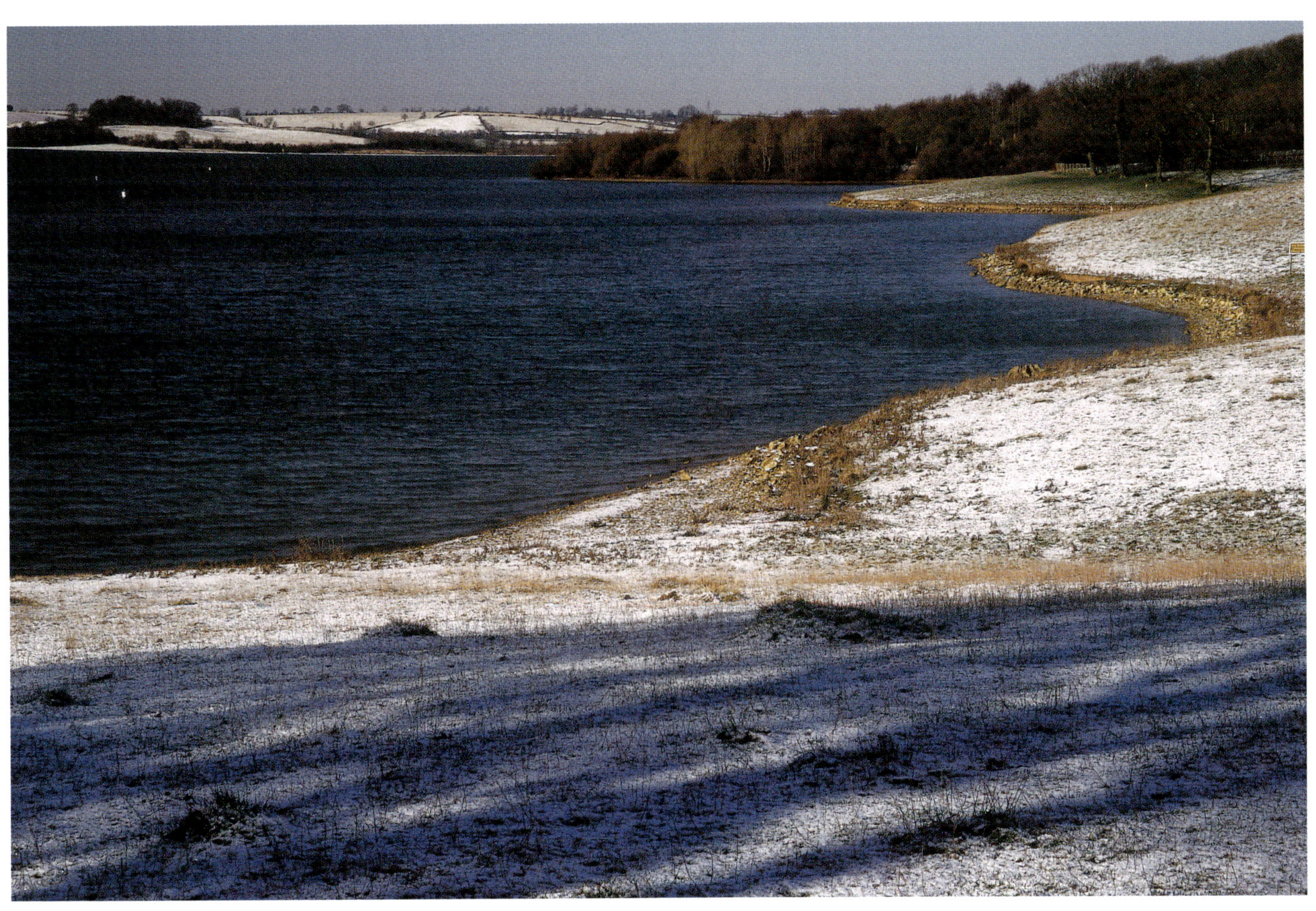
Deep blue water in February.

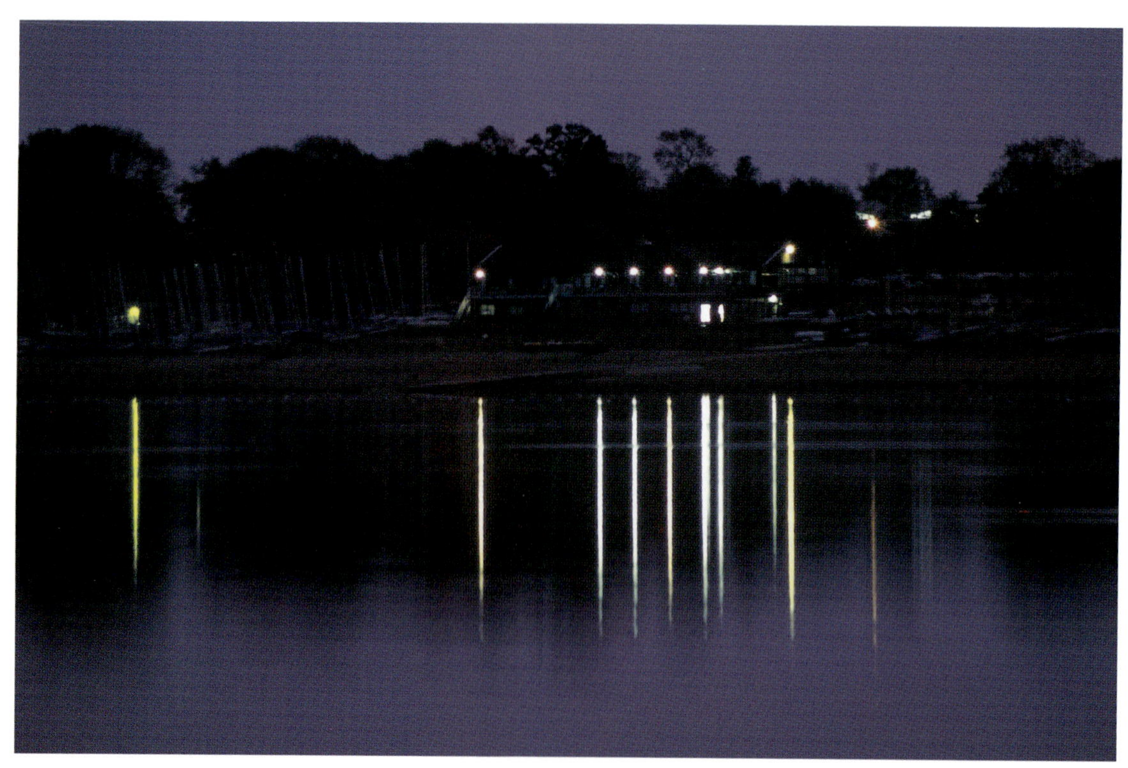

The lights of Rutland Sailing Club.

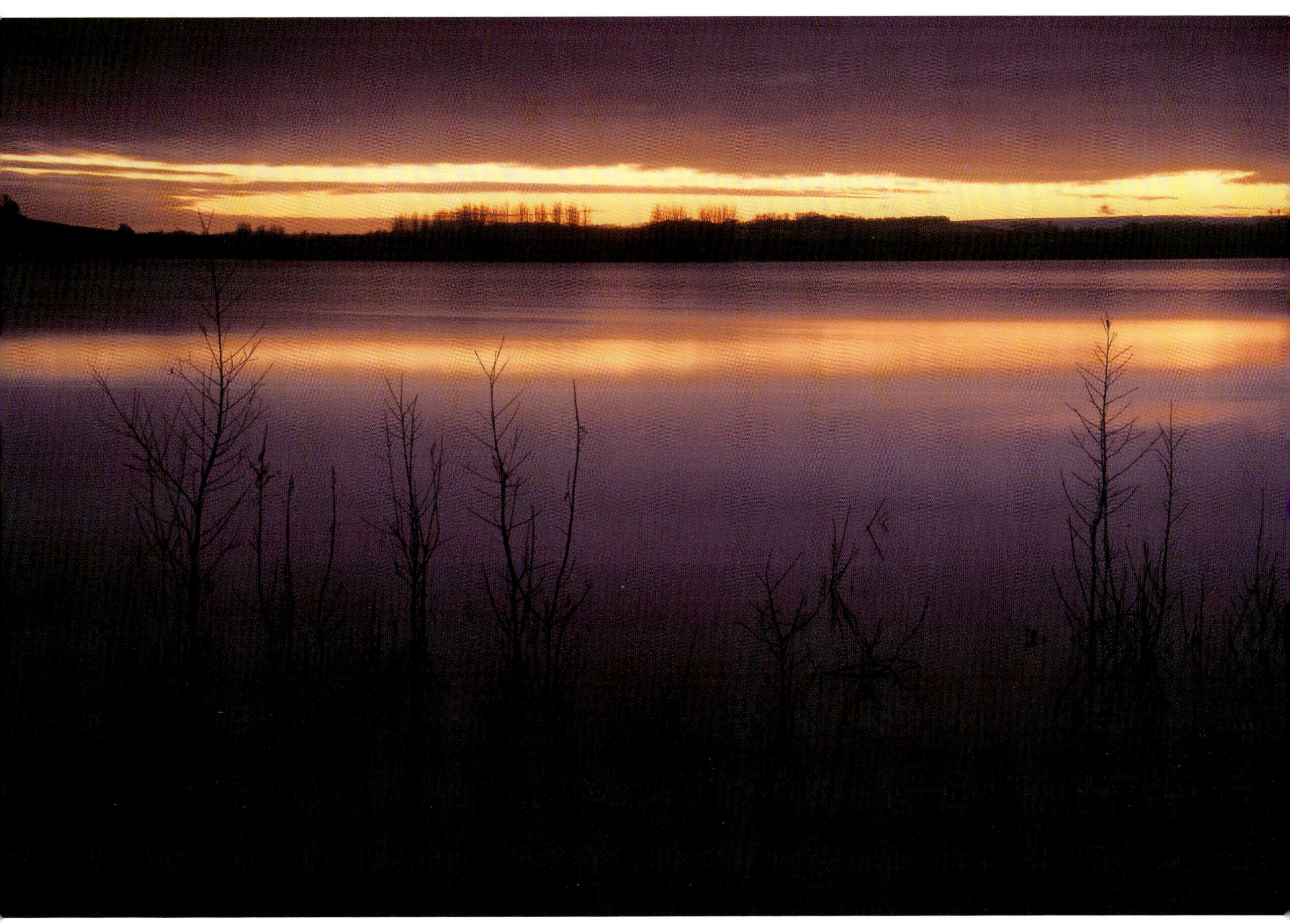

A view of the nature reserve.

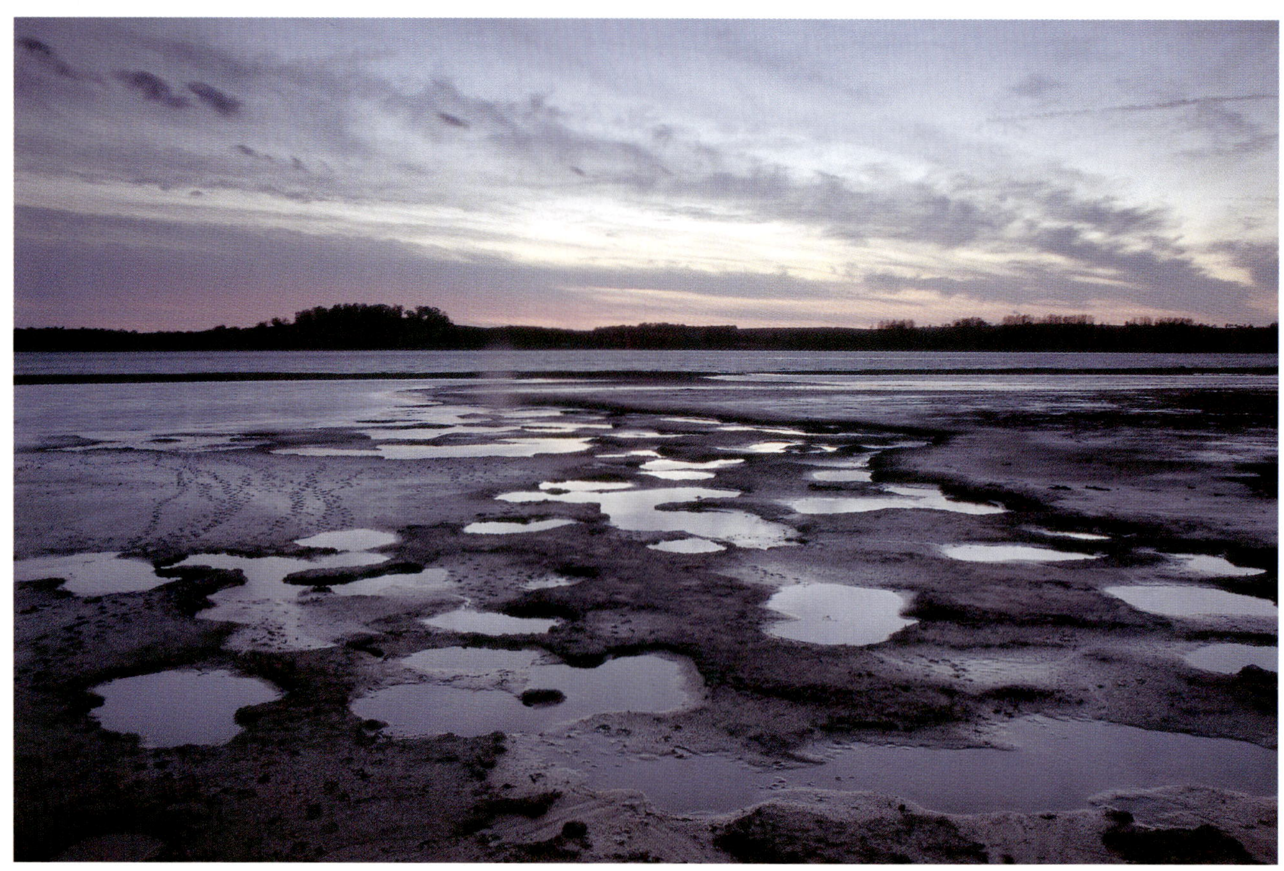

When the water levels are this low, the Water takes on an appearance of a coastline at low tide.

Opposite page: Pre dawn at Burley Reach.

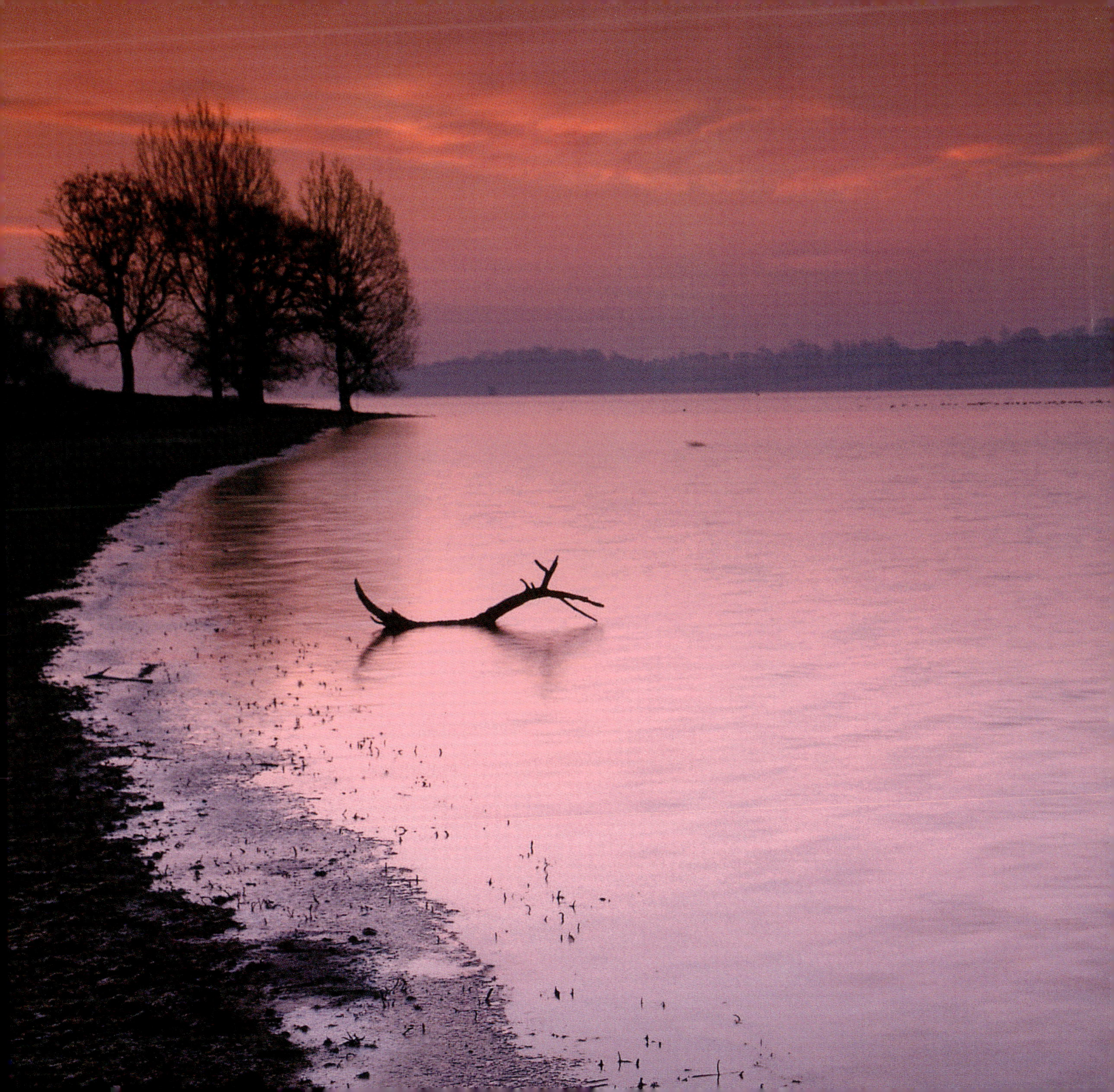

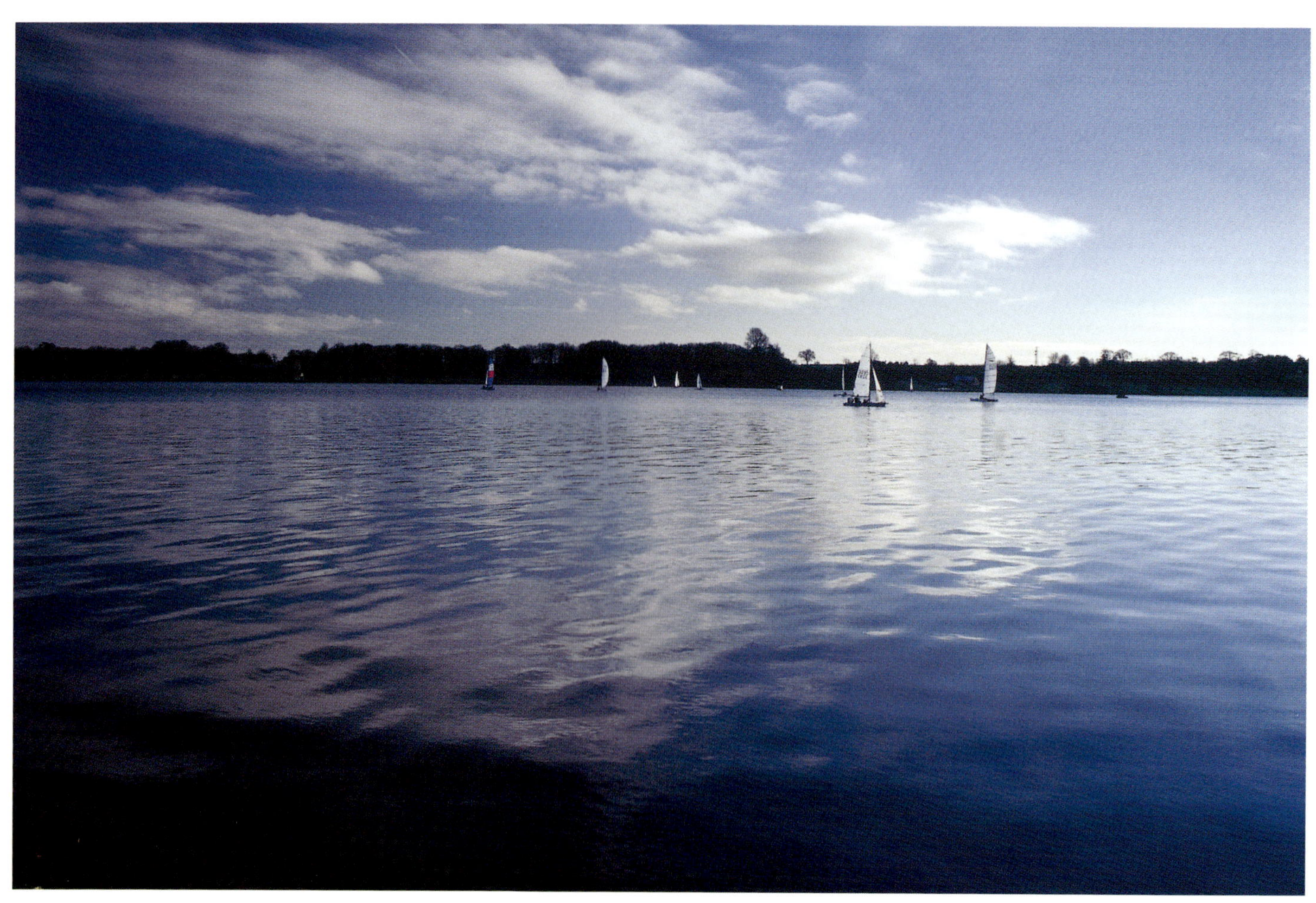

Even in early January, a clear sky can turn the water blue.

The 'waves' are seldom so pronounced
as on this very windy day.

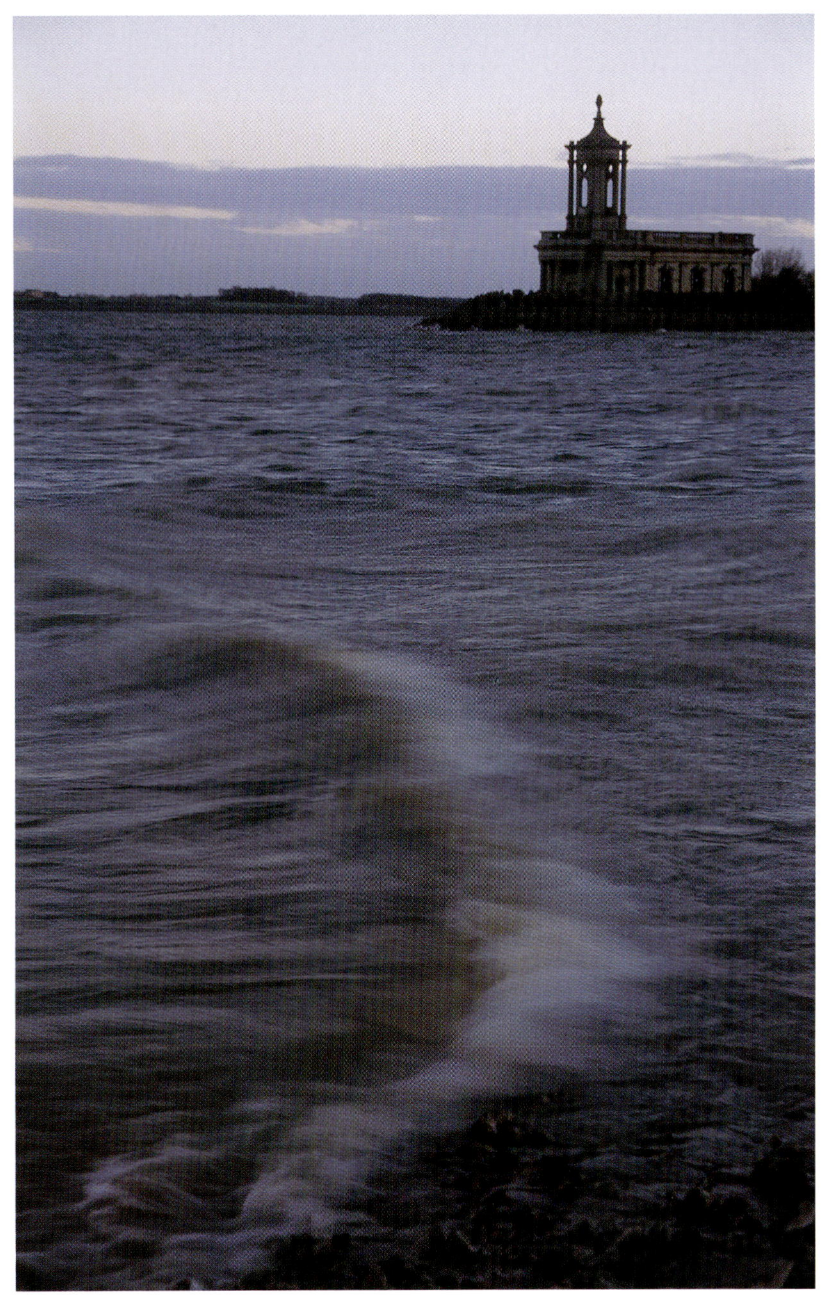

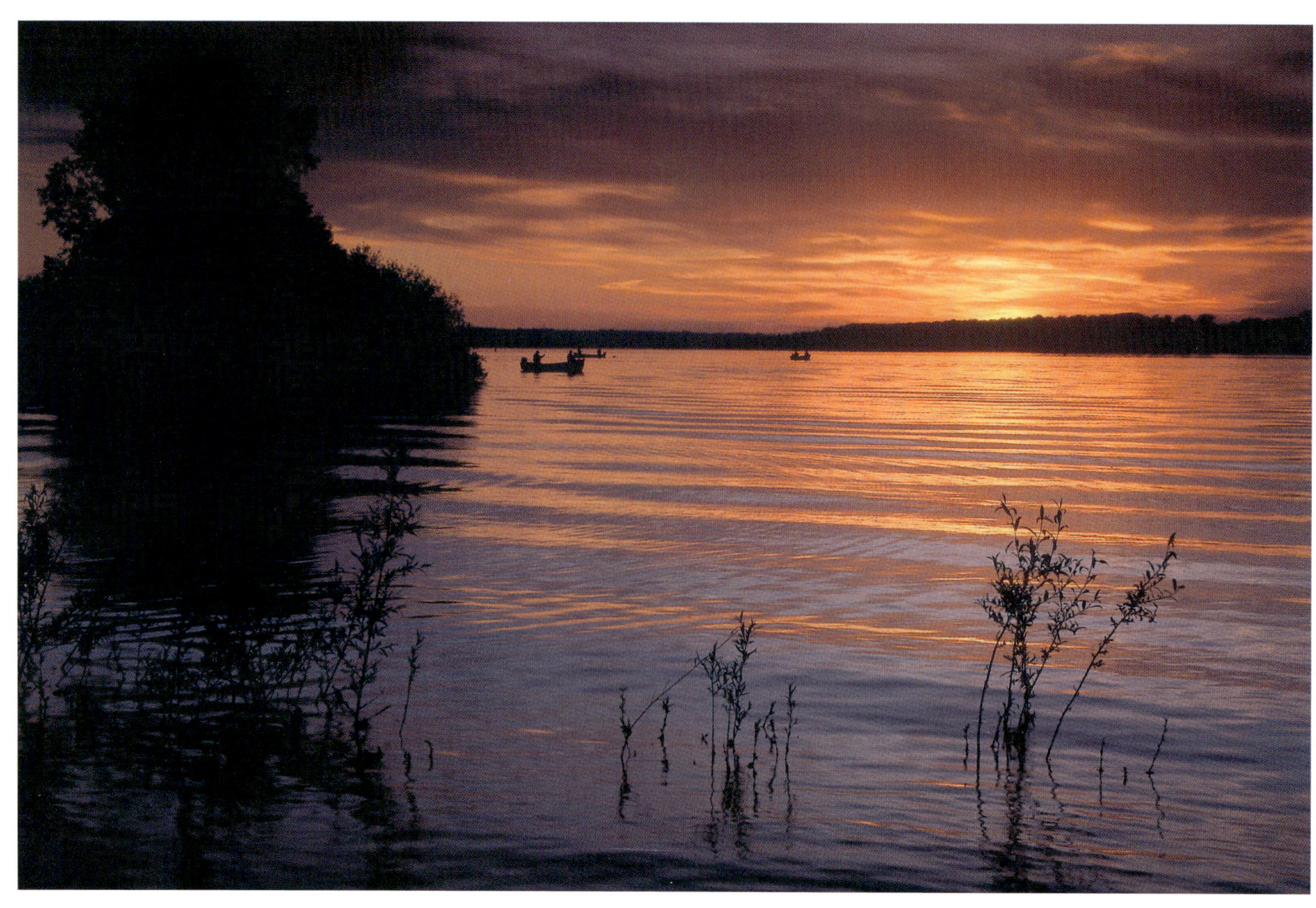

Sunset from the picnic area at Edith Weston.

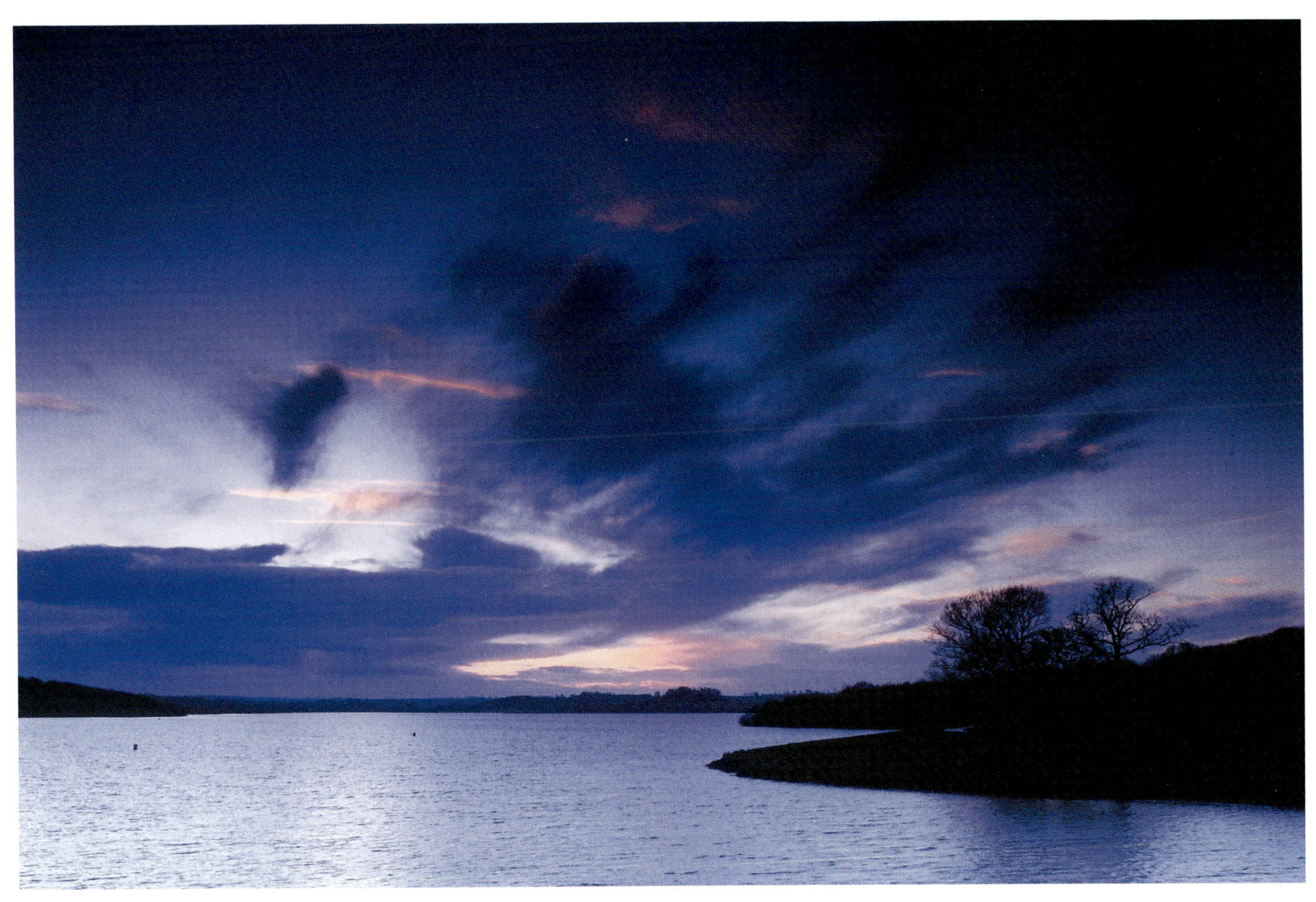

An alternative sunset.

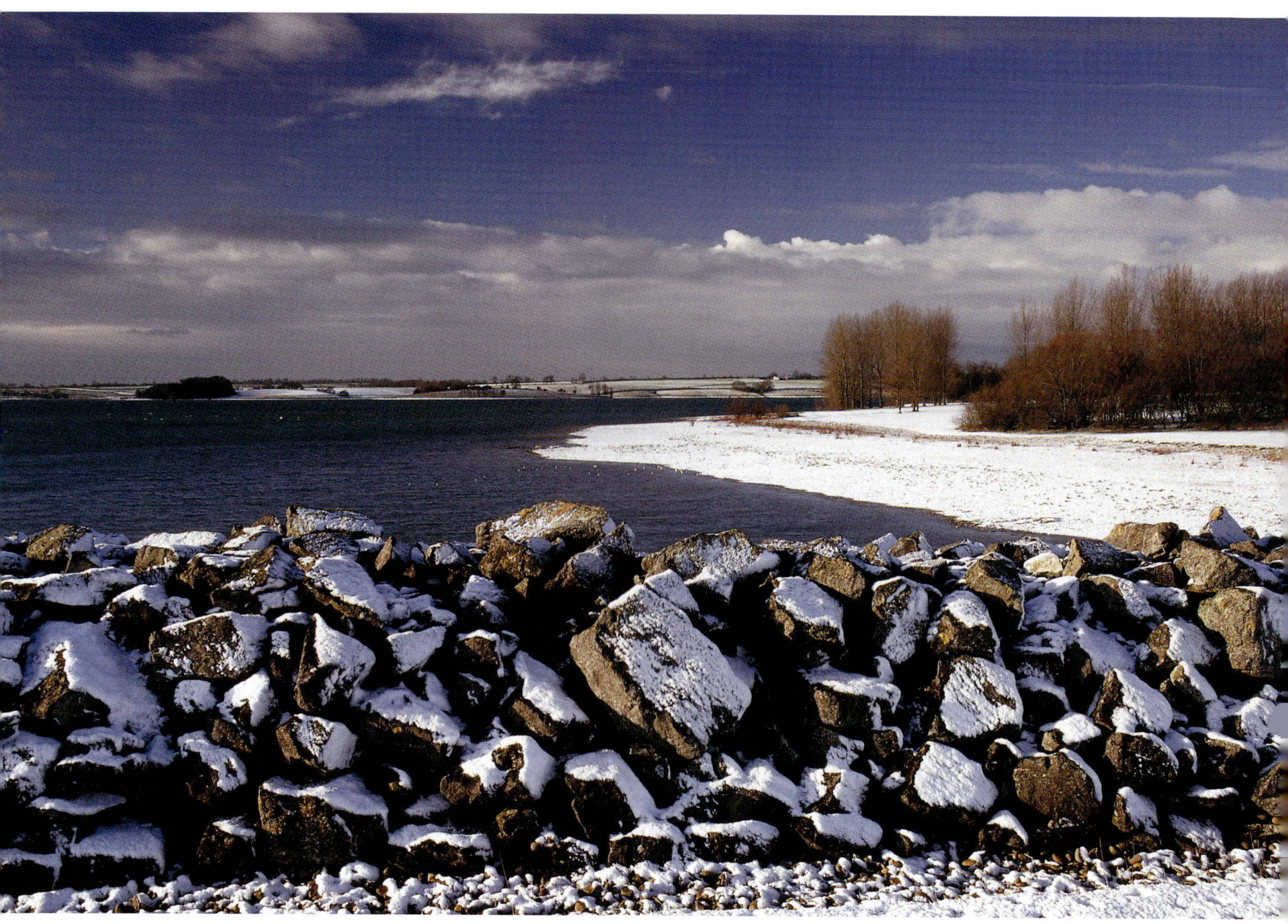

The dam in winter.

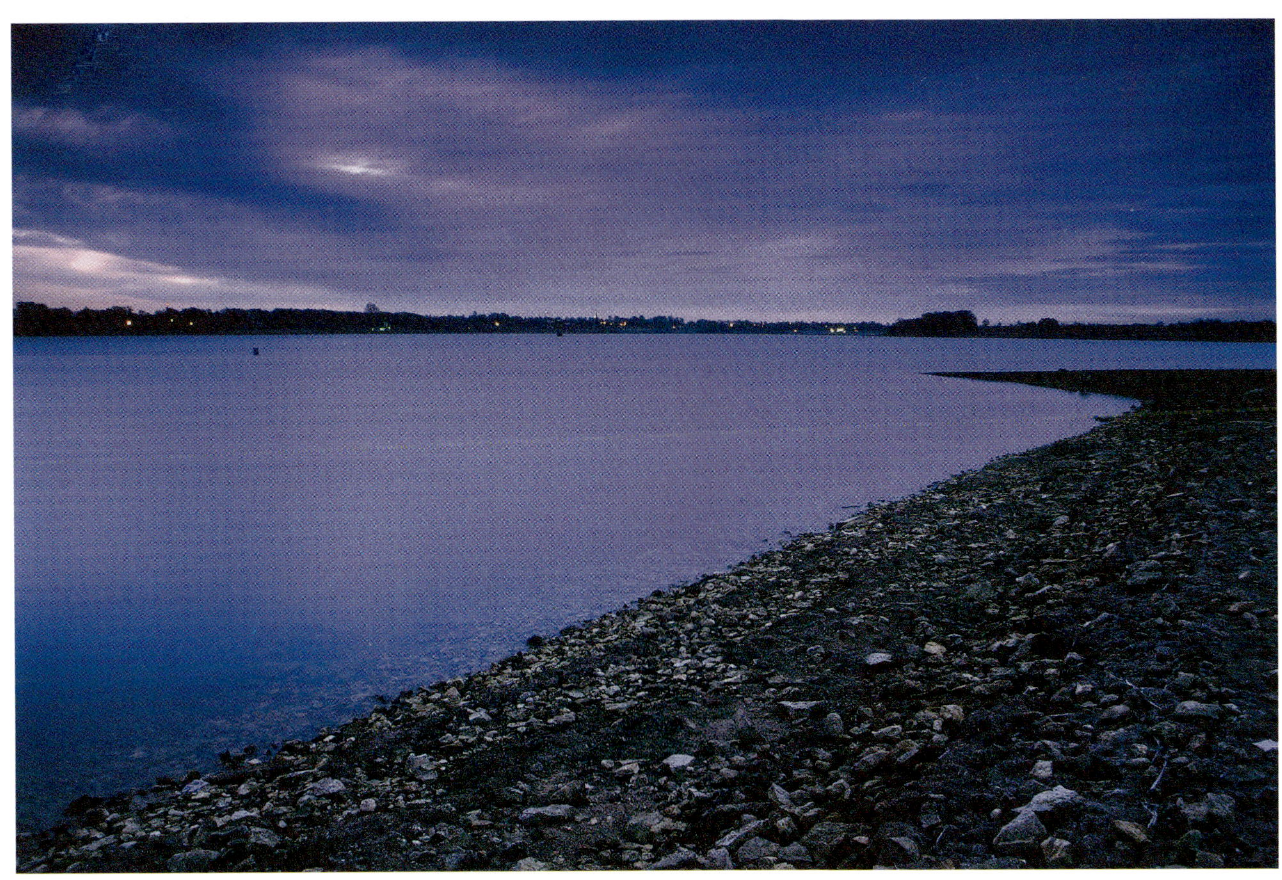

Whitwell shoreline with Oakham lights in the far distance.

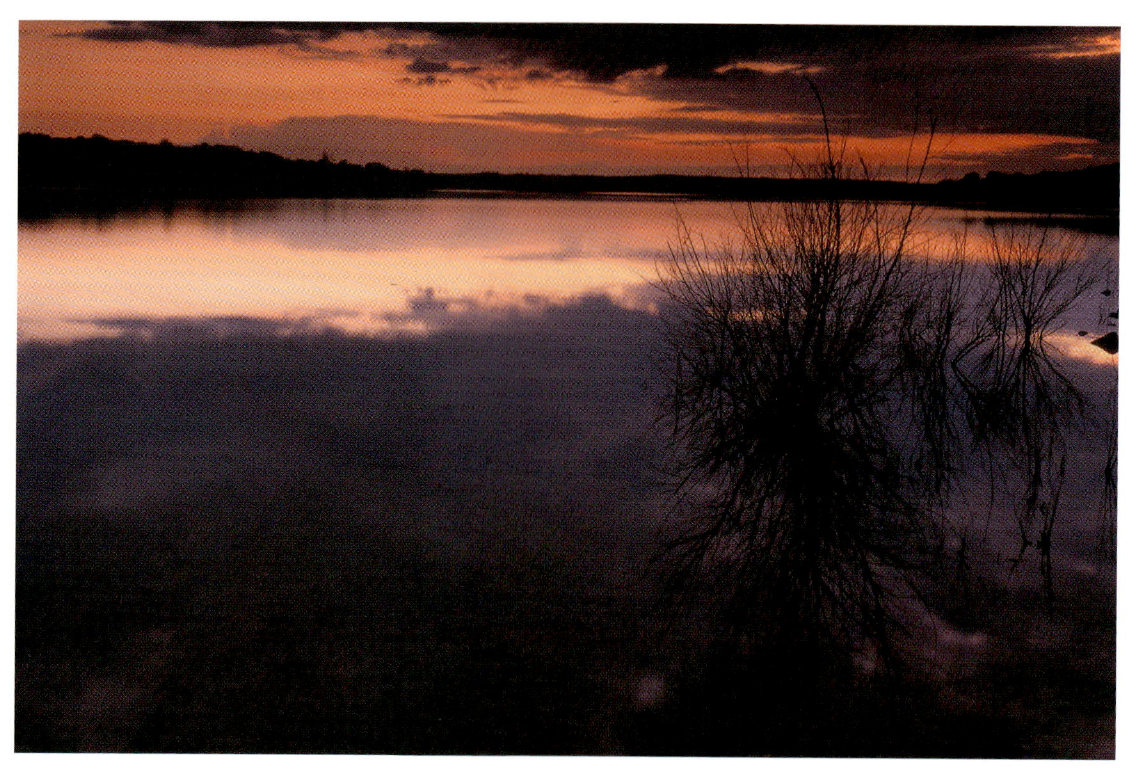

A view along the northern arm of the Water.

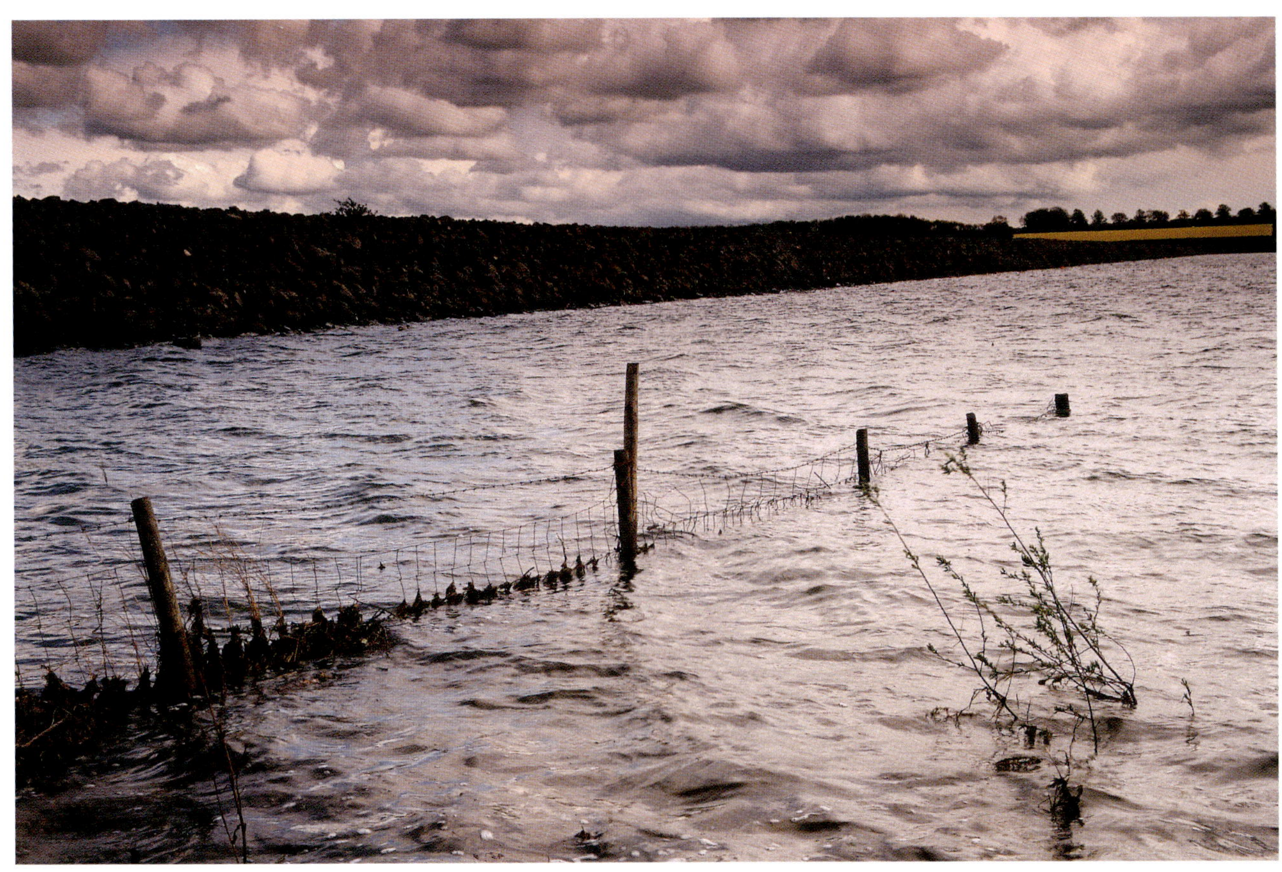

High water levels in May, drowning sheep fences.

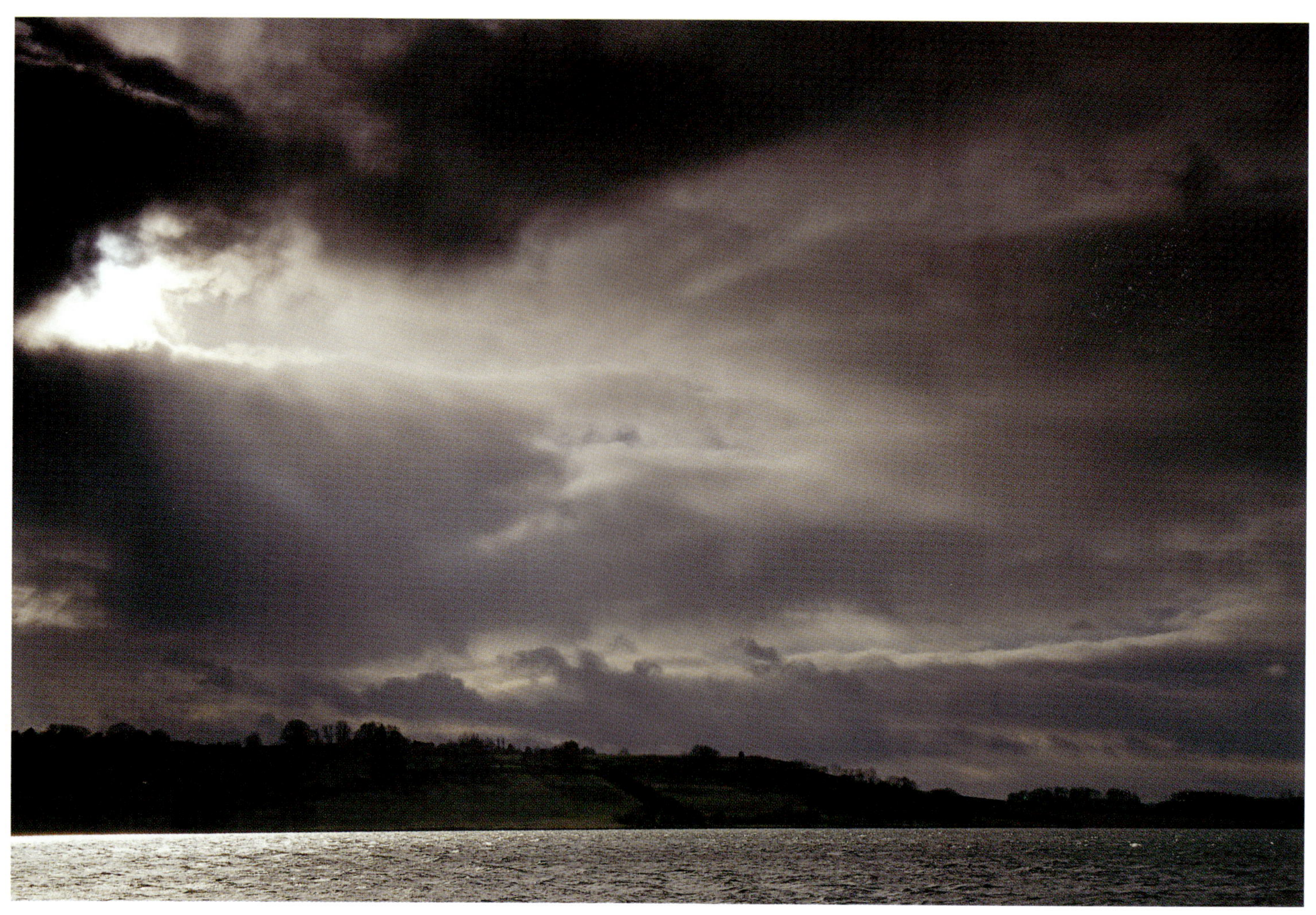

Wild skies above the Hambleton Peninsula.

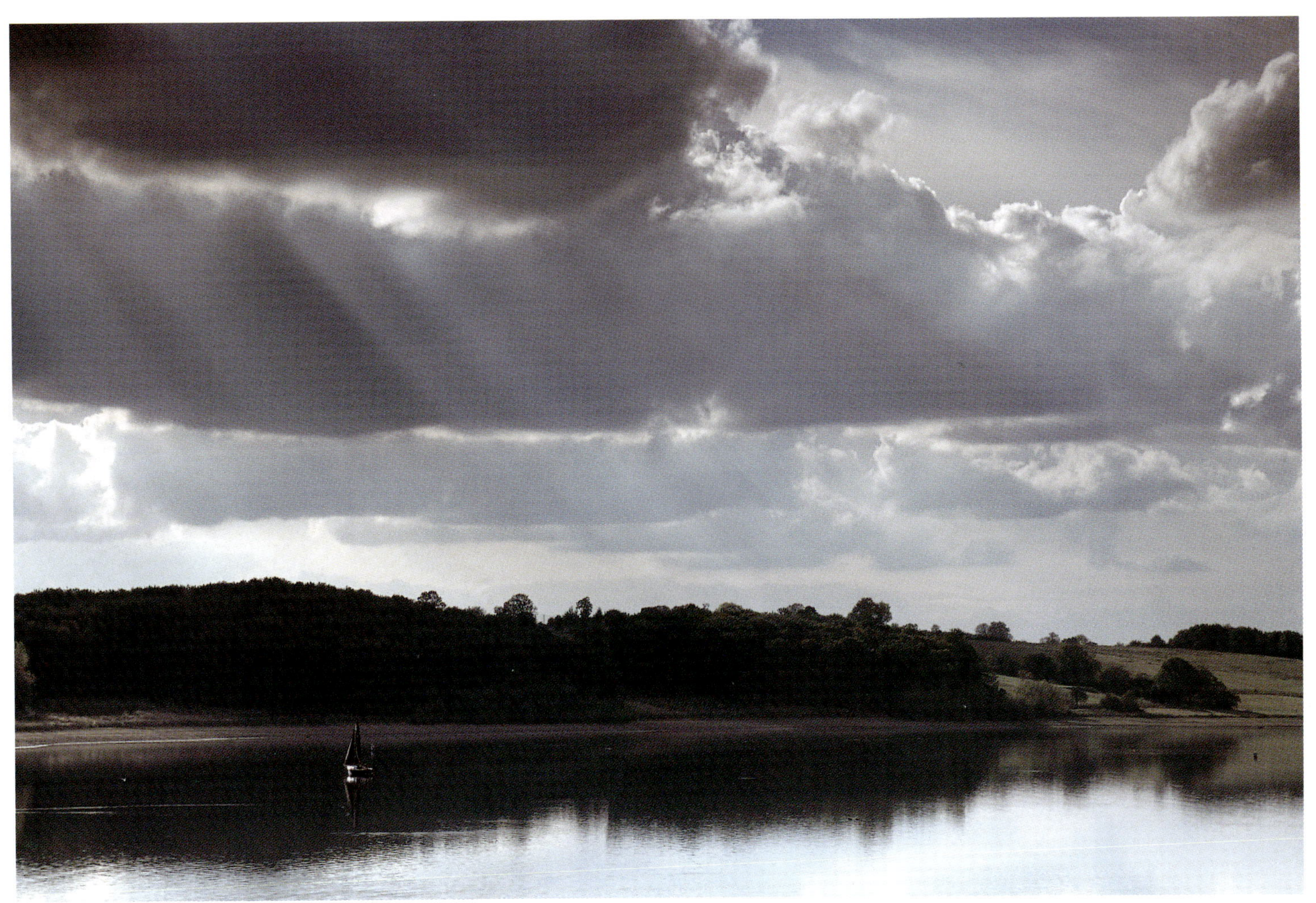

Becalmed.

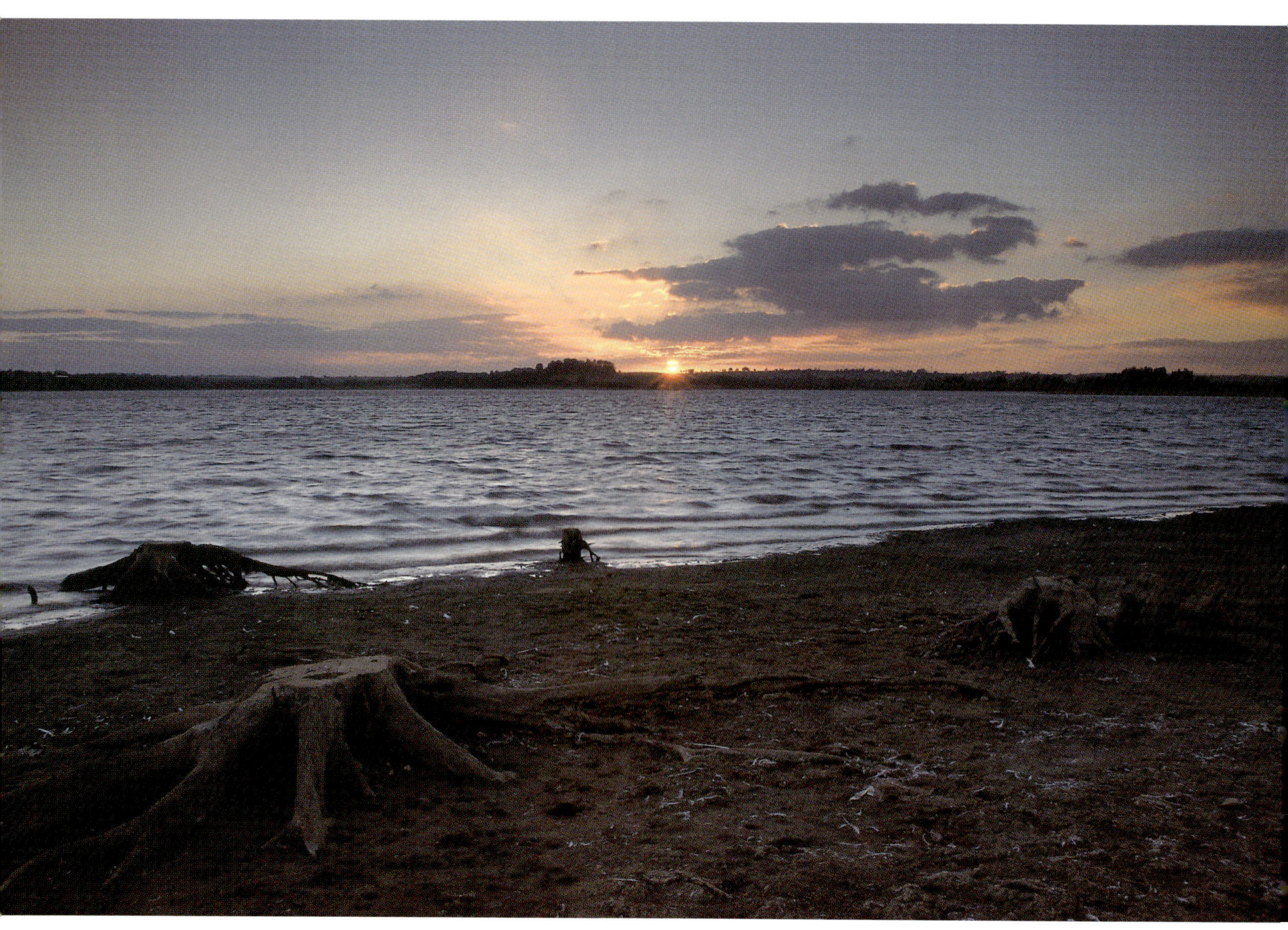

Below the normal shoreline at Hambleton Wood.

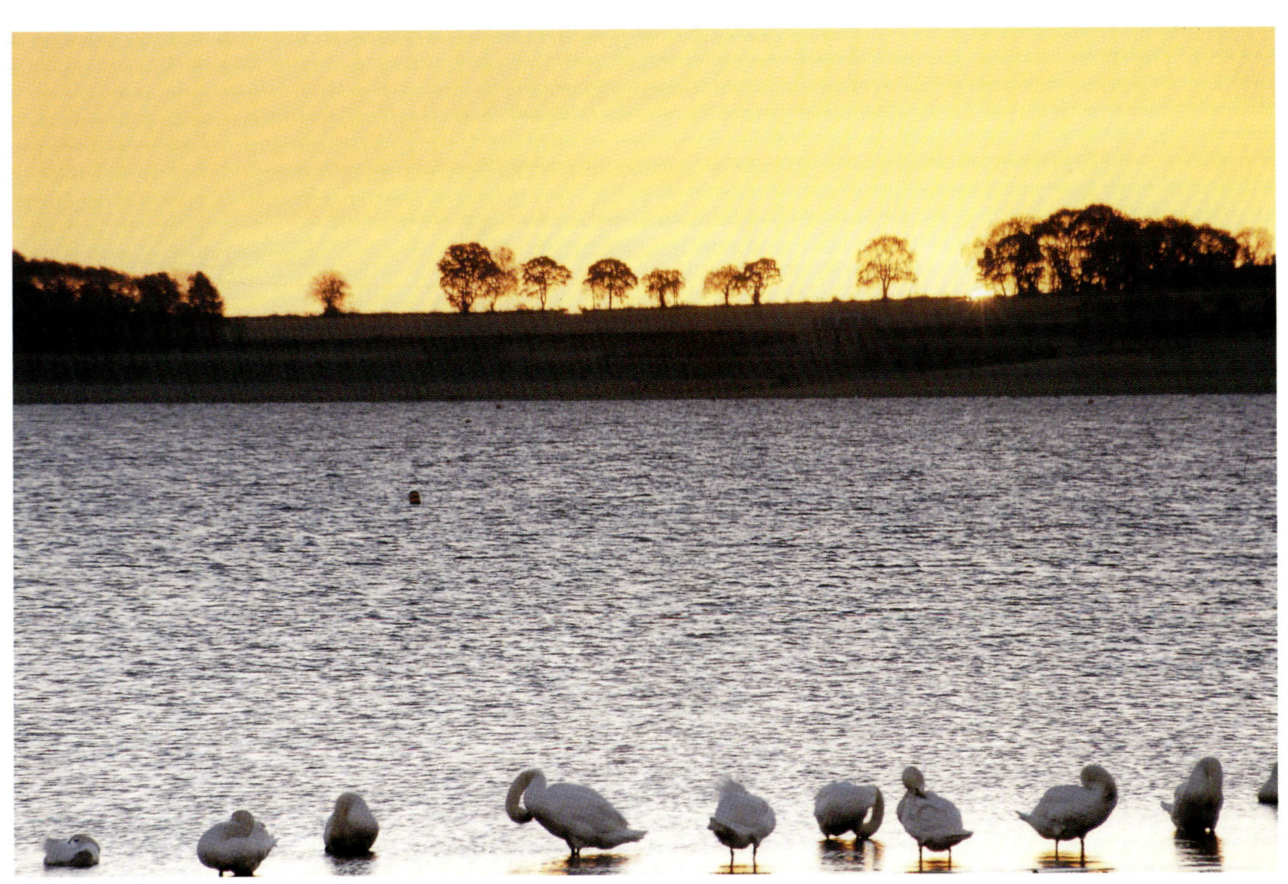

A sunrise, a long lens and it's almost possible to be in… Florida?

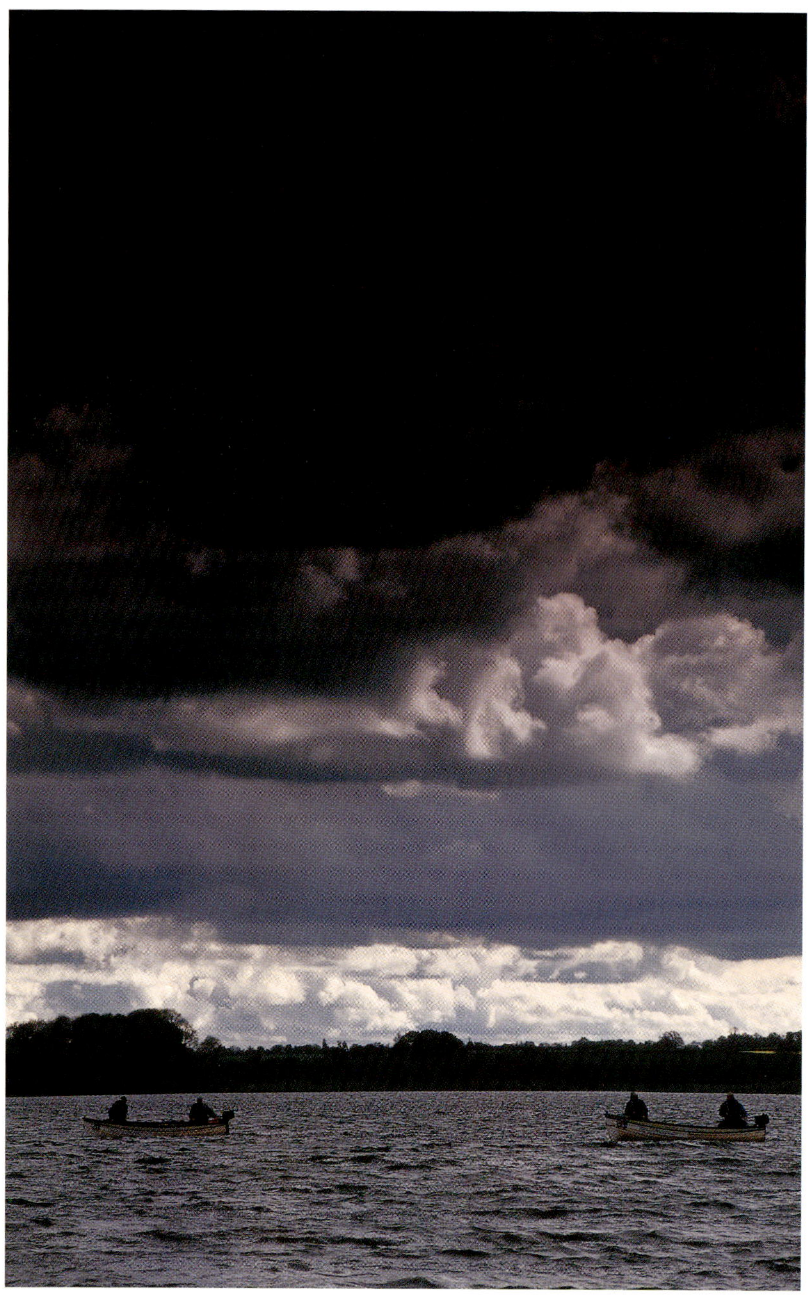

The fisherman were heading for shelter!

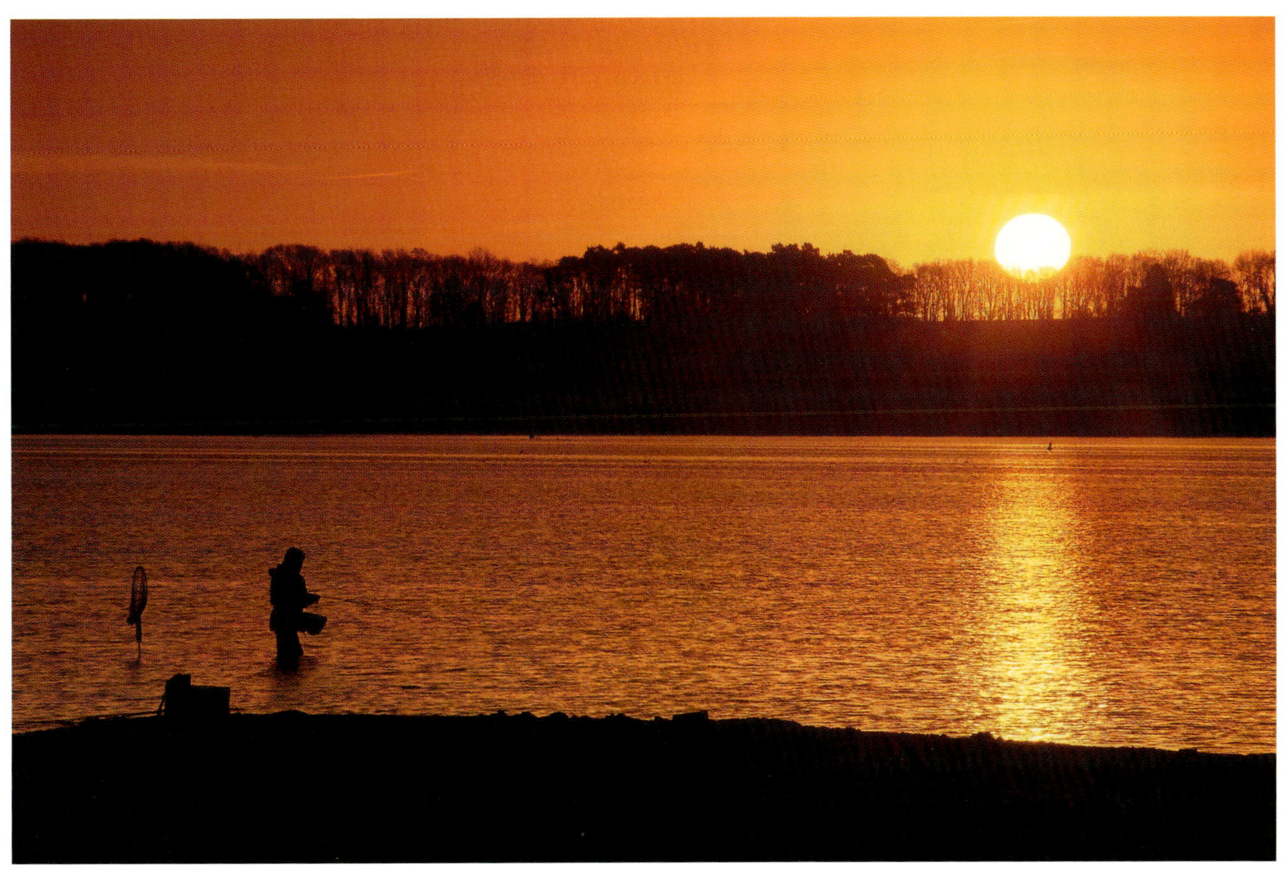

Fishing at first light.

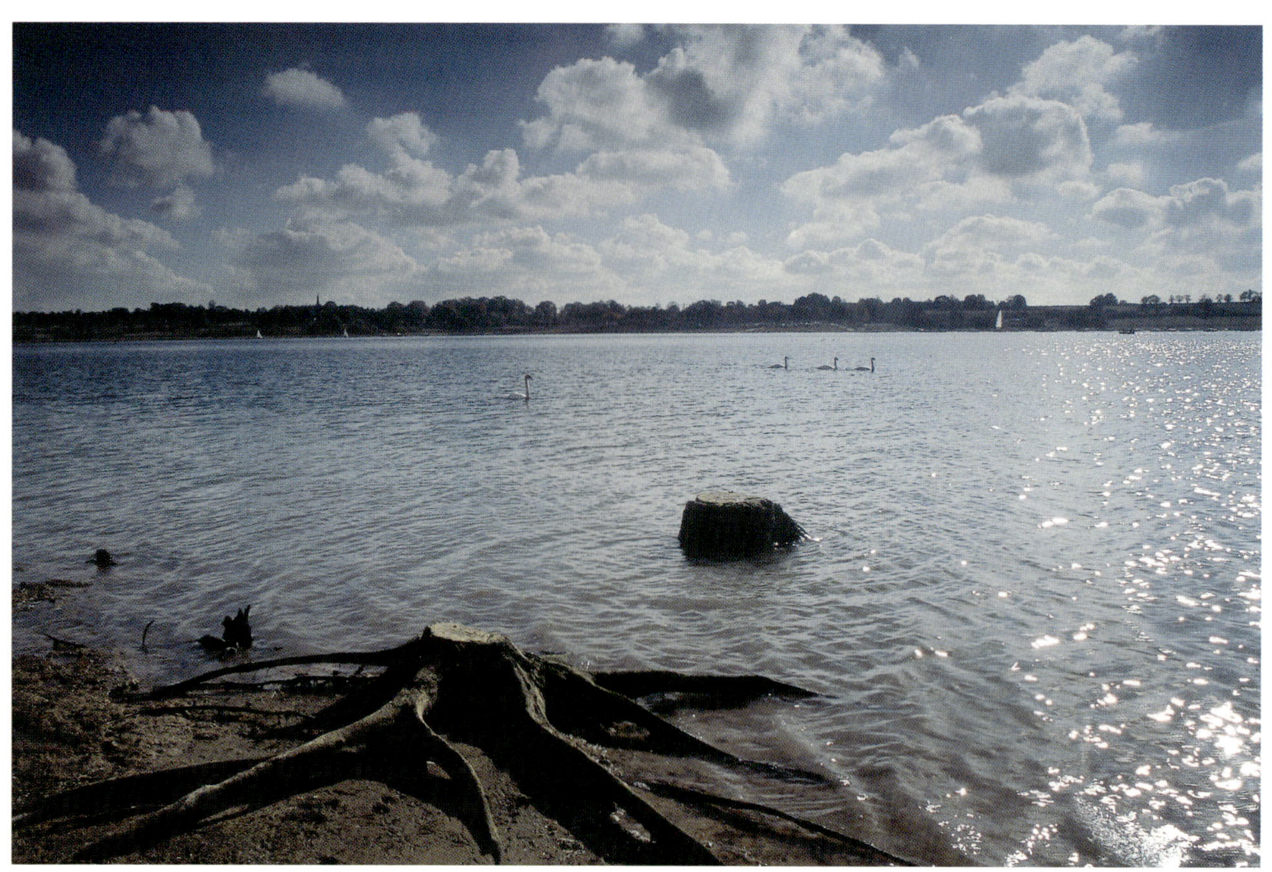

Wildlife glide past a tree stump submerged 25 years ago.

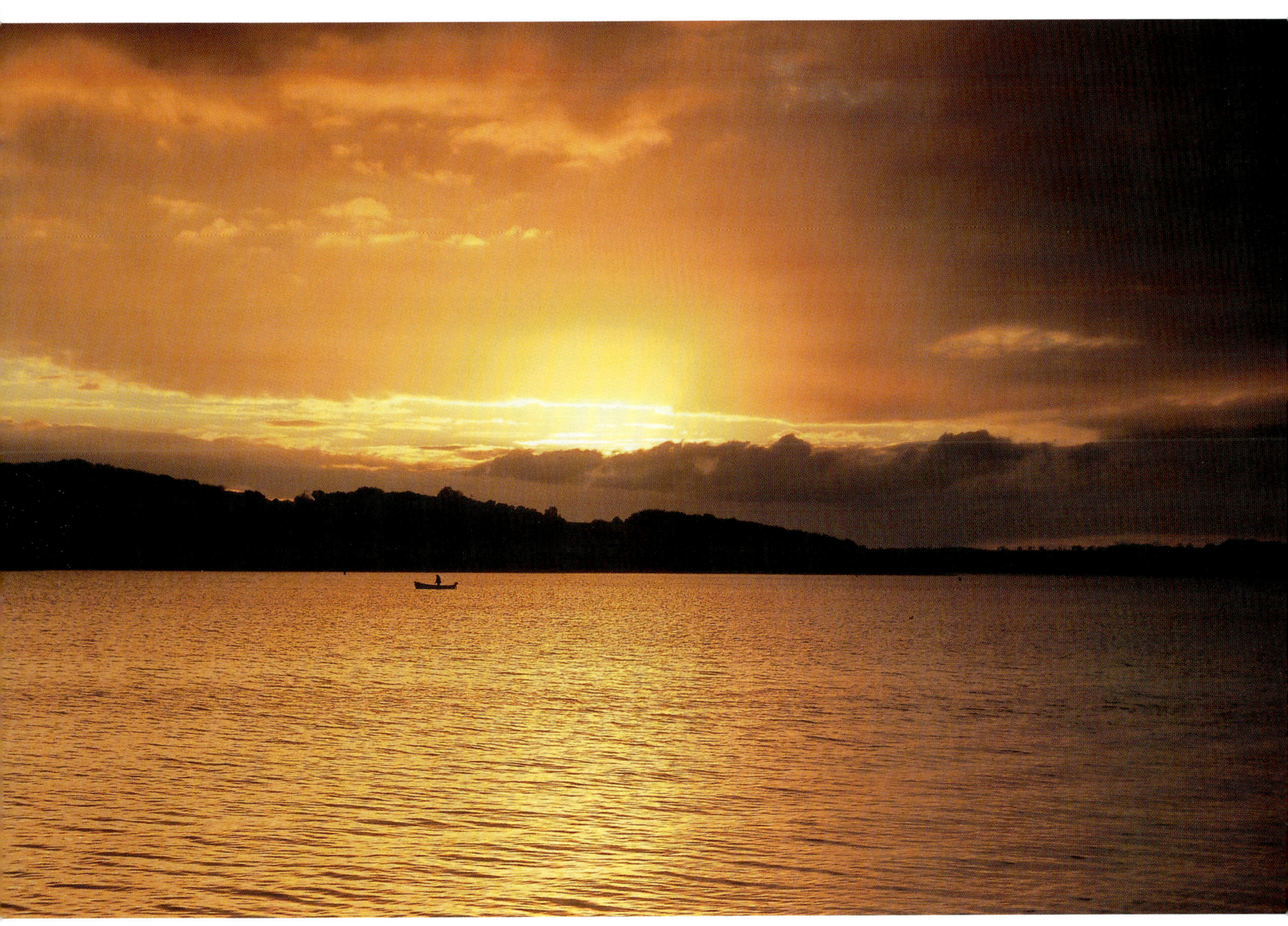

No matter how many I see, sunsets will always have a very special meaning.

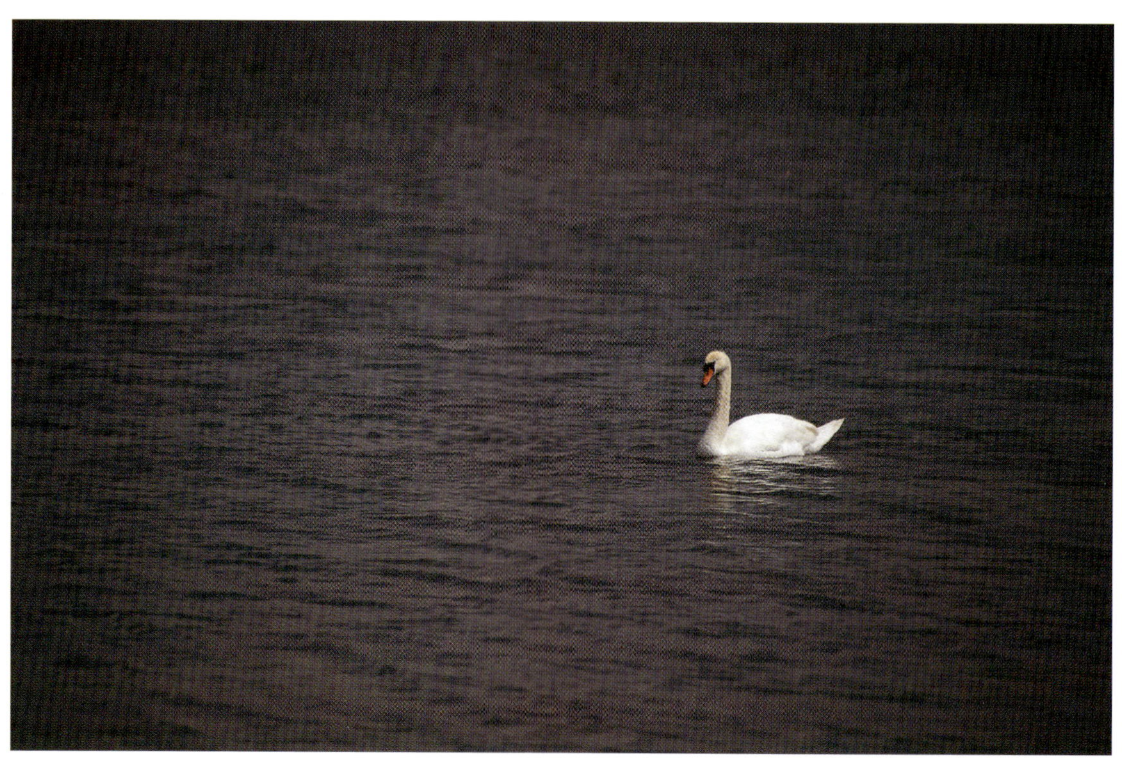

…and this resident has the freedom to stay a little longer.

PHOTOGRAPHIC NOTES

All the images in this book were taken with a Canon EOS5 auto-focus single-lens reflex, film camera. When introduced in 1992, it was revolutionary for a number of then groundbreaking innovations, of which virtually none are relevant for landscape photography, with the definite exception of the mirror lock-up facility which I always use in conjunction with a tripod. For landscapes, the camera is virtually always set to aperture-priority mode, very often with the setting at maximum aperture. The reason for this is to maximise the depth of field – the extent to which the image appears to be in focus, from the closest foreground to the furthest background.

However, the cost of making maximum depth of field the priority, is that the resulting shutter speed will invariably be slow and, except in the brightest of light conditions, too slow to hand hold the camera and avoid all effects of camera shake in the final image. Therefore all the images here have been taken with the aid of a tripod. In fact, the only significant equipment investment throughout this project was to upgrade my original tripod to a Manfrotto 055 'Tracker' fitted with an 029 standard head equipped with spirit levels. This is now my single most expensive (and heaviest) item of equipment.

For me, the use of a tripod is crucial to the whole picture taking process. It forces me to slow down, to concentrate on the elements of the landscape as seen through the viewfinder and it encourages me to wait for the combination of light, cloud and movement to do something special.

The only lenses used were two auto-focus Sigma zoom lenses: a 28-105mm and a 70-300mm. Occasionally the latter has been used in conjunction with a X 1.4 converter to increase the focal length to a maximum 420mm. The focal lengths given in the technical data following indicate the focal length that one of these lenses was adjusted to.

Personally, I find zoom lenses invaluable. Although fixed focal length lenses are normally of a better optical quality, the facility to adjust those elements of the landscape which are to be included in the final image, as viewed though the viewfinder, is a great stimulus to the creative part of picture-taking, the composition. It is sometimes not possible to stand in the ideal place for the desired composition – not least because there can be a large expanse of deep water between it and me. In such situations a zoom lens is the only method of adjusting the scale of the image. In any event, I find it much more satisfying to attempt to achieve the final image outdoors, 'in situ', rather than later by taking a pair of scissors to the print at a later stage. As a result, very few of the images here have been cropped, or altered in any way from the original transparency. The only cropping that has taken place is where the composition actually works better in a format other than the 35mm transparency shape.

No special effects filters have been used. The only filters used (all of which are part of the Cokin system) are graduated grey neutral density filters; the 81 series 'warm-up' filters and a polarising filter. These are the standard landscape photographer's filter tool kit and in fact, many of the images here would simply not have been possible without them.

For example, because the sky is almost always brighter than the land below it, very often the sky needs to be darkened to bring the different exposures needed for the sky and the land closer together and within the exposure range capability of slide film. This is typically achieved with a graduated grey neutral density filter which has no colour effect, but avoids either the sky being overexposed and lacking in detail or conversely the land being underexposed and lost in darkness. The 81 series warm-up filters are used to correct the tendency for a blue cast to appear when taking pictures in dull weather or in the shade. Also, in bright conditions with a blue sky, images can tend to have a colder feel than was actually experienced in reality and warm-up filters are used to correct this. Ideally, the use of any filter should be unnoticeable and it is interesting that my use of warm-up filters has decreased considerably since I made Fuji Velvia my standard film stock. The polarising filter is used mostly in sunny conditions and is invaluable for removing reflections and glare thereby increasing the true saturation of colours, including skies and, especially in this case, water.

I use the EOS5's internal meter to initially determine exposure. The main reasons for this are firstly that this method automatically takes account of the increase in exposure needed in respect of any filters fitted to the lens and secondly that I find the camera's metering system extremely reliable and have now become accustomed to the results that it gives in most circumstances. The spot metering facility can be used to provide additional information in difficult exposure situations (and to determine the strength of the graduated grey filter required) and in any event, if in doubt, I bracket the exposures. In certain situations, and definitely when I am taking shots of a view that I believe will make a great final image, I will bracket freely. I work on the assumption that I will never see this particular moment again and that therefore the small additional cost is well worth the investment to obtain a properly exposed single final image.

However, I almost always make some manual adjustment to the exposure recommended by the camera. After struggling for a long time to understand the textbook explanation of 'correct' exposure, I read a definition that described it as being that exposure which the photographer wishes it to be. From that moment on, I have freely adjusted the camera's recommended exposure to produce the image that I think best interprets my reaction to the view before me. Mostly, but not always, this involves a manual 'under-exposure' compared to the camera's 'correct' reading.

When I decided to take landscape photography seriously, I started to use slide film which has the benefit, amongst other technical considerations, of highlighting the photographer's weaknesses compared to the desensitised prints produced from print film. Originally I switched regularly between Fuji Sensia rated at ISO 100 and Kodak Elite Chrome also rated at ISO 100. Looking back, the very fact that I kept switching film must have meant that, subconsciously at least, I wasn't happy with the way the film was reflect-ing the landscaping I was photographing. I switched again, this time to Fujichrome Provia (also ISO 100) for almost a whole year and was much happier with the results. However, from the moment I received the processed slides back from my first roll of Fujichrome Velvia (ISO 50), I have never changed film again.

In the choice of film stock as in so many aspects of this learning process, I wish I knew then what I know now.

LOCATION AND TECHNICAL DATA

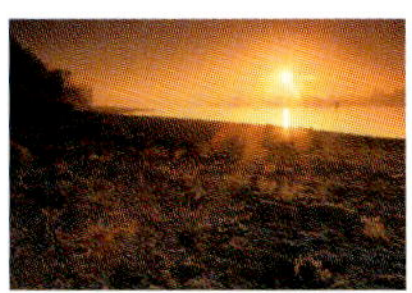

P.4. At low water levels, from the shore below the woods near Barnsdale Lodge, looking south-east.
8:34 am, 10th December
0.6 + 0.9ND grey grad. Fuji Velvia.
50mm, 1/2 second @ f/27.

P.7. From the track, at the very end of the road through the peninsula, looking south.
4:40 pm, 5th January
0.9ND grey grad. Kodak Elitechrome
70mm, 6 seconds @ f/11. Underexposed 1 stop

P.8. From near Mill Hill above Barleythorpe, looking due east over Oakham and its Church.
9:45 am, 10th July.
Polariser, 0.9ND grey grad. Fuji Sensia
300mm, 1/125 second @ f/8. Underexposed 0.5 stops

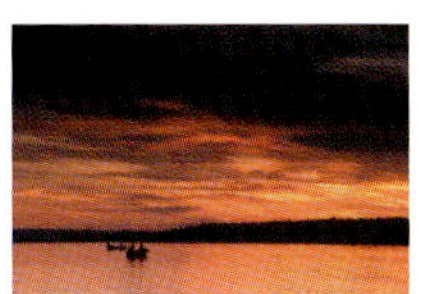

P.12. From the shoreline at Edith Weston picnic area, looking west.
9:02 pm, 18th May
0.9ND grey grad. Fuji Velvia.
105mm, 1/3 second @ f/11. Underexposed by 1 stop.

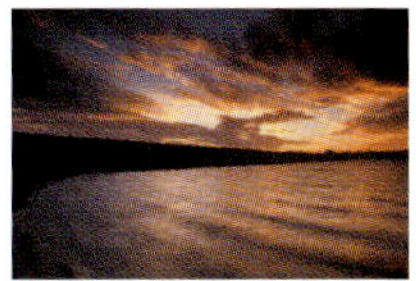

P.13. From the shore at the north end of the dam, looking along its length
8:20 am, 9th January
81A, 0.9ND grey grad. Fuji Velvia.
28mm, 0.7 second @ f/22. Overexposed by 0.5 stops.

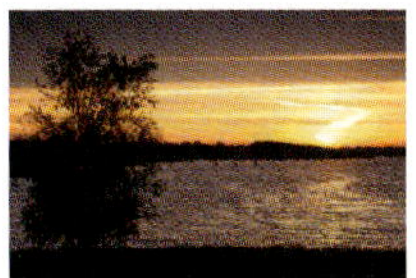

P.14. From the shoreline at Edith Weston picnic area, looking towards the sailing club.
7:13 pm, 15th September
0.9ND grey grad. Fuji Velvia.
65mm, 1/30 second @ f/8. Underexposed by 1 stop.

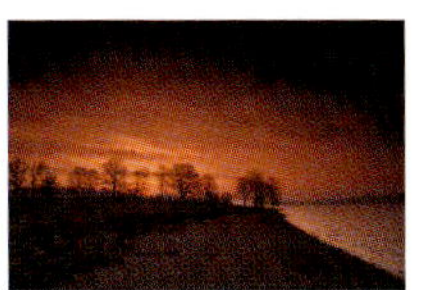

P.15. From the shoreline at Burley Reach on the north shore, looking east.
6:52 am, 3rd March
81A, 0.9ND grey grad. Fuji Velvia.
28mm, 1/6 second @ f/11. Underexposed by 1 stop.

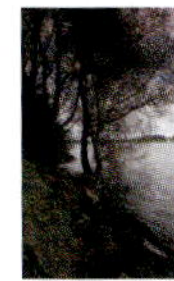

P.16. From the shore of the picnic area at Whitwell, looking south.
2:25 pm, 22nd April
Polariser, 81B, 0.9ND grey grad. Fuji Velvia.
45mm, 1/2 second @ f/22. Underexposed by 0.5 stops.

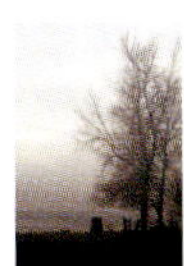

P.17. From the shore of the picnic area at Whitwell, looking south.
12:30 pm, 2nd December
81B, 0.6ND grey grad. Fuji Velvia.
40mm, 1/2 second @ f/22. Underexposed by 1 stop.

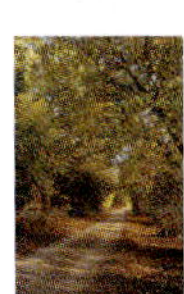

P.18. Hambleton Wood
3:22 pm, 27th October
Polariser. Fuji Provia
28mm, 1.5 seconds @ f/22. Underexposed 0.5 stops

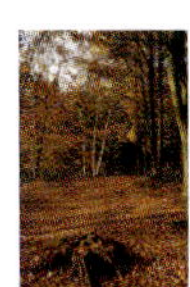

P.19. Barnsdale Wood
1:22 pm, 4th November
Fuji Velvia
28mm, 0.7 second @ f/22.

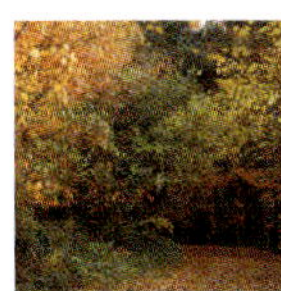

P.20. Barnsdale Wood
2:15 pm, 4th November
Fuji Velvia
28mm, 1 second @ f/16.

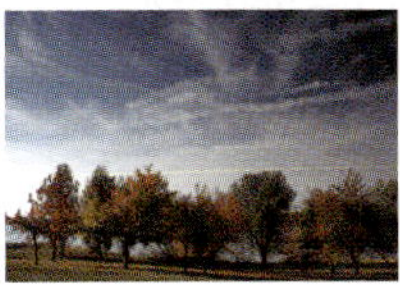

P.21. The 'camping field', just to the west of Whitwell car park.
10:18 am, 15th October
Polariser, 81C, 0.3ND grey grad. Fuji Provia
28mm, 1/10 second @ f/22. Underexposed 0.5 stops.

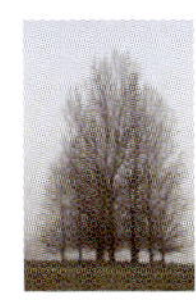

P. 22. From a postion near the Old Moat area on the end of the peninsula, looking north.
12:10 pm, 18th November
81B. Fuji Sensia
70mm, 1/45 second @ f/16. Underexposed 0.5 stops

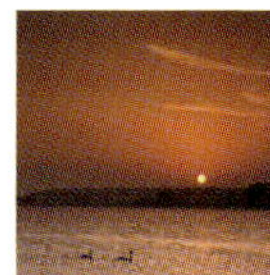

P.23. From Half Moon Spinney on the peninsula, looking towards Mowmires Reach.
6:56 am, 19th August
0.9ND grey grad. Fuji Provia
70mm, 1/60 second @ f/11. Underexposed 1.5 stops.

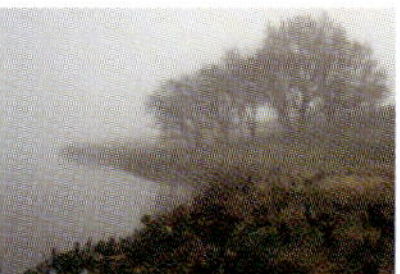

P.24. From Barnhill Creek on the peninsula, looking east.
11:35 am, 18th November
81B. Fuji Sensia
65mm, 1/15 second @ f/27. Underexposed 0.5 stops.

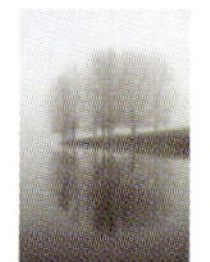

P.25. On the path on the north-eastern side of the peninsula, looking east.
1:25 pm, 18th November.
81B. Fuji Sensia
28mm, 1/15 second @ f/16. Underexposed 0.5 stops.

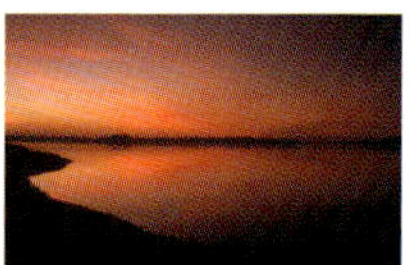

P.26. From the shore near Mowmires Reach, looking west.
5:16 pm, 5th December
81A, 0.3ND grey grad. Fuji Velvia.
28mm, 3 seconds @ f/22. Underexposed by 1 stop.

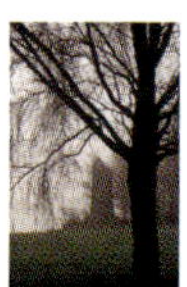

P.27. The Great Tower, at Syke's Lane
1:53 pm, 2nd December
81B. Fuji Velvia.
105mm, 1/6 second @ f/22. Underexposed by 0.5 stops.

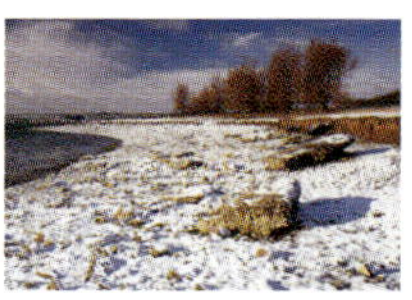

P.28. At Syke's Spinney, looking west.
10:14 am, 28th January
Polariser, 0.6ND grey grad. Fuji Velvia.
35mm, 1/3 second @ f/22. Overexposed by 1 stop.

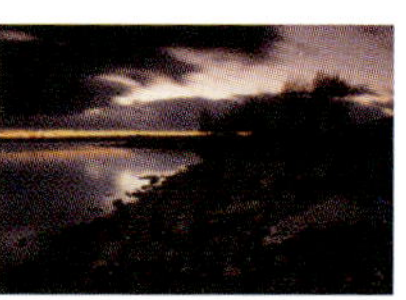

P.29. At Syke's Spinney, looking west.
5:20 pm, 8th February
81A, 0.9ND grey grad. Fuji Velvia.
28mm, 20 seconds @ f/22. Underexposed by 0.5 stops.

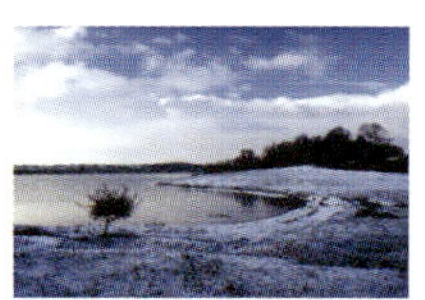

P.30. From the eastern end of the peninsula, on the southern side, towards Hinman's Spinney.
10:00 am, 9th January
Polariser. Kodak Elitechrome
28mm, 1/8 second @ f/22.

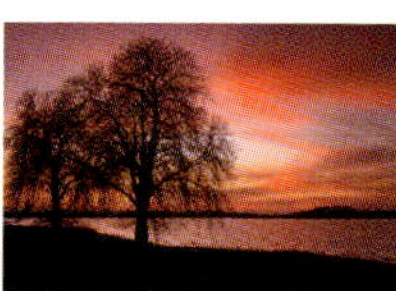

P.31. Near Mowmires Reach looking west.
4:46 pm, 27th January.
81B, 0.6ND grey grad. Fuji Velvia.
45mm, 0.7 second @ f/13. Underexposed by 0.5 stops.

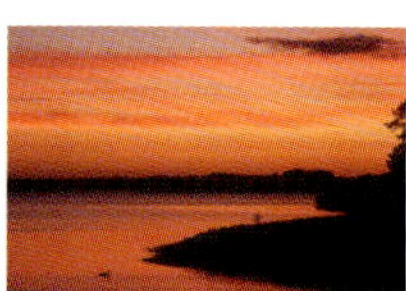

P.32. From the track on the southern side of the peninsula (below Lodge Farm) looking west.
6:11 pm, 18th October
0.6ND grey grad. Kodak Elitechrome
50mm, 30 second @ f/5.6. Underexposed 2 stops

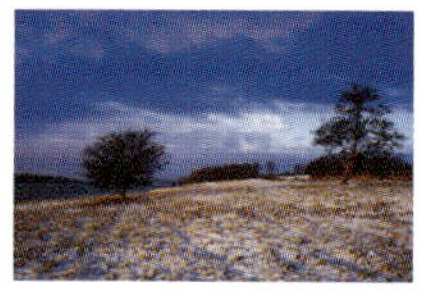

P.33. From the eastern end of the peninsula, on the southern side, looking to the west.
9:05 am, 9th January
Polariser. Kodak Elitechrome
28mm, 1/15 second @ f/22. Underexposed 1 stop

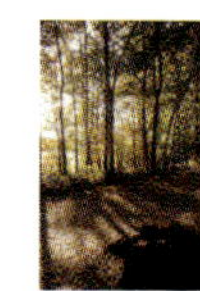

P.34. Along the path through Barnsdale Wood.
4:31 pm, 20th October
81B. Fuji Provia
28mm, 1/4 second @ f/16.

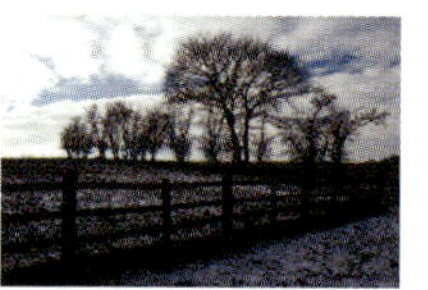

P.35. The south side of Barnhill Creek, on the peninsula.
Midday, 9th January
Polariser, 81B. Kodak Elitechrome
35mm, 1/10 second @ f/22.

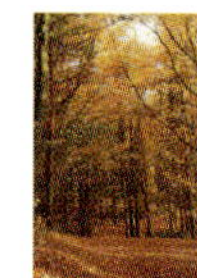

P. 36. Barnsdale Wood.
1:05 pm, 4th November
81B. Fuji Velvia
50mm, 1/2 second @ f/11.

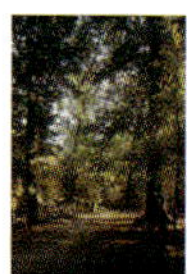

P.37. Approaching Berrybut Spinneys, from the west.
3:17 pm, 16th October
Polariser @ 50%, 81B. Fuji Provia
28mm, 1 second @ f/22. Underexposed 1 stop.

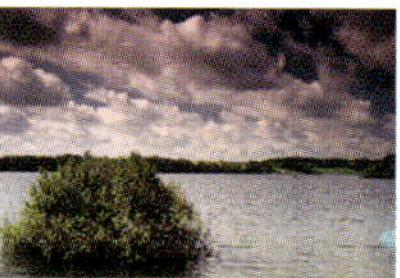

P.38. From the eastern corner of Barnsdale Creek, looking south-west.
10:41 am, 18th May
Polariser, 81B, 0.9ND grey grad. Fuji Velvia.
40mm, 1/6 second @ f/16. Underexposed by 0.5 stops.

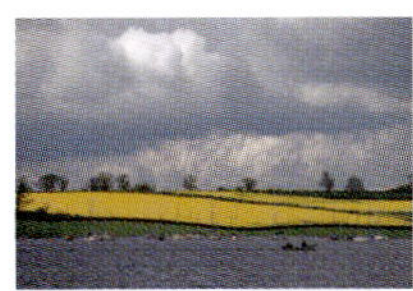

P.39. Looking just to the west of the sailing club from the south-eastern corner of the peninsula.
10:34 am, 6th May.
Polariser. Fuji Velvia.
200mm, 1/90 second @ f/8. Underexposed by 0.5 stops.

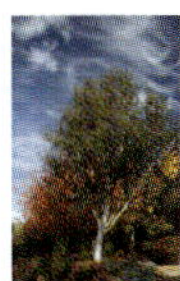

P.40. The Drought Garden, Barnsdale.
11:17 am, 15th October.
Polariser, 81B. Fuji Provia.
28mm, 1/8 second @ f/22. Underexposed 0.5 stops.

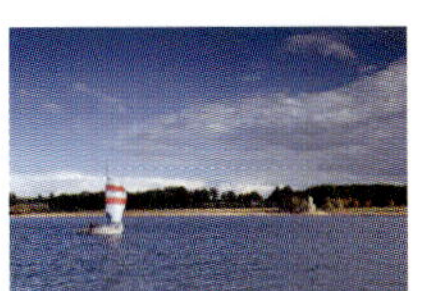

P.41. Between Hinman's Spinney and Half Moon Spinney on the peninsula, looking south-east.
2:35 pm, 26th October.
Polariser, 0.6ND grey grad. Fuji Provia.
60mm, 1/30 second @ f/11. Underexposed 0.5 stops.

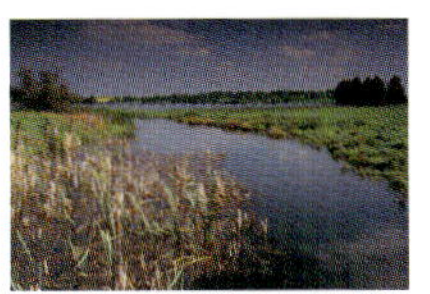

P.42. From the footpath at Lodge Inlet looking south-east.
5:27 pm, 18th May.
Polariser, 0.9ND grey grad. Fuji Velvia.
35mm, 1/4 second @ f/22. Underexposed by 0.5 stops

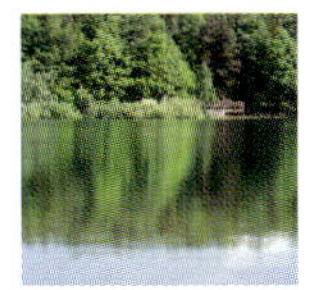

P.43. From the north side of the spit of land forming Barnsdale Creek, looking north.
9:42 am, 18th May.
Polariser. Fuji Velvia.
105mm, 1/2 second @ f/22. Underexposed by 0.5 stops.

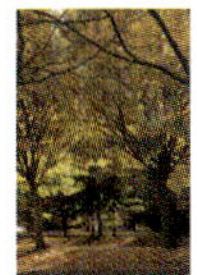

P.44. Whitwell car park.
3:07 pm, 20th October.
81B. Fuji Provia.
100mm, 1 second @ f/27. Underexposed 0.5 stops.

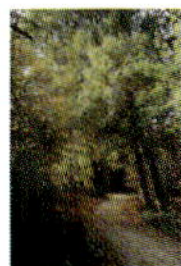

P.45. Approaching Berrybut Spinneys, from the east.
15:27 am, 16th October.
Polariser @ 50%, 81B. Fuji Provia.
28mm, 1.5 seconds @ f/22. Underexposed 1 stop.

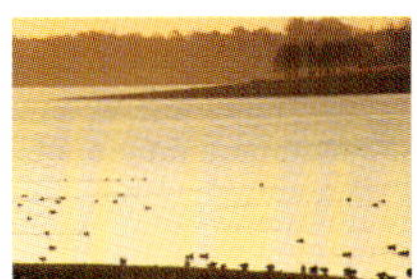

P.46. At low water levels, from the north side of Barnsdale Creek, looking south.
8:52 am, 7th December.
81B, 0.6ND grey grad. Fuji Velvia.
300mm, 1/30 second @ f/11. Underexposed by 0.5 stops.

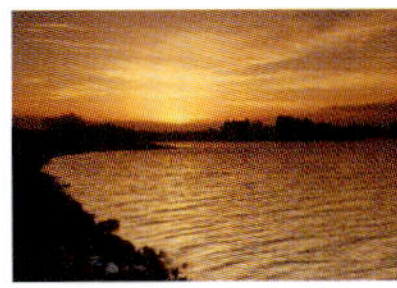

P.47. Along the southern shore of the peninsula, looking south-east towards the Old Hall.
8:25 am, 10th January.
81C, 0.9ND grey grad. Kodak Elitechrome.
50mm, 1/10 second @ f/22. Underexposed 0.5 stops.

P.48. From near the old jetty at Half Moon Spinney, looking almost due west.
7:01 am, 1st March.
0.9ND grey grad. Fuji Velvia.
230mm, 1/15 second @ f/8. Underexposed by 1 stop.

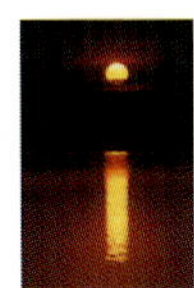

P.49. From near the old jetty at Half Moon Spinney, looking almost due west.
7:04 am, 1st March.
0.9ND grey grad. Fuji Velvia.
300mm, 1/180 second @ f/8. Underexposed by 1 stop.

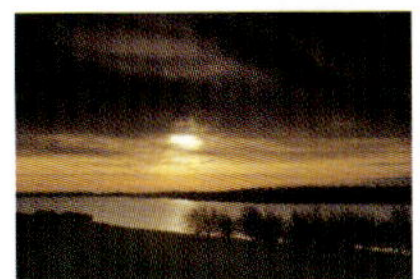

P.50. From the picnic area above Barnsdale Creek, looking towards the south-east.
9:15 am, 14th January.
81B, 0.6 + 0.9ND grey grad. Kodak Elitechrome.
35mm, 1/6 second @ f/22. Underexposed 0.5 stops.

P.51. Normanton Church, looking towards the sunset
6:50 9m, 24th September.
81C, 0.9ND grey grad. Fuji Provia.
28mm, 1/4 second @ f/22. Underexposed 0.5 stops.

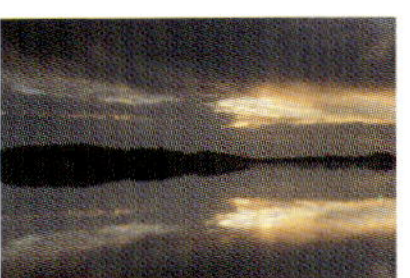

P.52. From just to the east of Hinman's Spinney, looking west.
6:40 pm, 21st October.
81B, 0.6ND grey grad. Fuji Provia.
40mm, 1/4 second @ f/22. Underexposed 1 stop.

P.53. Between Hinman's Spinney and Half Moon Spinney on the peninsula, looking south.
3:36 pm, 26th October.
0.6ND grey grad. Fuji Provia.
135mm, 1/60 second @ f/8. Underexposed 1 stop.

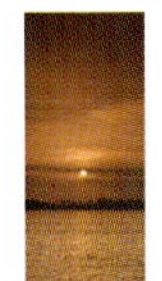

P.54. From the end of the spit of land at Whitwell Lodge, looking towards Mowmires Reach
8:00 am, 18th October.
81B + 81C, 0.9ND grey grad. Fuji Provia.
80mm, 1/45 second @ f/16. Underexposed 1 stop.

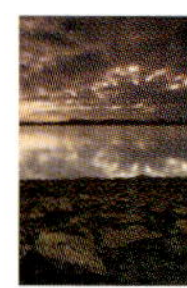

P.55. At low water levels, from the shore beside Syke's Spinney, looking south.
10:02 am, 4th January.
81A, 0.9ND grey grad. Fuji Velvia.
28mm, 1/4 second @ f/22. Underexposed by 0.5 stops.

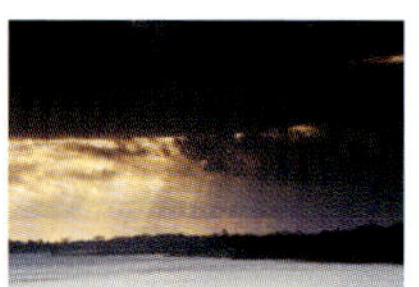

P.56. From the picnic area above Barnsdale Creek, towards the eastern end of the peninsula.
9:25 am, 17th January.
81B, 0.6 + 0.9ND grey grad. Kodak Elitechrome.
105mm, 1/4 second @ f/22. Underexposed 1 stop.

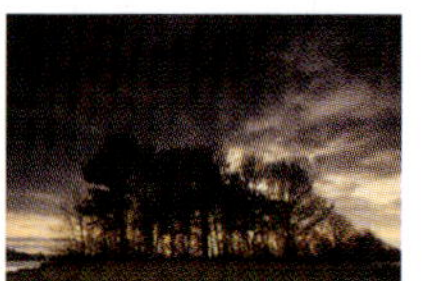

P.57. The small copse of trees on the tip of the land that forms Barnsdale Creek.
9:50 am, 14th January.
81B, 0.6 + 0.9ND grey grad. Kodak Elitechrome.
35mm, 1/8 second @ f/22. Underexposed 1.5 stops.

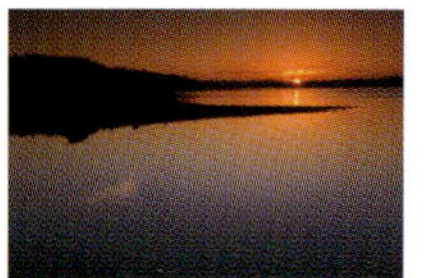

P.58. Near the Old Hall on the peninsula, looking towards Hambleton Wood.
8:15 am, 17th December.
0.9ND grey grad. Fuji Velvia.
28mm, 1/30 second @ f/6.7. Underexposed by 0.5 stops.

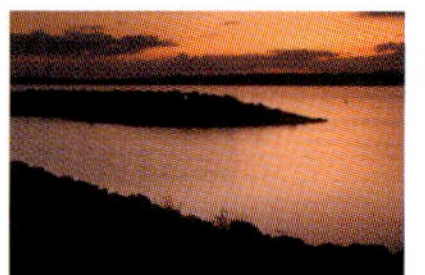

P.59. From the very south-easterly corner of the dam, looking west.
9:08 pm, 21st May.
81B, 0.6ND grey grad. Fuji Velvia.
60mm, 1 second @ f/27. Underexposed by 1 stop.

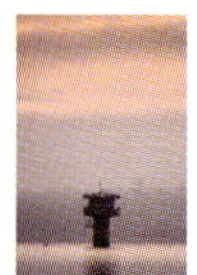

P.60. From the shore near Syke's Spinney, looking south.
12:10 pm, 2nd December.
0.6ND grey grad. Fuji Velvia.
300mm, with X 1.4 tele convertor, 1/60 second @ f/5.6. Underexposed by 1 stop.

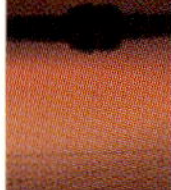

P.61. At the eastern edge of Gibbet Gorse, looking west.
5:54 pm, 1st March.
81A, 0.9ND grey grad. Fuji Velvia.
105mm, 1.5 seconds @ f/22. Underexposed by 1 stop.

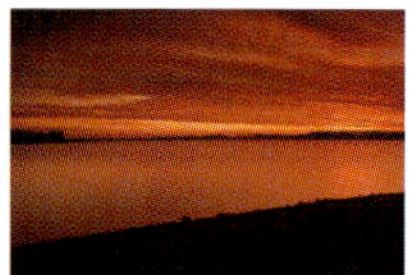

P.62. From the spit of land at Whitwell Creek, looking south-east.
8:02 am, 16th December.
81C, 0.9ND grey grad. Fuji Velvia.
35mm, 1 second @ f/22. Underexposed by 1 stop.

P.63. From near the picnic area at Whitwell, looking south-west towards Armley Lodge on the peninsula.
4:01 pm, 16th December.
0.9ND grey grad. Fuji Velvia.
105mm, 1/2 second @ f/8.

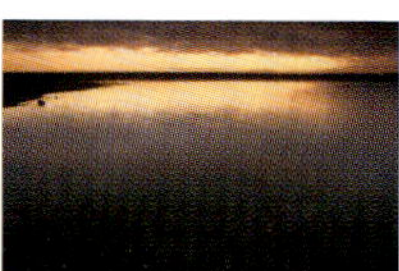

P.64. Near Syke's Lane picnic area, looking towards the dam (and a long way out from the normal shoreline!)
8:26 am, 4th January.
81B, 0.9ND grey grad. Fuji Velvia.
28mm, 2 seconds @ f/22.

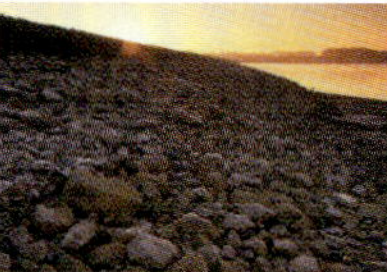

P.65. From the northern corner of the dam, at very low water levels.
8:24 am, 8th December.
0.9ND grey grad. Fuji Velvia.
35mm, 1 second @ f/22.

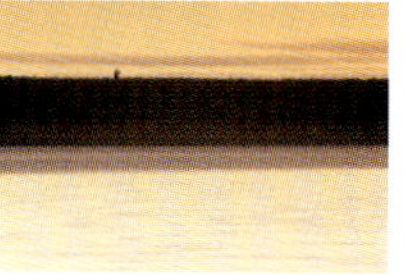

P.66. Looking towards the dam from the north at low water levels.
8:45 am, 4th January.
81B, 0.9ND grey grad. Fuji Velvia.
300mm, 2 seconds @ f/22. Underexposed by 1 stop.

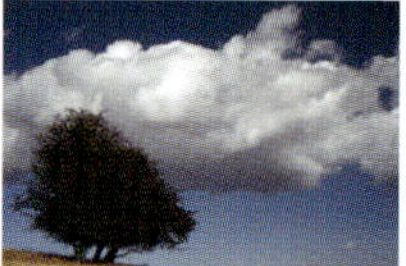

P.67. The isolated clump of trees on the north side of Barnhill Creek on the peninsula.
2:35 pm, 7th October.
Polariser, 81C. Fuji Provia.
50mm, 1/20 second @ f/22. Underexposed 0.5 stops.

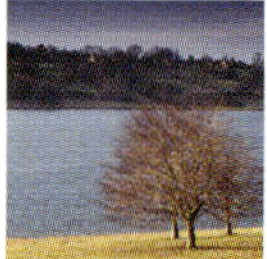

P.68. From just south of the top car park at Barnsdale, looking towards Hambleton village.
9:45 am, 16th January.
0.6 + 0.9ND grey grad. Kodak Elitechrome.
105mm, 1/3 second @ f/22. Underexposed 0.5 stops.

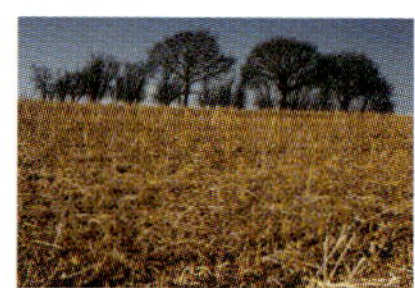

P.69. Just to the west of Half Moon Spinney on the peninsula.
3:10 pm, 21st February.
Polariser, 0.6ND grey grad. Fuji Provia.
70mm, 1/3 second @ f/32. Underexposed 1 stop.

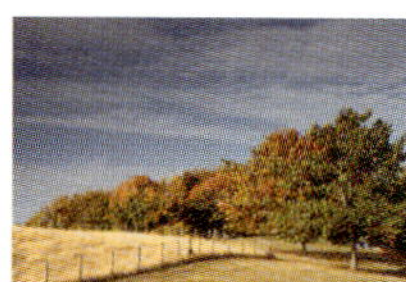

P.70. Looking back up the hill from near the Barnsdale entrance to Barnsdale Wood.
9:05 am, 14th October.
Polariser @ 50%, 81C, 0.3ND grey grad. Fuji Provia.
105mm, 1/6 second @ f/22. Underexposed 0.5 stops.

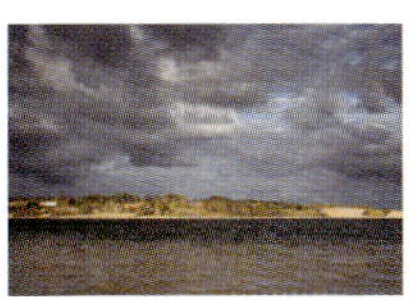

P.71. From near the car park at the bottom of the hill leading to Upper Hambleton, looking north.
4:45 pm, 19th October.
81B, 0.9ND grey grad. Fuji Provia.
50mm, 0.7 second @ f/27. Underexposed 0.5 stops.

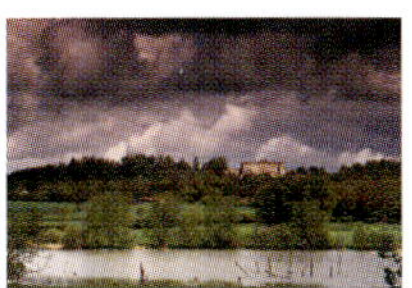

P.72. From the minor road leading to Rutland Water (North) Nature Reserve on the peninsula, looking due north.   11:43 am, 6th May.
81B, 0.9ND grey grad. Fuji Velvia.
105mm, 1/20 second @ f/19. Underexposed by 0.5 stops.

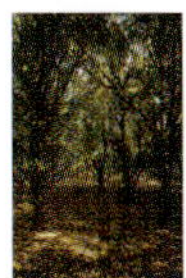

P.73. The Arboretum, Barnsdale.
11:49 am, 15th October.
Polariser @ 50%, 81B. Fuji Provia.
28mm, 2 seconds @ f/22. Underexposed 1 stop.

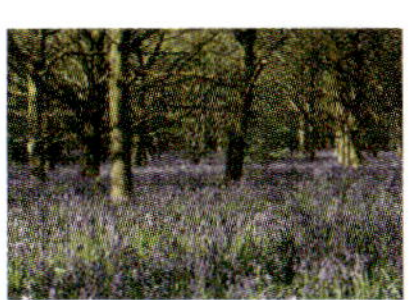

P.74. 'Bluebell Wood' within Hambleton Wood.
4:50 pm, 26th April.
81B. Fuji Provia.
70mm, 1/30 second @ f/16. Underexposed 1.5 stops.

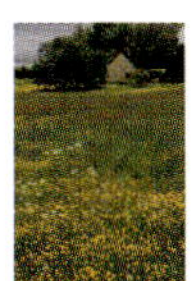

P.75. From the footpath at the top of the hill due north of the Old Hall on the peninsula.
3:16 pm, 21st May.
Polariser, 81B. Fuji Velvia.
100mm, 1/4 second @ f/27. Underexposed by 0.5 stops.

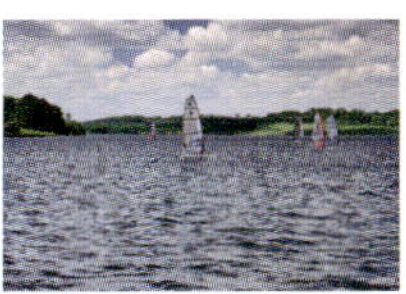

P.76. From the shoreline near the Moat on the peninsula, looking north-west, along the northern arm of the water.   2:06 pm, 22nd May.
Polariser, 0.6ND grey grad. Fuji Velvia.
80mm, 1/15 second @ f/11. Underexposed by 0.5 stops.

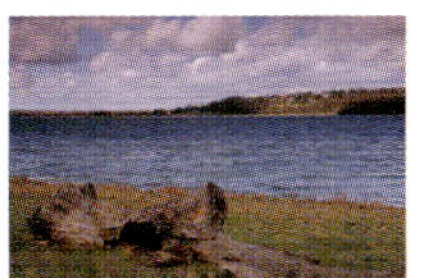

P.77. From the open land to the east of Berrybut Spinneys.
12:15 pm, 19th March.
81A, 0.9ND grey grad. Fuji Velvia.
60mm, 1/6 second @ f/22. Underexposed by 0.5 stops.

P.78. Lax Hill, from the south-eastern corner of the peninsula.
9:10 am, 10th January.
Polariser, 81A, 0.9ND grey grad. Kodak Elitechrome.
50mm, 1/4 second @ f /22. Underexposed 0.5 stops.

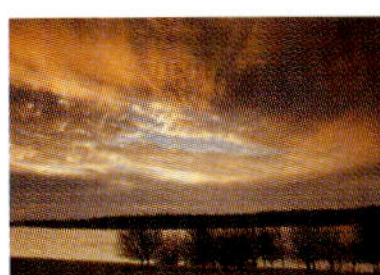

P.79. The field to the south-west of the top Barnsdale car park, looking south-west.
8:25 am, 15th January.
81B, 0.9ND grey grad. Kodak Elitechrome.
28mm, 1/15 second @ f/11. Underexposed 0.5 stops.

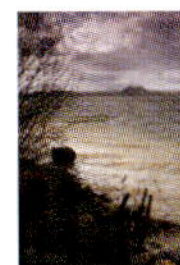

P.80. At the eastern edge of Gibbet Gorse, looking west.
2:28 pm, 19th March.
81B, 0.9ND grey grad. Fuji Velvia.
40mm, 1/10 second @ f/16. Underexposed by 0.5 stops.

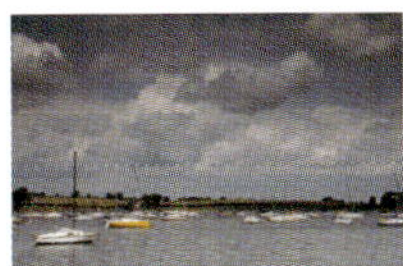

P.81. From the fields near the slipways at Rutland Water Sailing Club, looking towards the peninsula.
1:00 pm, 18th July.
Polariser, 81B, 0.6ND grey grad. Fuji Sensia.
70mm, 1/8 second @ f/27. Underexposed 1 stop.

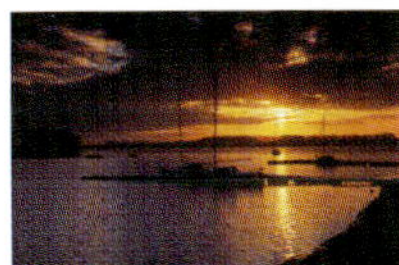

P.82. Whitwell Sailing Club rescue centre, looking towards the rising sun in the south-east.
8:40 am, 7th January.
0.9ND grey grad. Kodak Elitechrome.
60mm, 1/8 second @ f/27. Underexposed 0.5 stops.

P.83. From the northern shoreline of the peninsula, near the car park at the bottom of the hill, looking north.
10:34 pm, 18th May.
0.9ND grey grad. Fuji Velvia.
28mm, 6 seconds @ f/8. Underexposed by 2 stops.

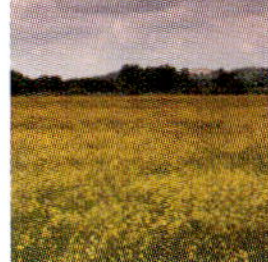

P.84. In the meadows around Egleton Bird Watching Centre, looking north.
2:09 pm, 2nd June.
81B, 0.9ND grey grad. Fuji Velvia.
70mm, 1/6 second @ f/22. Underexposed by 0.5 stops.

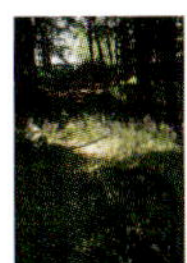

P.85. From behind the bench in the bluebell area of Barnsdale Wood.
1:17 pm, 18th May.
0.9ND grey grad. Fuji Velvia.
70mm, 1/3 second @ f/8. Underexposed by 0.5 stops.

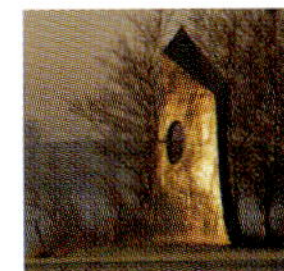

P.86. The picnic area at Syke's Lane.
8:54 am, 8th December.
Polariser, 81B. Fuji Velvia.
300mm, 1/8 second @ f/16. Underexposed by 0.5 stops.

P.87. Close to the Old Hall on the peninsula, looking south.
2:55 pm, 28th November.
81C, 0.9ND grey grad. Fuji Velvia.
105mm, 1 second @ f/22. Underexposed by 1 stop.

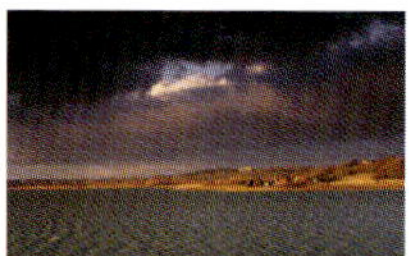

P.88. From between Gibbet Gorse and Berrybut Spinneys, looking towards the Old Hall on the peninsula.
3:24 pm, 13th January.
81A, 0.9ND grey grad. Fuji Velvia.
60mm, 1/6 second @ f/11. Underexposed by 1 stop.

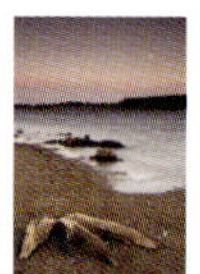

P.89. Below the normal shoreline at Hambleton Wood, looking south-east.
6:40 pm, 3rd October.
81C, 0.3 + 0.9ND grey grad. Fuji Provia.
40mm, 3 seconds @ f/22. Underexposed 0.5 stops.

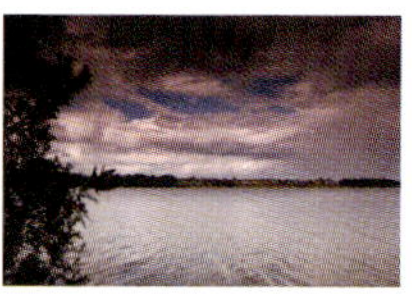

P.90. From the shoreline at Berrybut Spinneys, looking towards Lodge Farm on the peninsula.
3:03 pm, 2nd July.
81B, 0.9ND grey grad. Fuji Velvia.
28mm, 1/15 second @ f/22. Underexposed by 0.5 stops.

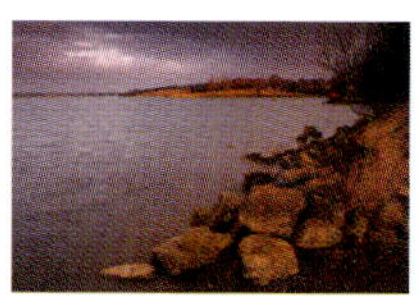

P.91. From the shoreline at Whitwell picnic area, looking west.
6:47 am, 15th March.
81B, 0.9ND grey grad. Fuji Velvia.
30mm, 1 second @ f/22. Underexposed by 0.5 stops.

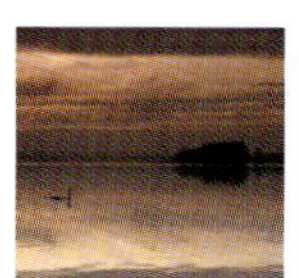

P.92. From the shore near Syke's Spinney, looking towards the mouth of Whitwell Creek.
11:45 am, 2nd December.
Polariser @ 50%, 81B, 0.3ND grey grad. Fuji Velvia.
70mm, 1/15 second @ f/11. Underexposed by 1 stop.

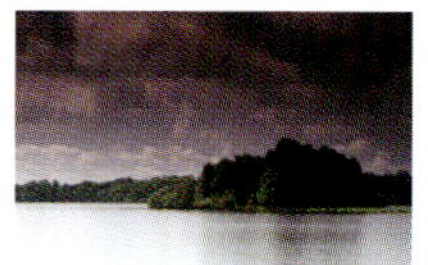

P.93. From the shore on the north side of Barnsdale Creek, looking south.
10:15 am, 18th May.
Polariser, 0.6 + 0.9ND grey grad. Fuji Velvia.
70mm, 0.7 second @ f/22. Underexposed by 0.5 stops.

P-94 From the jetty at the very eastern end of the peninsula, looking across the Water.
10:05 am, 18th November.
0.6ND grey grad. Fuji Sensia.
50mm, 1/30 second @ f/22. Underexposed 0.5 stops.

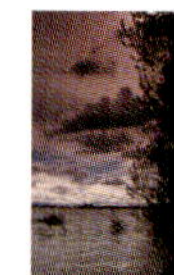

P.95. From the shoreline at Syke's Lane, near the north end of the dam, looking south-west.
3:29 pm, 5th May.
81B, 0.9ND grey grad. Fuji Velvia.
35mm, 1/45 second @ f/16. Underexposed by 0.5 stops.

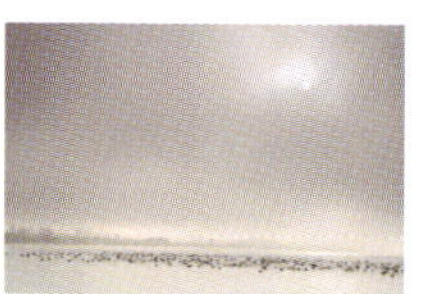

P.96 From the picnic area at Syke's Lane, looking towards Normanton.
1:18 pm, 2nd December.
0.6ND grey grad. Fuji Velvia.
60mm, 1/45 second @ f /9.5.

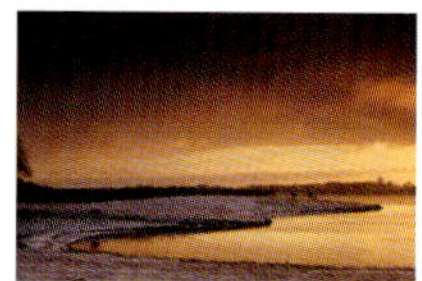

P.97. On the peninsula, from the field to the east of Hinman's Spinney, looking south-east.
8:40 am, 9th January.
0.9ND grey grad. Kodak Elitechrome.
28mm, 1/10 second @ f/22. Underexposed 0.5 stops.

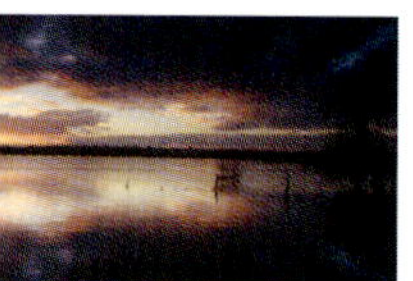

P.98. Looking towards Brown's Island from the extreme south-eastern corner of the peninsula.
4:00 pm, 9th January.
0.6ND grey grad. Kodak Elitechrome.
35mm, 1/6 second @ f/22. Underexposed 0.5 stops.

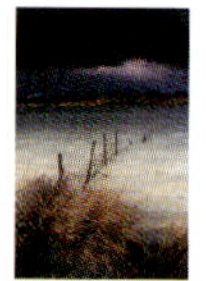

P.99. On the north shore of the peninsula north of the village, looking due north.
1:10 pm, 8th April.
0.9ND grey grad. Fuji Velvia.
50mm, 1/4 second @ f /22. Underexposed by 1 stop.

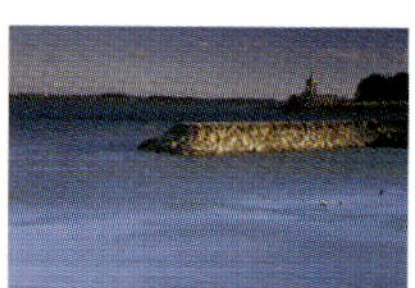

P.100. Above the Anglian Water boat park at Edith Weston picnic area, looking towards Normanton Church.
9:22 am, 13th January.
Polariser, 0.9ND grey grad. Fuji Velvia.
70mm, 1/4 second @ f/11. Underexposed by 1 stop.

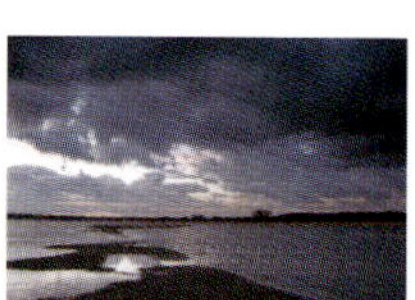

P.101. From the area know as Middle Hambleton, at very low water levels, looking due west.
6:05 pm, 20th October.
0.6ND grey grad. Fuji Provia.
28mm, 0.7 second @ f/16. Underexposed 1 stop.

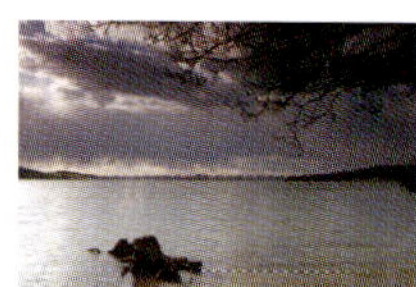

P.102. From the shoreline below Hinman's Spinney on the peninsula, looking west.
3:26 pm, 25th February.
0.9ND grey grad. Fuji Velvia.
35mm, 1/3 second @ f/22. Underexposed by 0.5 stops.

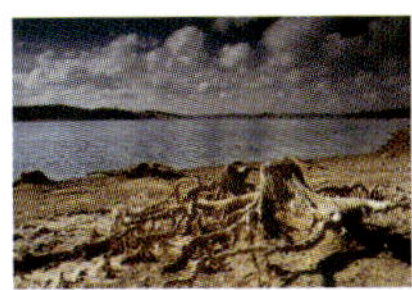

P.103. From below the normal shoreline during low water levels near Hambleton Wood, looking west.
12:55 pm, 21st October.
Polariser, 0.9ND grey grad. Fuji Provia.
28mm, 1/10 second @ f/22. Underexposed 0.5 stops.

P.104. From the very south-easterly corner of the dam, looking north.
9:10 pm, 21st May.
81B, 0.6ND grey grad. Fuji Velvia.
105mm, 1/3 second @ f/6.7. Underexposed by 1.5 stops.

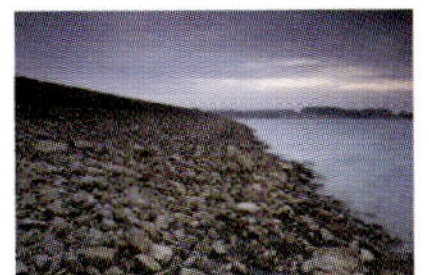

P.105. From the northern corner of the dam, at very low water levels.
8:13 am, 3rd January.
81A, 0.9ND grey grad. Fuji Velvia.
28mm, 10 seconds @ f/22. Underexposed by 0.5 stops.

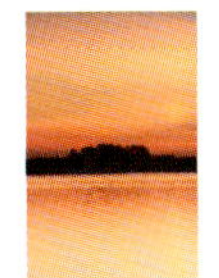

P.106. Lax Hill taken from near the Old Hall on the south shore of the peninsula.
5:07 pm, 27th October.
81C, 0.6ND grey grad. Fuji Provia.
140mm, 1.5 seconds @ f/11.

P.107. From Edith Weston picnic area looking north towards Half Moon Spinney at the end of the peninsula.
9:30 am, 17th May.
81B, 0.9ND grey grad. Fuji Velvia.
300mm, 20 seconds @ f/11. Underexposed by 2 stops.

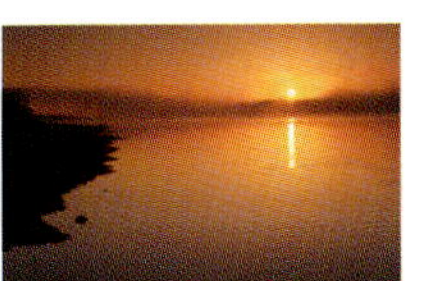

P.108. At low water levels, from the shore below the woods near Barnsdale Lodge, looking south-east.
8:23 am, 10th December.
0.6ND grey grad. Fuji Velvia.
50mm, 1/6 second @ f/27.

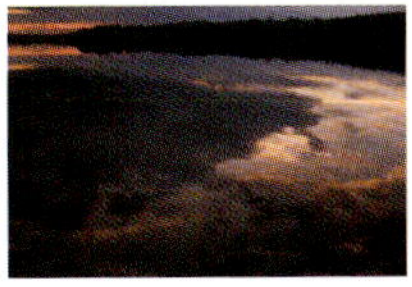

P.109. From the eastern end of Barnsdale Creek, looking back into the Creek.
8:23 pm, 6th May.
81B. Fuji Velvia.
28mm, 1/8 second @ f/8. Underexposed by 0.5 stops.

P.110. From between Gibbet Gorse and Berrybut Spinneys, looking towards the Old Hall on the peninsula.
3:22 pm, 13th January.
81A, 0.9ND grey grad. Fuji Velvia.
105mm, 1/10 second @ f/11. Underexposed by 1 stop.

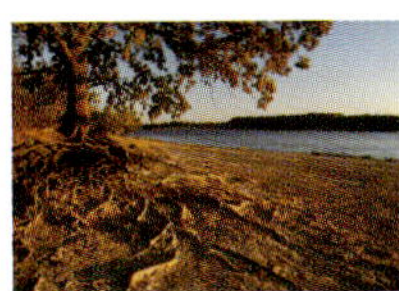

P.111. Below the normal shoreline at Hambleton Wood, looking south.
5:42 pm, 16th October.
Polariser, 81C. Fuji Provia.
28mm, 1 second @ f/22. Underexposed 0.5 stops.

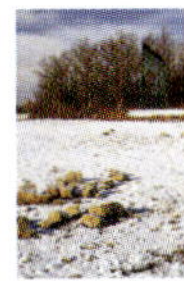

P.112. The low water shoreline at Syke's Lane.
10:02 am, 28th January.
Polariser. Fuji Velvia.
70mm, 1/4 second @ f/22. Overexposed by 1 stop.

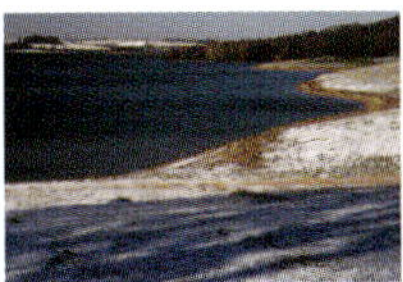

P.113. On the rise of the hill just to the west of Hinman's Spinney, on the peninsula, looking west.
9:48 am, 25th February.
Polariser @ 50%, 81A. Fuji Velvia.
70mm, 1/6 second @ f/32. Underexposed by 1.5 stops.

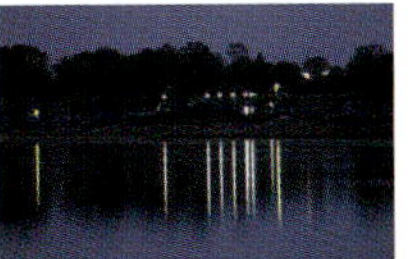

P.114. From just to the east of Hinman's Spinney, looking towards Rutland sailing Club.
7:28 pm, 21st October.
Fuji Provia.
300mm, 4 seconds @ f/8. Underexposed 2 stops.

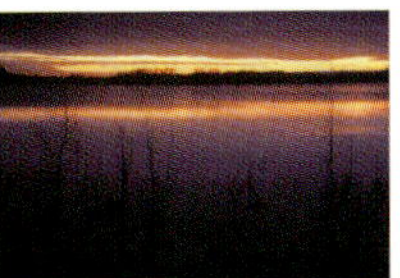

P.115. From the extreme south eastern corner of the peninsula, looking south-east.
4:40 pm, 9th January.
81B, 0.6ND grey grad. Kodak Elitechrome.
50mm, 1/20 second @ f/22. Underexposed 1 stop.

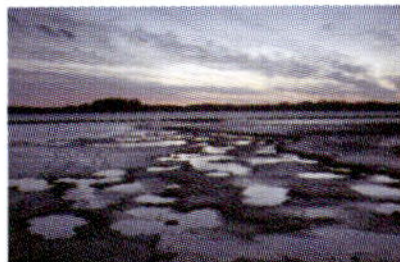

P.116. Towards Browns Island from Middleton Hambleton.
4:45 pm, 3rd November.
0.6ND grey grad. Fuji Provia.
28mm, 2 seconds @ f/22. Underexposed 0.5 stops.

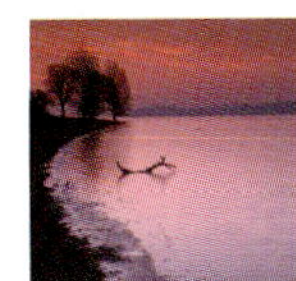

P.117. From the shoreline at Burley Reach on the north shore, looking south-east.
6:40 am, 3rd March.
0.9ND grey grad. Fuji Velvia.
50mm, 1 second @ f/16. Underexposed by 1 stop.

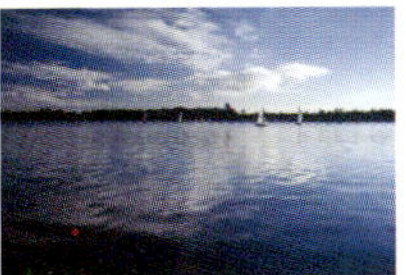

P.118. From the eastern end of the peninsula, on the southern side, looking towards Normanton.
12:10 pm, 5th January.
Polariser, 0.3ND grey grad. Kodak Elitechrome.
28mm, 1/10 second @ f/22. Underexposed 0.5 stops.

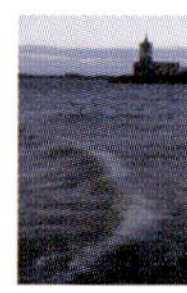

P.119. Normanton from Howell's Inlet at very low water.
8:22 am, 13th January.
81A. Fuji Velvia.
70mm, 1/8 second @ f/8. Underexposed by 0.5 stops.

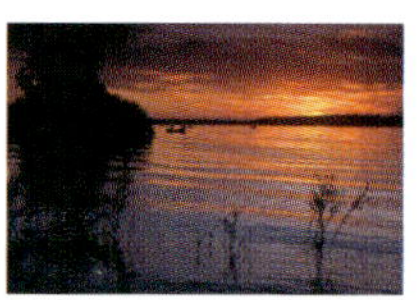

P.120. From the shoreline at Edith Weston picnic area, looking west.
8:54 pm, 18th May.
0.9ND grey grad. Fuji Velvia.
45mm, 1/10 second @ f/11. Underexposed by 1 stop.

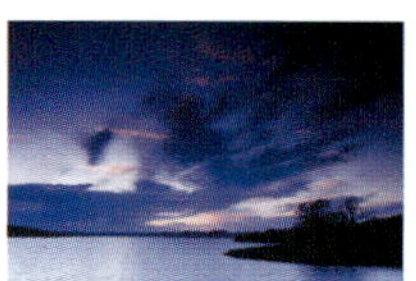

P.121. On the peninsula track, just south of Lodge Farm, looking towards Hambleton Wood.
4:25 pm, 19th January.
0.3 + 0.9ND grey grad. Kodak Elitechrome.
35mm, 1/6 second @ f/11. Underexposed 1.5 stops.

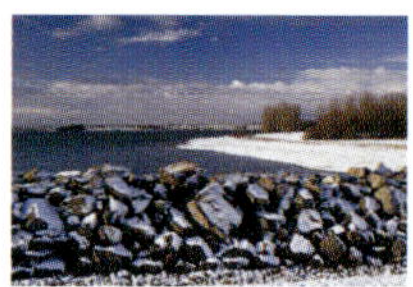

P.122. On the footpath at the northern end of the dam, looking west.
9:44 am, 28th January.
Polariser, 0.3ND grey grad. Fuji Velvia.
35mm, 1/2 second @ f/22. Overexposed by 1 stop.

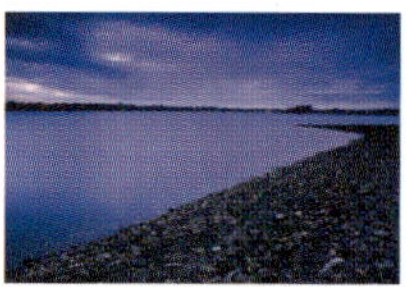

P.123. Along the shore at Whitwell, looking west towards Oakham.
4:20 pm, 17th December.
81B, 0.9ND grey grad. Fuji Velvia.
28mm, 30 seconds @ f/13. Underexposed by 1 stop.

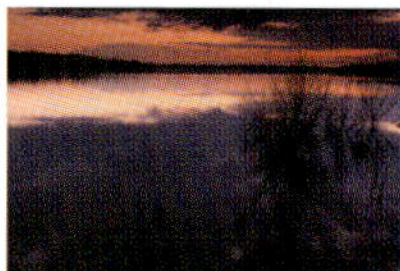

P.124. From the spit of land to the west of Whitwell picnic area, looking due west.
8:50 pm, 6th May.
81B, 0.3ND grey grad. Fuji Velvia.
40mm, 1.5 seconds @ f/8. Underexposed by 1 stop.

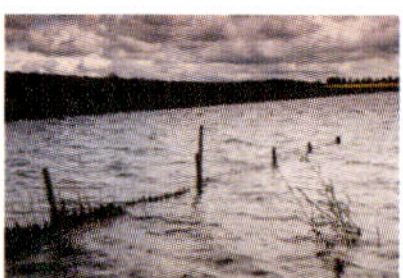

P.125. From the shoreline at Syke's Lane, near the north end of the dam.
3:17 pm, 5th May.
Polariser, 81B, 0.9ND grey grad. Fuji Velvia.
50mm, 1/20 second @ f/16. Underexposed by 0.5 stops.

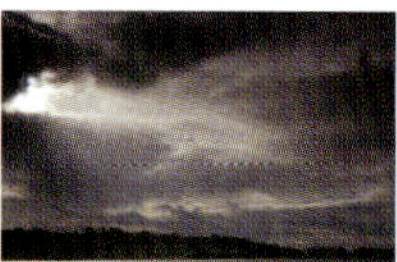

P.126. Hambleton on the peninsula, from the field below Barnsdale picnic area.
12:40 pm, 13th January.
0.9ND grey grad. Kodak Elitechrome.
50mm, 1/250 second @ f/11. Underexposed 0.5 stops.

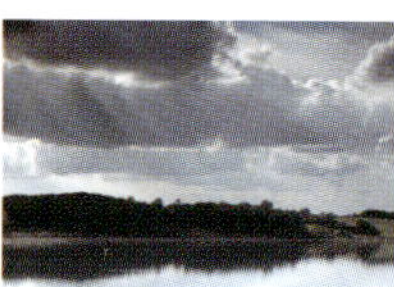

P.127. From the shoreline at Hambleton Wood, looking south-west.
2:58 pm, 21st October.
Polariser @ 50%, 0.9ND grey grad. Fuji Provia.
105mm, 1/90 second @ f/8. Underexposed 0.5 stops.

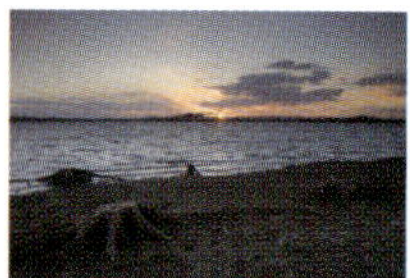

P.128. Below the normal shoreline at Hambleton Wood, looking south-west.
6:25 pm, 3rd October.
0.9ND grey grad. Fuji Provia.
28mm, 1/4 second @ f/22. Underexposed 0.5 stops.

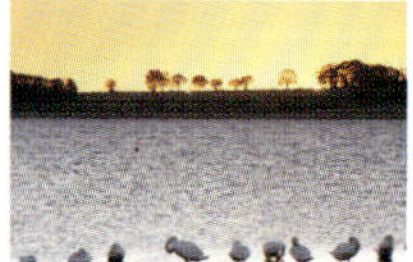

P.129. From the spit of land at Whitwell Creek, looking into the rising sun.
7:52 am, 25th October.
0.9ND grey grad. Fuji Provia.
300mm, 1/8 second @ f/11. Underexposed 0.5 stops.

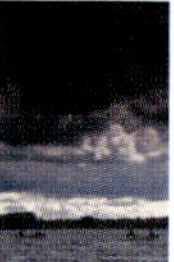

P.130. On the north shore near Whitwell Creek, looking south.
4:25 pm, 5th May.
0.6 + 0.9ND grey grad. Fuji Velvia.
120mm, 1/250 second @ f/8. Underexposed by 1.5 stops.

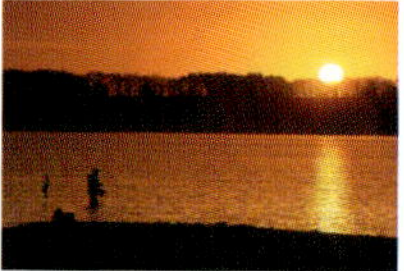

P.131. At low water levels, from the spit of land at the end of Whitwell Creek, at sunrise.
8:14 am, 7th December.
0.9ND grey grad. Fuji Velvia.
200mm, 1/8 second @ f/27. Underexposed by 1.5 stops.

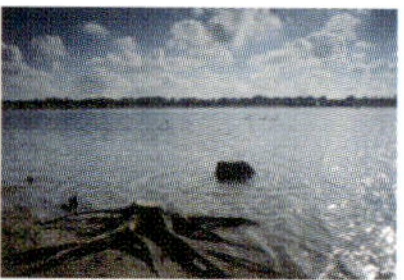

P.132. From below the normal shoreline during low water levels near Hambleton Wood looking south.
1:09 pm, 21st October.
0.9ND grey grad. 81B polarizer at 50%. Fuji Provia.
28mm, 1/20 second @ f/22. Underexposed 0.5 stops.

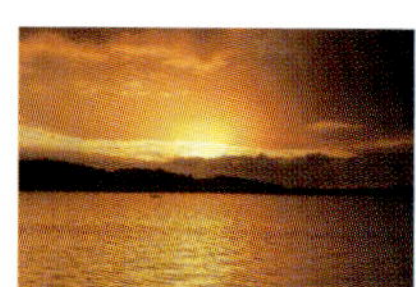

P.133. Between Hinman's Spinney and Half Moon Spinney on the peninsula, looking south-west.
4:40 pm, 26th October.
81B, 0.6ND grey grad. Fuji Provia.
50mm, 1/15 second @ f/8. Underexposed 0.5 stops.

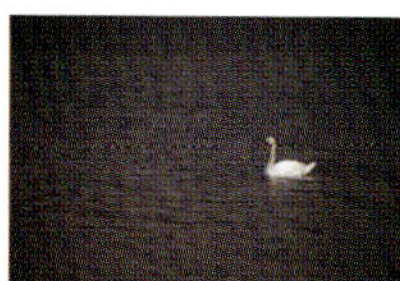

P.134. From 'Lapwing Hide', Egleton Bird Watching Centre.
3:02 pm, 2nd June.
Fuji Velvia.
300mm, 1/750 second @ f/5.6. Underexposed by 0.5 stops.